The 24 Laws of Storytelling

A Practical Handbook for Great Storytellers

Jonathan Baldie

First edition published in 2018 by Subject Zero Ltd.

ISBN 978-1-5272-2729-3

To the stories that gave me light on my darkest days.

Selected Bibliography

The 33 Strategies of War by Robert Greene; Profile. Copyright © Robert Greene and Joost Elffers, 2006.

All My Sons by Arthur Miller; Penguin Classics. Copyright © Arthur Miller, 1947 and 1975. Introduction copyright © Christopher Bigsby, 2000.

The Anatomy of Story by John Truby; Farrar, Straus and Giroux. Copyright © John Truby, 2007.

The Blind Assassin by Margaret Atwood; McClelland and Stewart. Copyright © Margaret Atwood, 2000.

The Book of Five Rings by Miyamoto Musashi; Shambhala Publications, Inc. Translation copyright © Thomas Cleary, 2005.

Carrie by Stephen King; Doubleday. Copyright © Stephen King, 1974.

Creating Character Arcs by K. M. Weiland; PenForASword Publishing. Copyright © K. M. Weiland, 2016.

The Dark Knight Returns by Frank Miller and Klaus Janson; DC Comics. Copyright © DC Comics, 1986.

Acknowledgements

First I would like to thank the many great storytellers and film-makers past and present who provided the endless material for this book. I don't have many friends, but films have always been there to keep me up in my lowest moments. I cannot properly express my gratitude in words.

My parents, Deborah and Nicholas Baldie, deserve thanks for their support. The excitement and pride they expressed when I first showed them my cover and manuscript is a moment of pure joy I will not forget.

And I must not forget to pay tribute to my dog Poppy, whose positive spirit helped keep me buoyant through the long nights of writing and editing.

I also want to thank the film critic Chris Stuckmann for rekindling my interest in stories several years ago. We have never met, but I cannot fail to mention his impact on my motivation for starting this project.

Finally, I would like to thank Alisha Moore at Damonza for her cover design and Rebecca Allen for editing the text.

About the Author

Jonathan Baldie is a writer and software developer. He has a degree in mathematics and lives in Stoke-on-Trent, England.

Spoiler Warning

It's inevitable that a book about storytelling should describe stories, and *The 24 Laws of Storytelling* is no exception. This book contains spoilers for many stories in literature and film. For a full list grouped by each of the 24 Laws, see the appendix.

Contents

Be Cruel to Your Characters

A story that fails to provide challenges for its characters does not deserve to exist. Too many stories fall flat due to the soft treatment of their characters. Obstacles drive stories. In general the crueller these obstacles are, the better. Be cruel to your characters by threatening what they treasure most dearly. This isn't to be sadistic—it makes your characters more likeable, relatable, and gives meaning to your story. Your audience will grow to respect you because your plot's unfortunate turns make it appear more realistic.

End Quickly at the Moment of Catharsis

A story's ending bears a special responsibility—if you fail to meet it, then you'll disappoint your audience and betray the trust they've invested in your story. The ending must provide ultimate catharsis, by releasing the main source of tension right at its highest point. Muddling up the release of tension and creating multiple false endings will only confuse your audience. The ending must also distil the essence of the story itself and provide the moral. Creating the perfect ending requires mastering the art of timing. End a story swiftly —the last act should be the shortest.

Law 3 · *page 27*

Trust Flaws More Than Strengths

Stories need conflict, and a perfect character without flaws is hard to challenge. It's difficult to make an exciting story about some awesome power longer than a paragraph or two. You can, however, make endless meaningful stories about what your characters cannot do. Don't think that writing your character as an untainted paragon of virtue will make them likeable—actually the opposite is true. People are attracted to each other's rough edges. Your readers will relate more with your hero if they show issues that taint their character.

Law 4 · *page 39*

Show, Don't Tell

As a storyteller your role is to immerse your audience in an experience, not to report events. Let your audience arrive at a conclusion themselves with clear evidence: real actions, dialogue, and atmosphere. As a rule of thumb, make your intention to illustrate a point, not to merely report it. By *evoking feelings and creating sensations, you bypass your reader's logical brain and let them effortlessly bathe in the rich worlds you build. Think of this as gently directing the natural flow of a river, as opposed to rigidly forcing a dam in its path.*

Law 5 · *page 53*

Reflect Reality in Fantasy

Even the most fantastical setting must be grounded firmly in reality. Rein in any attempts to add too many alien concepts into your story. Recognise now that these urges are self-indulgent—there is nothing good in confusing your audience. Characters, places, and objects with unpronounceable names will be forgotten. Use real-world names and concepts to inspire your world-building, and give your audience distinctive, relatable characters.

Law 6 · *page 73*

Make Your Villain the Hero of Their Own Story

Everyone sees themselves as the hero of their own story, even if they are the villain of someone else's. One-dimensional villains may suit simple minds, but to add deep nuance and rich emotional experiences to your story, write a complicated, relatable villain. Don't pull any punches—clearly justify their motivations with an impactful opening scene. The worst villains are negative, power-hungry, and one-dimensional—avoid these traits like the plague. No matter how you've written the antagonistic force in your story, it must be understandable and strongly argued.

Weave Foreshadowing Seamlessly into the Plot

Among their many traits, the best stories are unpredictable. Your audience wants to be led along a path with subtle breadcrumbs. In this regard, assume your reader is intelligent enough to recognise your clues. On the other hand, a twist ending will not be appreciated if it lacks any forewarning. You must learn the art of controlling potential energy— like a bow drawn fully taut, your plot must prepare its twist ending with a graduated series of clues.

Structure Your Story around Change

Whenever you think a story is boring, it's almost always because it lacks structure. An amorphous collection of scenes invariably feels unnatural—like one long, drawn-out scene rather than a complete story. Writers of these stories have failed to think properly about their characters and how they change with the plot. Story structure is, at its most distilled, the illustration of a character's single defining attribute.

Plan your story out into a finite number of acts, marking each with an irreversible action that shows an evolution in character.

Law 9 · *page 123*

Subvert Expectations

Audiences are good at recognising genre tropes. The only times you truly shock your audience will be in the moments your story subverts the expectations they have formed about the story's genre. Use this fact to your advantage. Pick a story trope, hint at it a little, only to completely subvert it—you can repeat this trick endlessly. Lead your reader down a road they think they know. As they recognise the ostensible ending in the distance and walk towards it, they don't see the unexpected hidden trap you've laid at their feet.

Law 10 · *page 133*

Conflict Is Everything—Guard It at All Costs

Stories don't require a lot of material to work well. Do not underestimate the simple power of playing host to a cast of likeable characters all in conflict with one another. Most of us feel timid in our daily lives, afraid to rock the boat—this may work in real life, but in storytelling it is suicide. The most reliable way to improve any story is to dial up the conflict between its characters. No one wants to read a story about sweet characters on the same wavelength who agree on everything. Create sparks and don't be afraid to start a fire.

Law 11 · *page 145*

Characters Must Learn from Their Mistakes

No one likes people who bumble carelessly through life, never learning from the variety of mistakes they make. Such people are lost causes, and we instinctively know to stay clear of them. In contrast, we admire people who learn from their mistakes and strive to improve themselves. People—and readers—are forgiving of flawed people making mistakes, but only so long as they see what they did wrong and never repeat it. Show your characters shaking off their old selves and stepping into new shoes. This metamorphosis can be the most significant source of the education that your story provides.

Law 12 · *page 167*

The Hero and Villain Must Share the Same Goal

For your story to have tension, you must create a legitimate threat to something that the characters care about. If your villain's motives don't spark any kind of real resistance from your hero, then there's no threat. To create real emotional resonance in your audience's hearts, your hero and villain must seek the same thing—this can be a literal object, or your villain can threaten something less tangible that your hero nevertheless deeply identifies with. Giving your hero and villain the same goal with opposing motives and alternate methods is a recipe for a great contest.

Law 13 · *page 183*

Series Are a Right, Not a Privilege

A series of stories can only stand on strong foundations, built from the ground up. Boundless sums of money have been wasted attempting to create shared story universes where no such right has been earned. A multi-part series of stories can only exist when its constituent stories are entertaining, when they develop likeable characters, and most importantly, are self-contained. Build investment in your characters, then put them through hardship, and finally allow them to achieve catharsis. Once again, you must master the art of controlling potential energy—the longer the tension is drawn out, the more satisfying the feeling of catharsis upon its release.

Law 14 · *page 211*

Make Bold Choices

Do not tread lightly when writing your plot's twists and turns. Your readers want to be grabbed roughly by the arm and hurled headlong into a good story—be the one storyteller out of a hundred to give them that pleasure. Too many authors make timid decisions that end up ruining their work. Timidity betrays weakness of thought and a lack of planning. Avoid this fate by firmly pushing your story in a definite direction. Your best work will polarise your audience. Accept this fate, and never fear being disliked for the fallout of your bold narrative choices—usually the opposite is true.

Law 15 · *page 223*

Tighten with Relentless Rigour

Cut anything from your story that does not serve it. Any unnecessary parts will distract the audience from the important parts of your story. The best way to avoid fluff is to plan well and have a definite goal in mind before you start drafting. When editing your drafts, your goal is to get to a point where to remove any single paragraph, sentence, or word would cause the story to not make sense. Be concise both in your writing and the plot itself. Create an elegant flow from scene to scene by tightening down on every necessary detail.

Law 16 · *page 243*

Humour Is Always Welcome

Regardless of genre, humour is always welcome. But a moment of levity is especially welcome when it distracts the reader away from a serious backdrop. A single, short, well-delivered line can make your audience forgive ten chapters of demure tragedy. Humour that pokes fun at your characters or some element of your story can be an indirect way of exposing some truth. It also reminds the audience they're here to enjoy themselves, and shows them that you don't take yourself too seriously.

Law 17 · *page 261*

Write along the Line of Greatest Intuition

Audiences are especially good at spotting when you try to force the plot. Realising that you need to place some artificial decision or event just to make your plot work is a bad sign. Nothing ruins an audience's immersion like an unrealistically idiotic decision by your character. Put yourself in the character's shoes. What is your first instinct? What would you do? Choose that action for your character.

Law 18 · *page 285*

Accord with Timeless Myths

History has shown us that the stories that come closest to humanity's timeless myths enjoy the strongest resonance with the audience, and thus the longest perennial success. Timeless myths can never be repeated too often because they touch on fundamental things about human psychology. As long as human nature ceases to change, these rules will continue to work. Accord with cultural myths and common human experiences to achieve a deep connection with your audience.

Law 19 · *page 305*

Build Tension with the "Bomb under the Table" Technique

Tension invariably grabs the audience's attention, and it is simple to manipulate to gain the maximum effect. Introduce a problem and let it build. Allow the tension to grow until it becomes unbearable. Your goal is to induce discomfort. At some point you must release the tension and allow your reader a chance to catch their breath, but only once the tension has been allowed to grow to a satisfactory level. This rule can be extended from single scenes right across entire series—see it as one of the most powerful tools in your storyteller's arsenal.

Law 20 · *page 323*

Concentrate Dramatic Impact

Too much circulation makes the perceived value go down. The less of a good character you show in the story, the more valuable they are. Only give characters or scenes as much space in the story as necessary and no more. This is a common stumbling block for sequels—the storyteller or the commercial interests behind them mistakes the audience's love for a character by giving too much away and diluting their once strong impact. Avoid this fate by resisting the urge to open Pandora's box—it'll only spoil your character's mystery. Instead, you must work hard to build tension and potential energy all the way through your story, delivering the knock-out punch when the time comes.

Law 21 · *page 341*

Description Is Telepathy

The most common mistake writers make when describing a character or a place is to exhaustively list every detail about them in as literal a way as possible. Contrary to intuition, this actually fails to convey the most important details because it constrains the reader's imagination. The best way to describe is to make your descriptions as brief and intuitive as possible. Give your audience a tidbit, and let them decide for themselves what the characters look like. That will help them to take ownership of the story and feel invested in its outcome. Unleash the raw cosmic power of your audience's imagination.

Law 22 · *page 361*

Great Dialogue Is About What's Not Said

Dialogue is the best way to illustrate conflict. Friction between characters is vital to any story, and one of the best ways to show it is through dialogue rich with conflicting motivations. Dialogue is not a reporting device, it is a manifestation of that character's state, and it must therefore rely on subtext. Use dialogue to encourage your audience to discern feelings and facts, not merely to explain facts or plot details.

Law 23 · *page 383*

Write Proactive Characters

Just as in real life, there is nothing more irritating than a character who acts like a wimp, giving up at the slightest difficulty, and doing nothing about the challenges that face them. Audiences relate to characters who are proactive. Make characters who act to create the plot, not the other way around. Great characters make your reader look up, not down. Leave your audience feeling more inspired than when they first pressed "play" on your story.

Law 24 · *page 399*

Point Everything to the End and Beyond

The best stories move with a deliberate pace. Not every story has to move fast, but every part of the story must build to the crescendo of your ending. The most lasting part of your story is the impression it leaves in the audience well after they've read the last page or left the cinema. You can achieve this most powerful of effects through the use of subtext—it is always better to leave the juiciest details unsaid and leave your audience thinking.

Preface

Stories have a unique ability to convey information—no other device can simultaneously entertain and educate. The ability to create a story and immerse an audience gives one great power, since stories capture our attention instantly, and we humans have an innate ability to extract lessons from them.

A good story takes us away from the difficulties of life and on a journey of discovery far from our daily experience, free of the boundaries our own lives place on us. We are instantly mesmerised and immersed inside the world created by the storyteller.

There is no greater feeling than recounting a story to friends who all hang on your every word. Captivating an audience in a story is like casting a spell—if you take the right steps, draw out the tension, and deliver a character arc well, then the audience follows you willingly and loves you for the experience. If you bungle by explaining too much or neglecting your characters and their interrelated dramas, then the magic is lost.

Think back to the last time you read a book or watched a film that had a deep impact on you. This story immersed you inside its world, taking you to faraway places with people who became to feel like good friends. It affected you emotionally, and by the end you were grinning, crying, laughing, or better: a combination of all three. With little more than a few pages or some images on a screen, you fell under the storyteller's spell. Storytelling is a form of seduction, and seducing your audience can be reduced to a series of timeless, reliable principles that anyone can learn.

With modern technology and widespread public education, the resources required to write and tell a story are within everyone's reach. For you the storyteller, there are no barriers to cross, only the effort required to spend on your creation. These resources are within you and solely under your control.

Whether you're writing a novel, creating a fictional story for your next script, or laying out a real-life story for a speaking engagement, there are long-established principles that always improve your audience's experience. History shows us patterns of these principles in the stories that have enjoyed enduring success and eternal loyalty from their audiences.

The 24 Laws of Storytelling is designed to identify and explain these storytelling principles in a practical way. Each law is explained not through abstract, pedantic definitions or unscrupulously dissected scene-by-scene autopsies, but instead through stories, both fictional and real. To do otherwise would be to have little faith in the very topic that this book covers.

Real-life or fantastical, all great stories immerse the audience in an experience that locks their attention and leads them on a journey of discovery. New perspectives, new emotions, and new thoughts are all possible from the art created by the storyteller. Stories aren't mere escapism—they directly affect the real world through the experiences they provide.

> *Fantasy is hardly an escape from reality. It's a*
> *way of understanding it.*
> —Lloyd Alexander, 1924-2007

In storytelling, you can't be nice. The best way to immerse the audience is to grab their heartstrings, and you can't do that with soft silk gloves. Threaten something the main character treasures to make them progress in a meaningful way—often the more cruel the threat, the more meaningful the journey, as you'll see in Law 1. Indeed, all of these storytelling principles can be boiled down to creating a character who the audience loves and then torturing them. There is of course more to storytelling than this, but it is the foundation of every story's structure.

Storytelling immersion can't happen without a premeditated story structure. The structure of a story forms its foundation, and just as any building with weak foundations will fall, a weakly structured story will meander and feel like a waste of time. Both the character movement and structure require adequate planning before you begin writing. The price of ignoring this advice is to experience writer's block on a daily basis and write a rambling tale that needs repeated rewrites. It is far better to discover an inconsistency or a plot hole at this early stage than after three months of meandering writing.

Your model is the military leader preparing the strategy for a grand campaign—you research and plan meticulously, and study past successes and blunders for the keys to victory. The lessons contained in stories that succeeded and blundered are there to be analysed, and you ignore them at your peril. Failure to study these lessons of history is to put yourself through unnecessary pain. Repeating the mistakes of others and publishing a rushed, mediocre story is to achieve either rank obscurity or to damage your reputation irreparably. Whatever your medium then, it is far better to learn from the vast wealth of knowledge of stories from the past than to bungle with writer's block. Instead of being blown about by the whims of fate, you take control of your writing.

To work on a film set with Alfred Hitchcock (1899-1980) for the first time was an unnerving experience. Film directors are usually balls of stress, barking out orders at their staff and arguing with their actors. They desperately try to exert control over every aspect of the film-making process. In contrast, Hitchcock would sit in his chair, say little, and sometimes doze off. New actors used to being coddled by other directors would find such hands-off control unsettling.

Hitchcock's Buddha-like demeanour was not a manifestation of any laziness. In truth, Hitchcock spent months before shooting in careful and rigorous contemplation, giving undivided focus to the planning of his films. He had done the majority of his work behind the scenes before production had even begun. As a young man, during his apprenticeship in film-making, Hitchcock had taught himself every aspect of the film-making process, from a film's lighting to its script writing, by getting involved wherever he could. Hitchcock developed an intimate understanding of every piece of the film-making puzzle and how they fit together.

Every single detail of the story, from the looks on the actors' faces to the colour of the lead actress's dress, was planned in painstaking detail. Hitchcock had absolute end-to-end control over the execution of the story, and his audiences felt the payoff when they watched his films, each one a classic of cinema. Hitchcock didn't need to waste valuable production time in a flurry of insecure panic as most directors usually did, reacting as his staff created fires to put out—instead, his months of planning gave him the serene air of confidence that he is known for today.

Do your story justice by embracing the planning phase as Hitchcock did—think deeply on how to design the moving parts, such as character development, the conflicting motives, and the gradual rise of tension. Like Hitchcock, you will save time and unneeded stress in the production phase. This is the beauty in giving the planning stage its deserved priority. When you cut out the countless wasted days of hesitation, procrastination, and rewrites, you'll be surprised by the amount of time left for crucial parts of the writing and editing processes. If you make your plans, write your notes, and come up with a structure, then you'll avoid writer's block and increase your productivity a thousandfold.

> *Strategy is the art of making use of time and space. I am less concerned about the latter than the former. Space we can recover, lost time never.*
>
> —Napoléon Bonaparte, 1769-1821

Do not worry about someone else stealing your ideas in this extra time you spend planning beforehand and tweaking your drafts afterwards. You are unique—

your story and the way you tell it are irreplaceable. No matter how talented your contemporary storytellers, none of them can write in your style. Understand: When you are writing with free creative expression, you have no competition.

As long as you're putting in the work, never give up on yourself. Few people will achieve what you have at your fingertips—a great novel or an inspiring speech will resonate with people and leave them with lasting positive effects. In your darkest moments, remind yourself of the positive ripple effect you can have on people. Dr Seuss's first story *And to Think That I Saw It on Mulberry Street* was rejected 27 times by different publishers. Stephen King threw away early drafts of *Carrie*, and the final manuscript of his horror novella was rejected 30 times by publishers. In either case, a slow start could not hold back lifetimes of success that continue without any signs of slowing down soon. In fact, both authors' works are accelerating in sales and popularity.

It's wise to practise writing on a daily basis, even if each session is brief. Writing may be an art form, but it is also a skill. Do not fall into the trap of taking too long away from looking at your story—such absences are dangerous because they can become habits. It is wise to observe your habits and figure out the optimal patterns—do you write better in the morning or at night? These variables may seem strange or irrelevant, but the body and mind operate in perfect harmony and their connections cannot be ignored. A small change in your writing routine can make a big impact, so experiment often and note the results.

Multi-bestselling author Ryan Holiday has urged writers to rely not on fits of inspiration but on treating writing like a job. You can't control when your bursts of genius rise forth, but you can quite easily sit yourself down at your desk each morning and address the work of the day. "Writers *write*," says Holiday in his classic *Perennial Seller*, reminding the reader of artist Austin Kleon's dictum that too many creators "want to *be* the noun without *doing* the verb." Make a pact with yourself to form a positive habit then—you'll develop a better feel for your story with focused daily effort than if you were to come back and forth at weekly intervals. If you want your story to be great, you need to treat writing more like a job than a light hobby—creating a timeless story requires nothing less than a dedication to the writing craft. It helps to choose genres or topics you are most enthusiastic about at the current point in your life —this can save you in your dark moments as you find it easier to summon forth the required creative energy.

The Milk Cow

A man had a cow; she gave each day a pot full of milk. The man invited a number of guests. To have as much milk as possible, he did not milk the cow for ten days. He thought that on the tenth day the cow would give him ten pitchers of milk. But the cow's milk went back, and she gave less milk than before.

—*Fables for Children* by Leo Tolstoy

It is all too easy to feel the seductive temptation to cut corners, neglecting the creative work to get the story out there as soon as possible. To rush your story in this manner is a sin that you will pay for with the contempt that your audience will deservedly give you. Whenever you feel a pang of panic to get your story published sooner rather than later, look at it this way—an extra week or month of editing or proofreading will seem insignificant a year after your publish date, but yield great benefits that you'd sorely miss otherwise. If you rush work out due to impatience or laziness, then you'll always regret it.

There is, however, a reversal to short time allowances. A harsh deadline, seen from the correct perspective, can spark untold creativity. Consistent daily writing becomes an even greater necessity and it gets easier for you to reach a flow state, forgetting time and the troubles of your normal daily life. Once you find that flow state, don't let go—keep going as long as you can.

Invest the necessary mental effort within a short time frame, and you can achieve in weeks what others do in months. Understand that there is little difference between the potential yield of a month and a week's worth of work. Given a month, you'll work at a leisurely pace. Given a week, you'll produce the same amount of content, and at a higher quality due to the immense pressure to perform. This fact may seem counter-intuitive, but the urgency of a tight deadline will awake endurance and mental powers you never knew you had. Creativity will come as necessity dictates it. Such high-density work time will deliver surprises day after day.

The Crow and the Pitcher

A crow perishing with thirst saw a pitcher, and hoping to find water, flew to it with delight. When he reached it, he discovered to his grief that it contained so little water that he could not possibly get at it. He tried everything he could think of to reach the water, but all his efforts were in vain. At last he collected as many stones as he could carry and dropped them one by one with his beak into the pitcher, until he brought the water within his reach and thus saved his life.

—*Aesop's Fables*, sixth century BC

See that time is relative, and effort can be adjusted accordingly—the amount of mental energy you spend on your story is entirely within your control. And your time is best spent analysing your story's structure and how well it fits together. The 24 Laws in this book will aid you in this process, helping you identify and understand the distilled elements of great stories and how you can harness their powers of immersion within your own creations.

If you take anything away from this book, let it be this: Doing a really good job is not only the right thing to do, but it's also the best marketing and sales decision you can make. Never cut corners, spend as much effort as you can perfecting your work, and people will find something in it to recommend to their friends— that is an absolute certainty. Whenever times are tough, think of the love with which your audience will cherish your work. Keep working on your creation until you are sure it is worthy of that love.

There is one type of story, that will rely on brute force marketing or the coat-tails of an established saga, that will make millions and give you your fifteen minutes of fame. There is another type of story, that will last for a timeless interval and fill you with pride and satisfaction for the rest of your life, and continue to enchant countless people after you're gone. One story charts a spike followed by a precipitous fall into obscurity; the other story charts a quiet beginning followed by an exponential rise.

If you feel conflicted by that choice, picture this: The Roman emperor Marcus Aurelius sat in a quiet room, writing personal notes to himself on how to be a good, hard-working, and generous person. Practically the king of the known world and worshipped as a god in his own lifetime, these notes were published into a book a thousand years after his death, titled *Meditations*. In that time, millions upon millions of people have read the book, wanting to learn from his wisdom and virtue.

People are not going to stop wanting to live good lives, and that is why *Meditations* has lasted through the ages. As a storyteller, you must also touch upon the most timeless aspects of the human condition, and aim for the type of perennial success that this long-dead Roman emperor will continue to drive for the next thousand years. Successes built from long, gradual rises last the longest—let the work speak for itself, and then even the gentlest of nudges can help your success gather momentum.

Artists have an interest in others' believing in sudden ideas, so-called inspirations; as if the idea of a work of art, of poetry, the fundamental thought of a philosophy shines down like a merciful light from heaven. In truth, the good artist's or thinker's imagination is continually producing things good, mediocre, and bad, but his power of judgement, highly sharpened and practiced, rejects, selects, joins together; thus we now see from Beethoven's notebooks that he gradually assembled the most glorious melodies and, to a degree, selected them out of disparate beginnings. The artist who separates less rigorously, liking to rely on his imitative memory, can in some circumstances become a great improviser; but artistic improvisation stands low in relation to artistic thoughts earnestly and laboriously chosen. All great men were great workers, untiring not only in invention but also in rejecting, sifting, reforming, arranging.

—Friedrich Nietzsche, 1844-1900

How to Use This Book

Consider *The 24 Laws of Storytelling* a kind of handbook on the art of creating immersive, joyful, and satisfying experiences for your audience through storytelling. By studying each chapter you will gain practical knowledge that you can use for any of your creative projects. This book will also add to your enjoyment of every book and film you go on to consume, because you'll gain a greater appreciation for the kind of hard work that has to go into their planning. But don't think that this material is only useful for novelists and screenwriters. The ability to captivate an audience, make them fall in love with a character, and take them on a rollercoaster of emotions are infinitely applicable in modern life.

By reading the book from cover to cover, you will thus gain a broad picture of storytelling in general. This approach is recommended the first time round. Not every one of the laws will apply to your given situation. But over the course of your writing career, it's likely that at some point, each one will come into play, and you can use *The 24 Laws of Storytelling* as your trusty companion along the way. This approach will work for you if your story has issues that you can't quite put your finger on. You're unsure if your story is quite how you want it, but you need some time to step back and read a series of simple, actionable guides on the aspects of a well-structured story.

A second approach is to select and dip into any one of the laws, digesting its lessons and making use of them. This may work best if you need a particular lesson to improve some aspect of your story. The structure of this book enables this method of consumption by decoupling each law from the overall book itself. You are not required to have read a previous section to understand another.

There are no prerequisites to reading this book. It is not structured like traditional books on storytelling. Those books merely take a linear journey through every facet of the storytelling process, each chapter prefaced with a dozen definitions and diving into detailed line-by-line autopsies of scenes. That approach limits the reader to set patterns, without giving them the wider perspective necessary to deliver an immersive experience to their audience. Theories are clean and simple, but situations rarely are.

In the German language, there is a distinction between two types of command: a *Befehl*, an order to be followed to the letter, and an *Auftrag*, a general statement of purpose. The latter approach, that of *Auftragstaktik*, gave 19th-century Prussian military officers latitude to achieve their missions in any reasonable way they saw fit. Granting junior officers this latitude not only saved time for their superiors by delegating the details, but it also gave the junior officers space to respond to circumstances, rather than having to rigidly obey established doctrine regardless of the problem they were facing. The French emperor Napoleon had exploited this failing of their predecessors in his masterful invasion of Prussia. The Prussian troops opposing his were exceptionally well drilled to the point of acting like simple robots—able to perform manoeuvres with attention to minute details, but unable to respond to events outside of their training.

Without a sense of the big picture, you may know where you will be tomorrow, but it's impossible to see where you're really going. If you are going to succeed as a storyteller, you must become a strategic planner. Individual storytelling tricks are useless when the big picture is blurry, because those tricks lack context. Understand that each failure of storytelling is really a failure in strategic planning. Character arcs must be charted out, events must be cohesive, and the theme must be consistent from start to finish—this can only be achieved by becoming a strategic storyteller.

Adopt and embrace an approach to writing that emphasises preparedness. Just as a leader doesn't declare war until he has gathered all the proper intelligence and his troops are drafted and trained, we as storytellers can't embark on our writing projects without a long and deliberate planning stage. The central theme of *The 24 Laws of Storytelling* is that only grand strategy can achieve grand results. Wading into the abyss without a map or a firm set of principles at hand may seem romantic, but in reality it's usually a recipe for disaster. To neglect this crucial piece of the writing job is also to neglect yourself and your audience. A poorly planned writing project can cause years of headache. Embarking on any long-term creative project with a goal and breaking the task into smaller parts will make it seem a lot more attainable. In essence, this book's goal is to make you take your writing seriously and plan your stories like a professional. This advice cannot be ignored. Teach a creative person how to plan, and you make them unstoppable.

> *In this context, I wrote three related pieces that became a book called* Encounters with the Archdruid. *To a bulletin board I had long since pinned a sheet of paper on which I had written, in large block letters, ABC/D. The letters represented the structure of a piece of writing, and when I put them on the wall I had no idea what the theme would be or who might be A or B or*

C, let alone the denominator D. They would be real people, certainly, and they would meet in real places, but everything else was initially abstract. That is no way to start a writing project, let me tell you. You begin with a subject, gather material, and work your way to structure from there. You pile up volumes of notes and then figure out what you are going to do with them, not the other way around.

—John McPhee, journalist and author

Each law of storytelling is supported by general examples that illustrate the lessons to the reader. By focusing on stories to express ideas and extract the appropriate the morals, the book stays true to the theme that it covers. For a book on storytelling to do otherwise would make no sense. In this book you will find detailed analyses of stories written by masters both old and new: Stephen King, Christopher Nolan, Arthur Miller, George Lucas, and Fyodor Dostoyevsky, among others. By studying these masters you will learn the same techniques they use to delight and inspire their audiences.

Certain acts almost always improve the audience's experience, an *observance* of the law, while others almost always decrease quality, a *transgression*. These are included in every chapter to give an example of the law's application. The use of positive examples and cautionary tales is a time-tested method of teaching, and great care has been taken to avoid neglecting that in this book.

> *From anecdotes, thought Prosper Mérimée, one "can distinguish a true picture of the customs and characters of any given period." Nietzsche was confident that "three anecdotes may suffice to paint a picture of a man." Isaac D'Israeli, whose Dissertation on Anecdotes affords a perfect reflection of his time's anecdotal preferences, thought anecdotes indices to character: "Opinions are fallible, but not examples." Says Ralph Waldo Emerson: "Ballads, bon mots, and anecdotes give us better insights into the depths of past centuries than grave and voluminous chronicles." His contemporary Ellery Channing agreed: "One anecdote of a man is worth a volume of biography."*
>
> —*The Little, Brown Book of Anecdotes*

Since we are dealing with works of creative art, most of them widely-known, there's a noticeably shallower pool of examples to draw from for the transgressions of each law. There is some inherent confirmation bias since failed stories generally don't make it to public consumption, not to mention the discomfort some may feel when creative works face criticism. Where such examples occur, the criticism is objective and well-founded, and no personal ill will is intended towards the creators of that work.

You'll also find further reflections on each law placed between sections. These authoritative quotes, anec-dotes, and short stories are intended to give more evid-ence for each law's truth.

Finally, this book can be enjoyed as a treatise on some of the best and worst stories ever told. Enjoy the stories told within the laws, take a step back to con-sider the lessons in them, and you may be inspired to create and tell your own someday—at which point, you hold in your hands the perfect companion to guide you on such a journey.

> *The people actually desire nothing more from tragedy than to be moved, to be able to cry their hearts out; an artist who sees a new tragedy, however, has his joy in its ingenious technical inventions and devices, in its manipulation and apportionment of the material, in its new use of old motifs, old thoughts.*
> —Friedrich Nietzsche, 1844-1900

Law 1

Be Cruel to Your Characters

A story that fails to provide challenges for its characters does not deserve to exist. Too many stories fall flat due to the soft treatment of their characters. Obstacles drive stories. In general the crueller these obstacles are, the better. Be cruel to your characters by threatening what they treasure most dearly. This isn't to be sadistic—it makes your characters more likeable, relatable, and gives meaning to your story. Your audience will grow to respect you because your plot's unfortunate turns make it appear more realistic.

Observance of the Law

In the 1959 epic *Ben-Hur*, Charlton Heston plays a Palestinian Jew, Judah Ben-Hur, who reigns as a wealthy prince at the time of occupation by the Roman Empire. His childhood friend Messala returns to Jerusalem with the Roman army as a newly appointed tribune, and commander of the Roman garrison in the ancient city.

In the time spent away from Jerusalem, Messala has developed a worship-like belief in the glory of Rome and its imperial power, distinguishing him from the kind and generous Judah, who believes in the freedom of the Jewish people. Though their reunion is joyful, within days an impassable rift forms between the two men, as Messala demands to imprison and execute the people whose identities Judah refuses to share.

Judah and his family go to watch the parade for the new governor of Judea. As they watch from the roof of their home, loose roof tiles fall and spook the governor's horse and nearly kill him. While clearly an accident, Messala sees in this an opportunity to further his political career by condemning Judah to slavery in the Roman galleys, sentencing his mother and sister to an indefinite time in prison.

With this cruel stroke he hopes to gain a reputation as a loyal servant of Rome and as a ruthless law-maker in the region. His goal is to impress the emperor and further his career back in Rome by succeeding over his predecessors and intimidating the people of Judea into accepting their subjugation.

Judah thus endures three years of hard and constant labour as a galley slave, losing his family, wealth, and status. But he silently accepts this fate, surviving a daily back-breaking ordeal that kills many others from exhaustion in less time. After these three years, the Roman consul Quintus Arrius discovers Judah while inspecting his vessel and its galley slaves ahead of a mission to destroy a fleet of Macedonian pirates.

Arrius is impressed by Judah's stoicism and endurance under such a heavy, sustained workload and offers to train him as a charioteer. The consul likes to dabble in such things outside of his official role at the head of the Roman army. Judah turns down his offer, citing his belief that God alone will help him in his quest for vengeance. The naval battle with the Macedonian pirates comes, and the Roman navy win, but at the cost of their ships. Separated from the battle in the midst of combat, Judah saves the consul's life when he tries to kill himself in the disgrace of their heavy losses. Judah refuses to allow Arrius this fate, quoting back to him his own words on the ship, "We keep you alive to serve this ship; so row well, and live."

Having changed his perspective on his return to Rome, Arrius realises his gratitude to Judah, and successfully petitions the Roman Emperor to grant the prince his freedom. Arrius even adopts Judah as his son, a common practice within Roman society. Over the course of the next year, Judah learns the Roman ways and becomes a celebrated charioteer, defeating all and gaining a reputation under his adoptive father's name.

Judah knows, however, that at some point he will have to return to Judea, as he promised himself years before. Arrius reluctantly allows him to return home, promising him that he is proud of him and his achievements.

Judah visits Messala's palace under the guise of his adoptive father's family name. He threatens Messala with the wrath of his anger, demanding to know the fate of his mother and sister. Intimidated by the man who now possesses all the imperial might of a consul, they agree to find the pair and assess their condition.

After finding the women in prison, Messala's officers discover that they have contracted leprosy—greatly stigmatised at the time—and expel them from the city. A former slave of Judah finds them, but they beg her to secrecy as to their condition. Pressed by Judah, but held to her promise, she lies to him, telling him they have died.

Now with nothing to live for, Judah decides to seek vengeance on Messala by defeating him in a chariot race. Judah wins the race, and a brutal collision breaks Messala's body. As the once-proud tribune lies dying in his final moments, he tells Judah he can find his family in the Valley of the Lepers. Judah thus finds his family, and the story culminates in Jesus Christ's crucifixion, miraculously curing them of their leprosy with his holy talents.

Interpretation

William Wyler's masterpiece of cinema spans a story of redemption in the face of overwhelming odds and incredible cruelty towards the titular character. It is widely considered to be among the best films ever made, not least due to the epic scale of its production for the time and its inspiring journey led by Judah.

Starting the story as wealthy prince loved by all, and being forcefully reduced to a galley slave, Judah's fall from grace is vast and sudden. Great care was taken at the start of the film to show Judah as a benevolent owner of his slaves, agreeing to free Esther, the daughter of his old friend and slave Simonides.

Thus he not only falls from a place of high material status but one of moral standing too. The audience cares about the character, having seen from his actions that he doesn't deserve his fate. In this method of storytelling, the audience isn't told about his goodness through dialogue or anecdotes. It's shown through Judah's refusal to give up his fellow Jews even to his old friend, and the benevolence with which he treats his slaves.

The ruthlessness and cruelty to which Judah and his family suffer in the story creates the opportunity for immense redemption—Judah faces his new fate with stoicism and strength, finding patience in the vengeance he wishes to exert on his nemesis Messala. It is this revelation of his incredible strength of character throughout the journey that *Ben-Hur* takes its audience that gives it the universally positive reception it has received. Had the story taken a less cruel turn, and not stripped Judah of so much from his former life, the journey of redemption would have had far less meaning.

Keys to Storytelling

Life is cruel, and bad things happen to us on a daily basis. A story without any adverse events has no meaning and no discernible lessons. You must be cruel to your characters and never pull the punches, because it's only in the face of this conflict that they'll show their true colours and progress as human beings.

You can write exposition through paragraphs of dialogue until you're blue in the face, but it'll never be as effective as showing the character forced into a choice between two options—one representing a regression to his old self, the other representing transcendence and positive growth.

The only way to show your character's moral fibre is to challenge them with something that threatens them right to the core. The most reliable technique to achieve this is to put yourself in your character's shoes and find the hardest decisions they can make. What person or thing is most important to them? Are they able to lose that person or thing? Will they stand by their moral code when it comes to losing a loved one? There's often not a definitive answer, so brainstorm some ideas and you'll be able to use one of them to set up a compelling moment of clarity for your character.

Once you've established what these decisions are, your story should force them to make those decisions. The best time to do this is usually in the latter half of the story, or the second story in a three-part series because this is when the stakes are highest for your main character.

In *The Empire Strikes Back*, when Luke Skywalker is beaten down and his hand severed by Darth Vader, the evil Sith Lord reveals he is Luke's father. Vader asks Luke to join him in overthrowing the Emperor and ruling the galaxy as father and son. On the precipice of anguish, Luke reveals his true character—he decides to reject his father's offer of power, preferring death to the dark side. We get a clear picture of Luke's trust in the Force, but he's only brought to this point by the extreme situation he is forced to face. This requirement is the essence of this law.

In *To Kill a Mockingbird*, Atticus Finch lives in the American South at a time when racial prejudice is the norm. Despite the pressure from the community to do otherwise, Atticus agrees to defend Tom Robinson in his criminal trial. The antagonist Bob Ewell offers plenty of cruelty to Atticus. He spits in Atticus's face during the trial, intimidates Tom's wife, and threatens Atticus's two children, Scout and Jem. Ewell wants to provoke a violent reaction out of Atticus, who stays measured and refuses to stoop to his level, providing a good example for anyone facing down a bully. We only see his stoicism and moral virtue because of the horrible treatment he is forced to face.

The true man is revealed in difficult times. So when trouble comes, think of yourself as a wrestler whom God, like a trainer, has paired with a tough young buck. For what purpose? To turn you into Olympic-class material. But this is going to take some sweat to accomplish. From my perspective, no one's difficulties ever gave him a better test than yours, if you are prepared to make use of them the way a wrestler makes use of an opponent in peak condition.

—*Discourses* by Epictetus

A story's rising conflict puts pressure on the characters to act in ways that force them out of their comfort zone and forge them into the people they need to be. As a muscle grows by being trained hard and torn down, a character develops through cruel opposition.

Such opposition only matters, though, once you've established the character's stable origin state and show what they value, which creates stakes for the conflict to threaten. The terrible chaos wrought in the story of 2008's *The Dark Knight* was only possible due to the investment in the characters built up by the origin story told in 2005's *Batman Begins*. We had to know who Bruce Wayne was before we could see his life torn apart by the ruthless Joker.

Start your story with an investment in your character's high stature. Give a display of their good morals, or how powerful they are within the sphere of their world. Then, think of the worst possible thing that could happen to him, and write that. Put yourself in his shoes, if that helps. Feel every ounce of emotion he feels.

Then ask, what choices does it force him to make? What opportunity does it give him to show his true colours? Stepping into your character's shoes and experiencing the dilemma will help you to write a more true-to-life depiction of his arc. What is the response? What is the pain? You need to provide concrete answers to these questions so that your audience can connect with your characters on a visceral level.

Misfortune is central to our sense of reality. It's why we feel an almost instinctual annoyance when stories subvert this expectation. Human cultures have not ignored this fact. The Chinese character for "crisis" is the character for "danger" in front of the character for "opportunity." All crises, no matter how hopeless they seem in the moment, are filled with hidden opportunities—in your stories, your characters must always see them and act.

Star Wars: The Last Jedi comes close to following this principle perfectly. The story seems to kill off General

Leia Organa, beloved leader of the Galactic Resistance. As Kylo Ren aims his sights on Leia's bridge, holding his hand to the trigger, we see a potential turn in his evil character. Kylo relaxes the trigger and decides not to kill his mother. But the shock of the sight of his First Order wingmen swooping in to destroy the Resistance ship's bridge captures his struggle between the light and dark sides of the Force brilliantly.

But after the explosion, the story saves Leia by having her pull herself back to the ship through her use of the Force. Had the writers decided to go with this bold story choice, killing off a beloved *Star Wars* character so early in the film, would have given the story an extra ounce of meaning and impact, and better served Kylo Ren's character development. Instead, audiences were left divided by the reversal of this plot point.

It's as the author Dennis Johnson said: "The stories of the fallen world, they excite us. That's the interesting stuff." Conflict drives movement, and movement drives stories. Without either, there isn't a story to be enjoyed. Take the following mantra when writing conflict for your stories: Everything will be alright in the end. If things aren't alright, you're not at the end.

> *Happiness is a garden walled with glass: there's no way in or out. In Paradise there are no stor-*

ies, because there are no journeys. It's loss and regret and misery and yearning that drive the story forward, along its twisted road.

—*The Blind Assassin* by Margaret Atwood

Reversal

A story with unending cruelty that lacks any catharsis or humour will suffer in quality because there's no release of tension. Your audience will put down the novel or leave the theatre having gained little from the ordeal, and will be reluctant to read any other stories you create.

Don't take this law at face value. Be cruel to your characters not for sadism, but to provide them with motivations for action and opportunities for growth. Understand that the role of cruel opposition is to portray the darkness before the dawn. Your story will always gain from injecting a little levity every now and then, some bit of comedy that lightens the tension. Remind your audience that you're trying to entertain them, not drag them through hours of drudgery. Your audience will forgive you ten chapters of cruelty if you give them a single line of well-timed humour (see Law 16, Humour Is Always Welcome).

Law 2

End Quickly at the Moment of Catharsis

A story's ending bears a special responsibility — if you fail to meet it, then you'll disappoint your audience and betray the trust they've invested in your story. The ending must provide ultimate catharsis, by releasing the main source of tension right at its highest point. Muddling up the release of tension and creating multiple false endings will only confuse your audience. The ending must also distil the essence of the story itself and provide the moral. Creating the perfect ending requires mastering the art of timing. End a story swiftly — the last act should be the shortest.

Observance of the Law, Part I

The original *Star Wars* film of 1977 follows the protagonist Luke Skywalker on a classic Hero's Journey. Luke starts the story as a whiny teenager, spurning his chores to go hang out with his friends. But on coming across two mysterious droids, and taking some lessons from the wise old hermit Ben Kenobi, secretly a former Jedi Knight, Luke begins a journey of maturation towards the film's climax.

The story pits the brave Rebel Alliance against a vast evil Empire, led by Darth Vader and Grand Moff Tarkin, who relentlessly tracked the Rebels to their secret base. One of the two droids from the beginning of the story carries secret plans on how to exploit a weakness in the Empire's new superweapon, the Death Star. As Tarkin threatens to use his Death Star to destroy the Rebel Alliance once and for all, Luke bravely dives into what seems an unlikely mission to destroy the monstrous contraption.

The tension builds to an unbearable level in the final act, as the Death Star comes tantalisingly close to the Rebels' base moon, and Luke and his wingmen gained closer on the weapon's structural weakness, hoping to destroy it. Then, Han Solo, the dashing freighter pilot, returns out of nowhere at the last minute, and Luke fires the proton torpedoes that destroyed the Empire's prized superweapon. At the height of the tension, the audience breathes a sigh of relief as the day is won for the Rebel Alliance. Within seconds of screen time, the heroes received their medals, and the story is over.

Interpretation

George Lucas's attempt at the Hero's Journey story paid off so well with audiences because of its immensely satisfying ending. Luke evolves from a whiny farm boy into a brave hero, fighting for the plucky Rebel Alliance against an evil Empire. The drama escalates throughout the story as Luke goes on daring adventures with a host of lovable characters.

The final act brings the tension to its pinnacle, as each side races against time to destroy the other. The Death Star gains closer and closer to the Rebel base. The Rebel fighters gained closer and closer to the weapon's structural weakness. And then Han Solo, who the audience believes has fled out of his own selfishness, returns at the moment he is most needed, clearing the path for Luke to destroy the Death Star. They returned to a hero's welcome, and at the high point of the relief and glory, the curtain closes.

The incredible rise in tension, the surprise, the relief of tension, and the glory, all happened in mere minutes of screen time. This precise brevity is what makes the

Star Wars ending so satisfying. The story has already spent two hours establishing the characters and setting up the conflict; all that is left is to resolve the tension in a climactic battle. There is no need to draw out the ending any longer. It is the perfect ending to the perfect Hero's Journey.

> *A hero ventures forth from the world of common day into a region of supernatural wonder. Fabulous forces are there encountered and a decisive victory is won.*
>
> —Joseph Campbell, 1904-1987

Observance of the Law, Part II

Christopher Nolan's *Dark Knight* trilogy reaches its high point in the 2008 film *The Dark Knight*. This part of the trilogy follows Batman and the Joker as they each fought for the soul of Gotham City.

The story begins with an optimistic tone, as Batman and district attorney Harvey Dent put hundreds of criminals behind bars in one fell swoop. But putting all the criminals in Gotham behind bars has an adverse effect. It creates a power vacuum in the city's criminal underworld, and the crime bosses hire the Joker in their desperation to get rid of Batman and resume their reign of terror over the city.

Through the course of the story, the Joker puts Batman through a series of impossible dilemmas, pushing the hero to the limits of his moral code. Each successive dilemma builds the tension up as the story reaches its climax—forcing Batman to give up his identity; to choose between Rachel, his love interest, and Harvey Dent; and to exploit the city's cell phone network.

In the end, after the Joker has ruined Harvey Dent, he sabotages two ferries attempting to leave the city, and gives each other the trigger to a bomb in the other ferry—otherwise, he'll blow them both up at midnight. Though the citizens of Gotham choose the side of good, and later call the Joker's bluff, the Joker laughs at Batman as he reveals he broke Harvey Dent, "Gotham's White Knight," and let him loose on a spree of murder.

Batman defeats Dent as he threatens to kill Commissioner Gordon and his family, only to realise that if the truth about Harvey gets out, that if Gotham finds out that their hero was broken down into one of the criminals he fought, everything they have won will be for nothing. So, Batman decides to take the blame for Dent's murders and rides into the distance as Gordon reluctantly sets the dogs on him. In this act of heroic sacrifice, Batman becomes the Dark Knight.

Interpretation

The culmination of this tragic story in heroic sacrifice is one of the most awe-inspiring endings in cinema. Its emotional weight comes right at the climax of the story's tension, right when the audience believes that the soul of Gotham has finally been lost to the Joker. But at the moment when the heroes realise all is lost in Harvey's death, Batman steps up and lives true to his morals, taking the fall for all of Dent's murders:

> *Commissioner James Gordon: The Joker won. All of Harvey's prosecutions, everything he fought for: undone. Whatever chance you gave us of fixing our city dies with Harvey's reputation. We bet it all on him. The Joker took the best of us and tore him down. People will lose hope.*
>
> *Batman: They won't. They must never know what he did.*
>
> *Commissioner James Gordon: Five dead, two of them cops—you can't sweep that up.*
>
> *Batman: But the Joker cannot win. Gotham needs its true hero.*
>
> *Commissioner James Gordon: No!*
>
> *Batman: "You either die a hero, or you live long enough to see yourself become the villain."*

I can do those things, because I'm not a hero, not like Dent. I killed those people, that's what I can be.

Commissioner James Gordon: No, you can't! You're not!

Batman: I'm whatever Gotham needs me to be. Call it in.

—*The Dark Knight*, 2008

Batman rides into the distance, and Gordon's son shouts after him, pleading with Batman not to sacrifice his identity, only to have his father explain it is the right thing to do for now:

James Gordon Jr: Batman? Batman! Why is he running, Dad?

Commissioner James Gordon: Because we have to chase him.

James Gordon Jr: He didn't do anything wrong.

Commissioner James Gordon: Because he's the hero Gotham deserves, but not the one it needs right now. So, we'll hunt him, because he can take it. Because he's not our hero. He's a silent guardian. A watchful protector. A Dark Knight.

—*The Dark Knight*, 2008

The ending is delivered with immense speed and weight, after a heavy tension-filled plot filled with emotional conflicts and impossible dilemmas. The character of the Joker knows that the only way Batman can stop him is to kill him, which would violate his one rule—to never kill—and reduce him to the likes of the criminals he's sworn to fight. Batman stays true to his morals throughout each dilemma, and does the same in the ending, sacrificing himself in the process.

Had Batman not made his final choice, had there been any doubt or lack of closure on the Joker's plan, or had less tension been built before the climax, then the ending would have been far less powerful. *The Dark Knight* gives us the perfect ending, delivered right at the climax of the story's tension, closing the film's curtain at the height of drama.

Keys to Storytelling

A story's ending must be the natural culmination of all the events that happen in its plot. The end must accord with both the rising tension and the characters' journeys. It must resolve all conflicts specific to that story and let the audience achieve catharsis. The ending is the last impression that your story will leave on your audience, and a story cannot be great without a perfect, fitting ending.

In life, too, the way you end any deed will be how it's remembered. You must plan any endeavour all the way to the ending, lest you come up against some impassable obstacle. What good is it to spend time writing a story, only to spoil it at the end? Leave your audience with a positive and satisfying feeling when they've finished with your story—they'll sit back, sigh, and smile, as all tension is released and all characters developed to exactly where they need to be. The essence of this law is to master the art of timing—all things must end, and you must use tension and character development to find the optimal time to end your story.

Time to Die

Ikkyu, the Zen master, was very clever even as a boy. His teacher had a precious teacup, a rare antique. Ikkyu happened to break this cup and was greatly perplexed. Hearing the footsteps of his teacher, he held the pieces of the cup behind him. When the master appeared, Ikkyu asked: "Why do people have to die?" "This is natural," explained the older man. "Everything has to die and has just so long to live." Ikkyu, producing the shattered cup, added: "It was time for your cup to die."

THE 24 LAWS OF STORYTELLING

—A Zen koan

Alexander the Great (356-323 BC) took Macedon from a small kingdom at the periphery of Greek affairs to one that dominated most of the known the world, extending from Greece to modern-day India. He inspired his army of men to win battle after battle, founding cities in modern-day Egypt and Asia that still bear his name, and did it all in his twenties. What's more impressive, is that he started his journey in the shadow of his father, Philip—who was already known as a cunning and powerful leader—since many children of great leaders fail to live up to their parents' records. History has not forgotten Alexander the Great's impressive feats, but his legacy is tinged by the hedonistic circumstances of his end—dying alone from malaria, resented by his exhausted troops, after his life had spiralled into booze-filled excess.

In stories as in real life, then, one must appreciate the everlasting impact of the ending. Alexander's story ended at a slow, low point of excess, unlike the dramatic pace of his conquests. In contrast, your story should end at a high point of tension, the great crescendo of a rising plot. Extend your story past its natural ending and it'll run out of steam, boring your audience. They'll fidget in their seats, wondering why events are still continuing, but unable to place their fingers on why that is. The pacing of your story should rise until it reaches a climax—end your story there.

There is a simple reason why most storytellers never know when to end the story: They neglect the planning stage and form no concrete idea of their goal. They write the story as they go, telling themselves that they're writing "organically." These are platitudes—what they're really doing is creating an incohesive mess that ends in a way not congruent to the rest of the story. Planning to avoid this is crucial—the crescendo of everything, from the plot itself to your characters' arcs, should fall at the precise moment your story ends.

If you feel like you're stuck on writing your ending, it's likely that you could have worked harder to plan out your story's outline beforehand. Resist the human tendency to react to everything thrown at you, and learn to step back, analyse your character arcs and the story structure, and the solution will come to you. All parts of the story matter and they tightly interrelate. The ending must always feel natural, then, and reflect the core message of the story.

It is a great sin to write an ending that is inconsistent with the tone or message of the story. The ending must reflect and underline the message of your story. Too many writers try to act clever and subvert the audience's expectation with a twist ending. Subversion isn't a bad thing in itself, but with the ending, you must keep it consistent with the body of the story. Otherwise, it won't feel like it has any connection to the real world, and it will be tossed aside as yet another deus ex machina.

An inexplicable twist ending, bearing no relation to anything foreshadowed in the story. is the most common and time-tested way to doom your story to oblivion. Your audience will not think you are clever for doing this—if you try to shoehorn in some inconsistent twist ending for no reason other than to feel smart, you'll only leave your audience feeling cheated of their time, and all too ready to give your work the negative reviews it deserves.

A successful reversal of this sin can only be achieved when the ostensible twist ending was foreshadowed earlier in the story. In *The Prestige* by Christopher Nolan, the ending is a twist, but it is consistent because of the repeated foreshadowing throughout the story. At first, we're shocked, but then we realise it affirms the core message of the film—the three-part magic trick culminating in the Prestige, the final act. The film feels like the completion of a circle. Is there any better way to end a story?

Reversal

What possible good can come from a fudged, ill-planned ending? Finishing your story on an inconsistent note betrays the audience's investment and reverts whatever message you wanted to tell. End your story quickly or you'll draw out all the tension, making your audience check their watches and head for the door.

Law 3

Trust Flaws More Than Strengths

Stories need conflict, and a perfect character without flaws is hard to challenge. It's difficult to make an exciting story about some awesome power longer than a paragraph or two. You can, however, make endless meaningful stories about what your characters cannot do. Don't think that writing your character as an untainted paragon of virtue will make them likeable—actually the opposite is true. People are attracted to each other's rough edges. Your readers will relate more with your hero if they show issues that taint their character.

Transgression and Observance of the Law

There has never been a more powerful fictional super-hero character than Superman. Countless stories have depicted him not only as a perfect, godlike being invincible to any attack but also noble in mind and spirit: an unstoppable force and an immovable object.

It's easy to write amazing spectacles such as flying vast distances at incredible speeds, feats of supernatural strength, and bullets bouncing off his Kryptonian skin like flower petals. Without any physical flaws to speak of, writers struggle to make exciting plots centred around Superman—how could one be expected to create conflict for an invincible character?

Their answer lies in three options. First, and most common, is Kryptonite. Superman's cells decay when exposed to the radioactive mineral from his home planet, reducing his strength to that of a normal man—this is usually how writers give his enemies a fighting chance. In other words, weaken the perfect character to force him down to the same level.

Second, they can write an antagonist even more powerful than Superman. The celestial god Darkseid often fills in this role, possessing vast powers of energy manipulation and instantaneous teleportation, while able to match and exceed Superman's strength and speed. This technique solves many problems in a simple way—why grapple with a perfect character's flaws when they can write in a supervillain even more powerful than he?

The third device is to give him problems that his powers alone can't solve. This technique involves an antagonist threatening Superman's love interest, Lois Lane. He may be invincible, but she isn't, and in these situations, wits and creativity are more valuable than brute strength. These indirect challenges create great emotional turmoil that is more interesting than a straight action fight scene.

The success of this final technique is why a lot of Superman stories spend more time focused on his human alter ego, Clark Kent, who lives an unsuspecting human life as a photojournalist for the fictional *Daily Planet*. The 1978 film *Superman* starring Christopher Reeve as the title character uses this theme, and that of the Hero's Journey, to spend more time showing Superman developing and discovering his powers than using them.

Each of the film's acts closely accords with the Hero's Journey story pattern, calling Superman to higher levels of heroism. The journey from Krypton to Earth in the first act, from Smallville to the Fortress of Solitude in the second act, and then from Metropolis to outer space in the third act. When humanity is in crisis,

Superman was torn in two by the wishes of his two fathers—his Kryptonian father Jor-El, commanding him not to meddle in human affairs, and his adoptive earthly father Jonathan Kent, encouraging him to embrace and use his powers to help humanity. This contrast between the godlike powers of the invincible Superman, and the plain, virtuous Clark Kent provides audiences with a great interpretation of the classic heroic tale.

On its release, the combination of the film's groundbreaking special effects and method of science fiction storytelling engrossed audiences and gave it near-universal critical acclaim.

Interpretation

Superman is perhaps the hardest character to write a story around because he has no flaws, physical or moral. He a powerful godlike being *and* has a noble and pure heart. The only way that writers have been able to write exciting stories about Superman is to use one, or a combination of the three classic Superman foils: Kryptonite, an even stronger foe, or a problem that his powers can't solve.

In every Superman story that's reached critical acclaim, there's had to be some artificial external conflict inserted into the story. Without it, Superman flies about unchallenged, dispatching criminals with ease, and there's no movement to the story at all. The 1978 *Superman* film succeeded by using two key story themes. First, it's an origin story, showing Superman discovering and developing his powers over time. Superman's journey of discovery echoes Joseph Campbell's Hero's Journey—he accepts the call to arms, leaves his comfortable human life behind, and achieves great feats of heroism.

Second, it creates conflict between Superman's home world and his adopted world through the opposing wishes of his two fathers—his biological father on Krypton wants him not to interfere in human history, while his adoptive father urges him to use his powers for good. In this way, the story creates a dilemma for the hero, rather than a problem. The difference between a dilemma and a problem is that with enough time and energy, he can solve a problem with little more than sweat and a bit of exertion—prime fodder for an invincible superhero. A dilemma, on the other hand, lacks such a clear solution, and there is no right answer. The hero has to make a choice that shows something about his character.

As a perfect being, no problem can stand up to Superman; but a dilemma shifts the balance of the conflict entirely. A moral struggle, and a chance to show whether his preconceived beliefs hold up in the face of such an obstacle, provide for an exciting story.

Keys to Storytelling

Characters need to lose battles to win their wars. There's no better technique for showing personal growth, setting up conflict, and building tension. The heroes that never fail and always win are flat, predictable, and provide no tension to a story. They're static, devoid of any movement, and will doom your story to ruin.

A hero who is "just that good" and knows it, is actually far less relatable and likeable than you might think, and many among your audience will hope he falls flat on his arrogant face. As little as we like to admit it, people generally want to see flawless people fail; it's a perverse law of human nature.

Flaws make your characters relatable. A fear of talking to people, stubbornness in the face of helpful advice, and acting based on confirmation bias rather than evidence are some examples of flaws that most people can relate to having. Give your characters such flaws to bridge the gap between audience and story—research common character flaws in books and online to help with this. You can also use flaws you've experienced in your own personal life to add to the realism.

Film director Joss Whedon has discussed the difficulties of putting together a *Justice League* movie together with Superman versus his own *Avengers* stories. Whedon pointed out that the Avengers are easier to write because they express relatable personal issues and are weak enough to write action scenes for. On the other hand, Justice League characters like Superman and Wonder Woman are in practical terms gods without flaws. Other less powerful characters in that universe such as Green Lantern and the Flash are still powerful in their own right and make it difficult to write convincing threats for the group.

Batman, on the other hand, is a shining example of storytelling potential within the superhero genre. In spite of his access to untold wealth and futuristic technology, he is still a vulnerable human being, relying on his intelligence and capacity for hard work to achieve his goals. Superman can fly, throw mountains, and shoot lasers out of his eyes with little effort, while Batman can't do anything beyond what his technology can do.

Up against some villain, Batman's stories will typically show him losing the first encounter, getting beaten up near to the point of death. He escapes, has a moment of self-doubt, and returns to the Batcave. After spending time researching the new foe and training his body, he wins round two. The stakes and the dramatic tension are higher for this final fight because we know the villain beat him the first time. We feel as though we can aspire to be like him because his "powers" are real and rooted in reality. It's precisely his flaws that make him more of a hero than any unbeatable, godlike character can ever be.

Batman's moral code defines his character, and he stands by his moral code in stories like the 2008 film *The Dark Knight* where he sacrifices his heroic image for the greater good of the city he swore to defend. Batman stories have enjoyed consistent critical acclaim because his vulnerabilities are contrasted against his unflappable moral character in the face of often brutal obstacles. He has flaws and often loses, so there's legitimate doubt about whether he'll win. All of this has made Batman more popular than Superman.

> *"Enter by the narrow gate. For the gate is wide and the way is easy that leads to destruction, and those who enter by it are many. For the gate is narrow and the way is hard that leads to life, and those who find it are few."*
>
> —Matthew 7:13-14

The same must be true for your story's characters. Save yourself the headaches of creating artificial challenges for an invincible god, and instead start with a flawed yet loveable hero and work from there. Create opportunities for your characters' flaws to be exploited. State their moral values upfront, and offer a dilemma to challenge those values. We the audience face these choices more often than we might think—that makes such dilemmas all the more interesting.

In less fantastical settings, the *Die Hard* series of films have shown that vulnerability and flaws are great strengths in the action genre. The main character John McClane's likeability stems from his cocky tough guy persona. However, the weariness, despair, and depression arising from the demands of his personal life undercut John's ostensible arrogance. He wasn't on his way to the big city to kick butt, he was there to try to rebuild his failing marriage. The start of film establishes this by showing John's real concern about this to the audience in simple ways, such as his nervousness and fear of flying. Establishing a character's relatable flaws first can be an efficient way of setting up the plot while also creating a real human connection with the audience.

Once the action gets going in the Nakatomi Plaza, every bit of blood on his arms as he crawls through broken glass, and every added moment of exhaustion, shows the audience the clear threat to his safety, and we question if he will make it through the night. But we enjoy watching it because we love John McClane, who is emblematic of the endearing underdog hero.

But as time progressed and the series reached its fifth entry, *A Good Day to Die Hard*, John McClane had become an invincible action hero, losing all the virtuous qualities that made him endearing in the original film. He's shooting people all over the place, stealing a car, and putting innocent people in danger. *Die Hard 5* is a pale shadow of the original *Die Hard* because it forgot the storytelling notes that it had so perfectly struck.

> *I offered them Utopia, but they fought for the right to live in Hell.*
> —*Superman: Red Son* by Mark Millar, Dave Johnson, and Walden Wong

Reversal

You may be tempted to turn your main character into a kick-ass hero who exposes no physical flaws, and it might make for some fun action scenes here and there. But such stories are consumed once and promptly forgotten. Flawless characters are forgettable because they're one-dimensional—there's no room for them to develop. Nothing challenges them to grow in any way. Flaws expose a weak point for your villain to attack and make the character learn a valuable lesson. Character growth is of utmost importance to any story, and therefore you ignore this critical law at your peril.

A flawless hero not subjected to any apparent threats can only form a minor part of an exciting story, notwithstanding an artificial external plot device to provide some manufactured threat. Your story must have a legitimate threat and conflict for the main characters. Don't fool yourself into thinking that your audience likes to see invincible gods for long—they seem impressive to begin with, but are devoid of tension. Thus there is no possible reversal to this critical law.

Law 4

Show, Don't Tell

As a storyteller your role is to immerse your audience in an experience, not to report events. Let your audience arrive at a conclusion themselves with clear evidence: real actions, dialogue, and atmosphere. As a rule of thumb, make your intention to illustrate a point, not to merely report it. By evoking feelings and creating sensations, you bypass your reader's logical brain and let them effortlessly bathe in the rich worlds you build. Think of this as gently directing the natural flow of a river, as opposed to rigidly forcing a dam in its path.

Transgression of the Law

George Lucas's *Star Wars* prequel trilogy came with hype and excitement never seen before in cinema history. Almost twenty years had passed since the iconic original trilogy graced cinema screens, creating a world of potential for story creators in science fiction fantasy. So it was with great fanfare and anticipation that the first of the prequel trilogy, *The Phantom Menace*, ruined all expectations and disappointed loyal *Star Wars* fans, who were left divided and confused by its ambiguous story, reliance on computer-generated scenes, and weak dialogue.

The story begins with Obi-Wan Kenobi and Qui-Gon Jinn being accosted by the corrupt Trade Federation. They discover that the Federation is planning an invasion of the planet Naboo for unknown reasons. The Jedi go down to the planet with the invading force in secret, instead of the more common-sense route of alerting the Republic and the Naboo. The plot of the film is explained by way of exposition scenes, offering little movement or character development along the way. Most exchanges of dialogue are emotionless and lack weight.

The sequel, *Attack of the Clones*, suffered similar problems due to the same narrative sins. What Lucas intended to be a love story to make the audience invested in

Anakin Skywalker's personal development ahead of his fall to the dark side of the Force in the original trilogy, ended up being an awkward and unrealistic romance between two weird characters who seem to fall in love in spite of everything either of them do in the plot.

Audiences were grateful for the prequel trilogy, but an underlying resentment and disappointment boiled to the surface, in stark contrast to the blind denial of the film's poor structure by many. Film critic Chris Stuckmann described this phenomenon by coining the term "Phantom Menacing" for any blind, hype-driven denial of a film's poor quality. Spurning simplicity, common sense, and the vast wealth of feedback from the first prequel, the direction of the plot once again prioritised computer-generated scenery over an emotionally resonant love story.

> *A silly and talkative woman had been boring Lucien Guitry with her vacuous chatter. "You know, I simply talk the way I think," she burbled. "Yes, but more often," he replied.*
> —*The Little, Brown Book of Anecdotes*

Interpretation

Throughout *The Phantom Menace* and its sequel *Attack of the Clones*, every other scene shows characters strolling in front of a computer-generated background, explaining the plot, their feelings, and the conflict in literal terms to the audience. In other words, they are *told* the plot; not once does the film bother to *show* any of these things to the audience. This results in a passive experience with zero emotional resonance.

Had Obi-Wan Kenobi been shown to be an impetuous young Jedi Knight through action, instead of this being literally explained in glib dialogue by his master Qui-Gon Jinn, we would have gained a much stronger sense of this character trait. Instead, we see little of Kenobi's supposed impetuosity. In fact, through his actions, the film shows him being one of the more calm, patient, and clear-headed members of the Jedi-led strike team.

This blatant contradiction in characterisation is one of the film's many plot holes. To make sure your story is taken seriously, never use plot to artificially mould the story to your liking. Instead, rely on atmosphere, tension, and subtext—they're infinitely more effective at communicating your desired theme or character trait. If you fail to show character traits to the audience, then don't try to ram it down their throats through literal exposition—it never works.

In *Attack of the Clones*, had we seen Anakin and Padmé go on dangerous adventures together, developing sexual tension with increasing heat, the story would have been a lot more powerful and believable. Instead, the characters literally *tell* the audience they are in love. A love story requires two characters who spark off one another—the lovers-to-be need to both have opposing viewpoints and ample opportunity to express them. Just like any other form of character interaction, it must be shown through conflict-filled dialogue that conveys the subtext of that interaction—make your audience *feel* the characters' mutual fears and motives.

> *Don't tell me the moon is shining; show me the glint of light on broken glass.*
> —Anton Chekhov, 1860-1904

Keys to Storytelling

The audience will not be fooled by literal descriptions of the plot through exposition. Your story cannot immerse the audience if it reports facts. Even news reporters, whose literal job it is to report facts, often seek the *story* that best hits a resonant tone. You can only guide the audience using subtext: by the movement your story takes, the choices your characters make, and the context of the plot. To report facts is to miss the point of what a story is; your audience wants exciting, immersive drama, not reportage.

Don't aim to communicate a literal picture of the scene in minute detail. Instead, prioritise the details that best convey the atmosphere of the scene—think of what your audience can infer through their intuition. In real life, when someone is angry, we know it without being told—we watch them burst into the room, not looking anyone in the eye, breathing heavily through their nostrils, and the subtext of their behaviour is clear.

Gillian Flynn does a good job in her 2012 novel *Gone Girl* by showing Nick Dunne's feelings about his wife, Amy, by using detailed descriptions:

> *Her brain, all those coils, and her thoughts shuttling through those coils like fast, frantic centipedes. Like a child, I picture opening her skull, unspooling her brain and sifting through it, trying to catch and pin down her thoughts. What are you thinking, Amy? The question I've asked most often during our marriage, if not out loud.*
>
> —*Gone Girl* by Gillian Flynn

Instead of being told "Nick felt intense resentment towards his wife," the audience gets a clear picture of
Nick's frustration through this nightmarish image.
Conveying feeling in this indirect manner causes the
audience to think further and ask questions, driving
their curiosity in your story's outcome. We wonder if
he would carry out this violent act if given the opportunity to do it and get away with it. We wonder what
this says about his character. Is he capable of such violence? Is Amy that crazy? Would he be justified in carrying this dream through?

By showing his dream, not commenting further, and
leaving it open for interpretation, the audience conjures
up a thousand deeper questions about the story. To tell
is to report a fact—nothing is communicated between
the lines and the audience is unmoved. To show, on the
other hand, is to convey an experience and allow the
audience to interpret that in their own way.

Dialogue is the strongest showing device in your arsenal. In Jane Austen's *Pride and Prejudice*, Fitzwilliam
Darcy goes for a stroll with the self-absorbed and superficial Caroline Bingley in the Netherfield grounds
before meeting the story's heroine, Lizzy Bennet.

> *"You used us abominably ill," said Mrs Hurst,*
> *"running away without telling us that you*

were coming out." Taking the disengaged arm of Mr Darcy, she left Elizabeth to walk by herself. The path just admitted three. Mr Darcy felt their rudeness and immediately said, "This walk is not wide enough for our party. We had better go into the avenue." But Elizabeth, who had not the least inclination to remain with them, laughingly answered, "No, no; stay where you are. You are charmingly grouped, and appear to uncommon advantage. The picturesque would be spoilt by admitting a fourth. Good-bye." She then ran gaily off.

—*Pride and Prejudice* by Jane Austen

This scene shows much about Mrs Hurst's snobbery in this brief exchange of dialogue, Darcy reveals his real character by speaking out, and Lizzy reveals how little this criticism affects her by teasing about appearances. Lizzy as the heroine is endeared to us by this one simple reaction to a nasty character. Had Austen told the reader that Lizzy was playful and mischievous, it would have failed to create anything like this level of conflict. We can't make up our minds about one of Lizzie's defining character traits without seeing her nature for ourselves.

Dialogue works so well as a showing mechanism because it's the most natural opportunity for characters to express themselves (see Law 22, Great Dialogue Is About What's Not Said). We often talk about how actions speak louder than words, but words with feeling that express conflicting, relatable motives speak louder than factual statements.

This law has infinite applications in everyday life—most of all in learning. The least effective way to learn any subject is to sit through a lecture delivered in a monotonous tone, the teacher reading dictionary notes verbatim from reference material. Rote learning may do well in passing exams, but it's terrible when it comes to creativity or application. A well-delivered story, on the other hand, will hook your audience's attention and show them what you're trying to teach. Teach your children morals through historical examples and ancient fables instead of scolding them— it'll keep their attention far better and produce less shame and guilt. Seeing an application of the lesson play out in a realistic scenario always resonates far deeper than any dictionary definition.

A Mother's Advice
　　Jiun, a Shingon master, was a well-known Sanskrit scholar of the Tokugawa era. When he

was young he used to deliver lectures to his brother students. His mother heard about this and wrote him a letter: "Son, I do not think you became a devotee of the Buddha because you desired to turn into a walking dictionary for others. There is no end to information and commendation, glory and honour. I wish you would stop this lecture business. Shut yourself up in a little temple in a remote part of the mountain. Devote your time to meditation and in this way attain true realisation."

—A Zen koan

At the age of five, Alfred Hitchcock misbehaved and earned himself a reprimand from his father. Expecting the thrashing to end all thrashings, his father instead quietly sent him to the local police station with a note. The officer on duty read it and locked the young Hitchcock up in one of the holding cells. Terrified and confused, he watched as the officer read out his father's message on the note: "This is what we do to naughty boys." Though he only remained locked in the cell for five minutes, this short, sharp, visceral shock had a more significant impact on Hitchcock's life than any shouting or thrashing could have had.

Hitchcock's early experience may have terrified him, but it taught him that people respond more deeply when shown rather than told. Give people a taste of their own medicine and see how more effective it is at correcting their bad behaviour than merely yelling at them. In his later career, on a film set, instead of shouting at actors who weren't doing their jobs properly, he would suddenly throw a china cup against a wall or smash a lightbulb on the floor. Nothing was said, but his crew knew what he meant and got back to work. This is the highest application of the Show, Don't Tell principle. Study Hitchcock's approach—it will reap untold benefits for your storytelling.

> *I arrived in Berlin knowing not a single word of German. My job was art director, and I worked side by side with a German draftsman. The only way we could communicate was by pencil — drawing things so we could understand each other. The other man looked a little bit like Harpo Marx. We were both designing titles and sets, and finally I was forced to learn the language. Germany was beginning to fall into chaos. Yet the movies thrived. The Germans placed emphasis on telling the story visually — if possible with no titles or at least very few. The*

> Last Laugh *was almost the perfect film. It told its story even without subtitles—from begin-ning to end entirely by the use of imagery, and that had a tremendous influence on me.*
>
> —Alfred Hitchcock, 1899-1980

In war, the ancient Chinese strategist Sun Tzu believed that listening to speeches was too passive an experi-ence to have any deep impact on soldiers. It bored them and didn't create any measurable effect on their skill or bravery. Instead, he advocated making the stakes more real for soldiers by placing armies on a psychological "death ground"—a place, physical or moral, that strikes the gravity of the situation into the soldiers' minds. In the most literal example, a general could make his soldiers fight to the bitter end by pla-cing them near the edge of a precipice or eliminating all forms of escape from the battle—they are forced to fight for their lives by the real threat of death on all sides. A lecture by a leader may be as rousing as he can write it, but it can never have the same impact on his army as a well-timed blast from the opposing force.

As in war, we are profoundly affected by our envir-onment and what we see and feel around us. If those around us are tense and simmering with rage, this re-flects onto us. If those around us are relaxed and casual, then this reflects onto us. Military instructors drill the motto "calm is contagious" into their soldiers' minds to keep them focused in stressful situations. In real life, people don't literally say that they are feeling these emotions outside of therapy sessions. Instead we intuit those feelings from them through the subtext of their resultant behaviour. It's in our nature; it's not something we have to try to do. We crave emotional highs and lows, and to varying degrees we can access these feelings by being present in our environment.

The effect of this law, then, is to make your audience active participants in your story. Telling your audience pieces of information makes them passive participants. While acceptable in small sporadic doses, massive dumps of information will achieve little except bore your audience and detach their attention from the story. The best method of storytelling is to make your audience experience the story themselves—they'll feel all the conflict, tension, and catharsis your characters feel, and the lessons you have to show will be real to them.

> *All this happened in much less time than it takes to tell, since I am trying to interpret for you into slow speech the instantaneous effect of visual impressions.*

—*Lord Jim* by Joseph Conrad

Reversal

Relying on exposition to drive your story forward is like building your house on a foundation of soft sand —it might stand up, but it's not solid enough to keep it there for long. But often it is hard to do no telling at all —it's story*telling* after all. When kept in its place, telling is an efficient technique to set the stage for a new scene. Tell when you're establishing a new scene, chapter, or character, but keep it brief. Use telling to bring the audience up to speed when there is no need for drama, just the necessary facts.

Law 5

Reflect Reality in Fantasy

Even the most fantastical setting must be grounded firmly in reality. Rein in any attempts to add too many alien concepts into your story. Recognise now that these urges are self-indulgent—there is nothing good in confusing your audience. Characters, places, and objects with unpronounceable names will be forgotten. Use real-world names and concepts to inspire your world-building, and give your audience distinctive, relatable characters.

Transgression of the Law

After the wild success of English writer J. R. R. Tolkien's *The Hobbit*, his publisher asked him to write a sequel. Tolkien sent his publisher an early draft of *The Silmarillion* but, due to a misunderstanding, he rejected it without fully reading it.

Thus Tolkien began work on what would later be known as *The Lord of the Rings*, which gained him further fame as a celebrated writer. This three-part series bowled over audiences with its rich, dangerous world and strong characters. Having the commercial success of *The Lord of the Rings* under his belt, Tolkien could return to writing his second novel *The Silmarillion* once more.

Tolkien admitted many times to be more a linguist than a writer, and that his stories were a creative way for him to express the fictional languages he'd created, such as Elvish, which features heavily in all of his Middle-earth stories.

Despite the creative avenues it opened up for him, Tolkien never did complete *The Silmarillion*. But it did delve further into the mythology of Middle-earth than his previous books, forming an extensive narrative that describes the universe of Eä in rigorous detail. The entire origin story of all the gods, angels, and lands in Middle-earth, and that of all of Tolkien's languages are taken apart and each described in pages and pages of detail.

At the time of its final release, critics accused *The Silmarillion* of lacking the same kind of levity as *The Hobbit* and *The Lord of the Rings*. Most of all, though, its most significant criticism was that it gave excessive focus on difficult-to-read archaic languages and many challenging and hard-to-remember names.

Robert M. Adams of *The New York Times Review of Books* called *The Silmarillion* "an empty and pompous bore," and even claimed that the main reason for its "enormous sales" was the "Tolkien cult" created by the popularity of *The Hobbit* and *The Lord of the Rings*, predicting that more people would buy *The Silmarillion* than would ever read it.

Interpretation

The Silmarillion was a critical failure upon its release not because it was a weak piece of writing, but because for the average reader it was like reading about some alien culture in a foreign language.

> *In the beginning Eru, the One, who in the Elvish tongue is named Ilúvatar, made the Ainur of his thought; and they made a great Music before him. In this Music the World was begun;*

for Ilúvatar made visible the song of the Ainur, and they beheld it as a light in the darkness. And many among them became enamoured of its beauty, and of its history which they saw beginning and unfolding as in a vision. Therefore Ilúvatar gave to their vision Being, and set it amid the Void, and the Secret Fire was sent to burn at the heart of the World; and it was called Eä... The Great among these spirits the Elves name the Valar, the Powers of Arda, and Men have often called them gods. The Lords of the Valar are seven; and the Valier, the Queens of the Valar, are seven also. These were their names in the Elvish tongue as it was spoken in Valinor, though they have other names in the speech of the Elves in Middle-earth, and their names among Men are manifold. The names of the Lords in due order are: Manwë, Ulmo, Aulë, Oromë, Mandos, Lórien, and Tulkas; and the names of the Queens are: Varda, Yavanna, Nienna, Estë, Vairë, Vána, and Nessa. Melkor is counted no longer among the Valar, and his name is not spoken upon Earth.

—*The Silmarillion* by J. R. R. Tolkien

The book reads like an encyclopaedic text, with no discernible protagonists or antagonists—most of the characters in the book are all-powerful gods or angels. Close this book and attempt to recite the names of five characters and their races from the above passage. Hard, isn't it? Without personalities and driving motives for us to latch onto, characters are just forgettable names on a page.

To a die-hard fan of Tolkien's series, *The Silmarillion* is a new, fertile frontier to discover in Middle-earth. But to the average reader, none of the characters' names bear any relation whatsoever to names audiences are used to in the real world, especially at the time of its release. This problem ensures that readers cannot discern any concurrent story from the text and that all its characters and their names are forgotten.

In a modern world filled teeming with science-fiction worlds and stories in shared universes, *The Silmarillion* constitutes what we would today call "fan service." If you find success as a fantasy writer, then it's likely that your audience will fall in love with the world you've built in your stories. You can choose to reward the most eager of your fans with a book like *The Silmarillion* if you want. But avoid writing in its exhaustive, terse style when establishing your career—instead be concise and make each character stand out.

Nobody believes me when I say that my long book is an attempt to create a world in which a form of language agreeable to my personal aesthetic might seem real. But it is true.

—J. R. R. Tolkien, 1892-1973

Observance of the Law, Part I

If Tolkien's work on *The Silmarillion* was a flop, that cannot be said for his two earlier works *The Hobbit* and *The Lord of the Rings*. *The Hobbit* takes audiences on a journey of discovery with the likeable Bilbo Baggins, an unassuming hobbit from the Shire.

Bilbo begins the story as a provincial everyman content to live a stress-free life in his comfortable home, trying his best to avoid being bothered by anyone. But Gandalf the wizard and a band of dwarves, led by their deposed king Thorin Oakenshield, turn up at Bilbo's house. The lost dwarves hope to recruit Bilbo as a burglar for their mission to recover their lands taken by the dragon Smaug. A hobbit, they reasoned, will be smaller, quieter, and lighter of foot than a big, clumsy dwarf, and therefore the ideal burglar.

Bilbo is not amused at this rowdy band of dwarves turning up at his home unannounced, eating all his food, and demanding he join them on a dangerous adventure. It seems like it will yield little reward for the likely threat of a gruesome, fiery death. But after much cajoling he agrees to join the quest, realising this is his one great chance to go on an adventure.

However, Gandalf's real reason for choosing Bilbo is because he sees deep inside the hobbit a rare level of courage and determination. This makes him ideal for such a dangerous quest—but it will require a series of perilous dangers to draw it out. At the start of the journey, Bilbo proves his skills as a burglar by saving the dwarves from a pair of murderous trolls who have imprisoned them and stolen their horses. Bilbo, using his wits, keeps the trolls bickering about how to cook them all. Their furious discussion lasts until the sun rises the next morning, turning them both to stone, allowing Bilbo and the dwarves to escape. The dwarves have indeed found their ideal burglar.

Interpretation

The Hobbit captivates its audiences with tales of fun characters exploring a new and exciting world of wizards, magic, and dragons. But it is Bilbo Baggins's character that has the greatest positive impact. Bilbo resembles the British everyman, understatedly brave and fiercely proud of his home. His pragmatism and down-to-earth nature gave the audience a reason to connect with him, and displays of his bravery give him admirable personality traits that audiences can aspire to.

Bilbo, once content to live in comfort in the idyllic rolling fields of the Shire, finds his courage. The story's challenges make him realise the strength inside him he never knew he had. The fantasy and world-building in *The Hobbit* are subordinate to a timeless story of the reluctant hero on an uncertain yet exciting journey—something most people imagine themselves doing one day.

The Hobbit became a classic in children's literature because it mixes the fantastical elements of the world it created with a positive message that all audiences can enjoy, because of the main character's personality: down-to-earth, likeable, and relatable. Write a Bilbo Baggins in your story, and you'll give your audience the chance to place themselves in whatever fantasy world you choose to create.

> *Every moment of a science fiction story must represent the triumph of writing over world-building. World building is dull. World building literalises the urge to invent. World building gives an unnecessary permission for acts of writing (indeed, for acts of reading). World building numbs the reader's ability to fulfil their*

part of the bargain, because it believes that it has to do everything around here if anything is going to get done. Above all, world building is not technically necessary. It is the great clomping foot of nerdism. It is the attempt to exhaustively survey a place that isn't there. A good writer would never try to do that, even with a place that is there. It isn't possible, and if it was the results wouldn't be readable: they would constitute not a book but the biggest library ever built, a hallowed place of dedication and lifelong study. This gives us a clue to the psychological type of the world builder and the world builder's victim, and makes us very afraid.

—M. John Harrison, author and critic

Observance of the Law, Part II

The Marvel Cinematic Universe was born in 2008 with the release of *Iron Man*, a superhero movie about the genius inventor Tony Stark. Stark is a billionaire playboy who has inherited his father's company, Stark Industries, which sells high-tech weaponry to armed forces around the world. Stark demonstrates their latest weapon, a missile called "the Jericho," to the US Army in war-torn Afghanistan—he proudly stretches his arms wide as his deadly creation obliterates the acres of land behind him. Stark's confidence and pride in the display radiate out of him, and he bowls over his military audience. They leave the battered site in triumph, all laughing and joking together, feeding off Stark's good vibes.

After the demonstration, a group of attackers ambushed the military convoy, killing all the soldiers protecting Stark. Waking up hours later in an underground cell, Stark realises that the attackers have used his own company's rocket-propelled grenades against him and his own country's soldiers. This revelation sparks a 180-degree turn in Stark's worldview, and he vows to help people, not hurt and kill them—but for now, he needs to escape, and his shrapnel wounds are killing him. Stark and a fellow captive build an arc reactor to power an electromagnet to keep the pieces of shrapnel away from his heart. They build an iron suit to help destroy the terrorist base.

On his return, Stark designs an even more powerful arc reactor that will power a new, sleeker version of the iron suit. Stark learns from the intelligence agency S.H.I.E.L.D. that his trusted advisor, Obadiah Stane, has been arms trafficking to criminal mercenaries and terrorist groups across the globe. Finding out about an imminent attack from the same terrorist group that attacked him, Stark flies to Afghanistan in his new iron suit and saves a village from his company's Jericho weapon, using the suit's impressive weaponry. This scene combines great action with some slapstick comedy, as Stark struggles to get used to his new body armour.

Stark defeats Stane in the end and the following day, against the wishes of S.H.I.E.L.D., he announces at a press conference that "I am Iron Man." The final scene cuts to the press going crazy at Stark's feet, the billionaire once again on top of the world.

That night, at his home, a mysterious figure emerges from the shadows. It is S.H.I.E.L.D. director Nick Fury, played by Samuel L. Jackson, sporting the character's trademark black eyepatch. Fury explains to Stark that he wants to discuss the formation of the "Avenger Initiative." The Marvel Cinematic Universe is born, with dozens of great stories of similar fun and excitement to follow.

Interpretation

What makes *Iron Man* and the following Marvel superhero films different wasn't only the journeys of self-discovery taken by their protagonists, but also the cast of likeable characters set in a real, relatable world. The characters do not have the same magical, mystical powers of their comic book sources, but instead rely on technology in a world resembling our own—with smartphones, computers, and the Internet. Actor Robert Downey Jr is perfect for the role of Tony Stark, the cocky yet charming billionaire playboy. In spite of their antics, we all love this type of rogue in real life, and characters like them always work well in stories.

Iron Man was notable at the time for its levity, making many jokes at Stark's expense, even in what seemed to be the film's darkest moments. Its genius is in keeping the conflict and tension at an increasing level throughout the film, while keeping a frame-breaking joke handy to keep the audience engaged. The film also includes many improvised scenes, one of which has Stark eating pizza with his colleagues, all of them joking and having a good time. Audiences respond well to unscripted scenes such as this, because they can bring even the most powerful comic book hero characters down to earth—who doesn't like having fun with their friends while eating pizza?

More importantly, *Iron Man* set a precedent for all the Marvel films that followed. In these stories, little emphasis is put on world-building the shared universe behind the stories, which is surprising given the loyalty of the fans to the source material. Whenever the narrative strays too far into world-building, exploring some lore behind the story, some joke always bursts the scene's seriousness. In the 2011 Marvel film *Thor*, the title character spends most of the screen time on Earth, away from his heavenly homeworld of Asgard. The film follows Thor around as he bumbles around New York City, passers-by weirded out by his medieval-looking armour. There's a famous scene in which the main characters enjoy coffee in a diner, only for Thor to smash his mug onto the floor demanding "Another!"

This trend is not just confined to the film series' heroes. *Thor*'s main villain, Loki, the protagonist's underappreciated brother, is a convincing villain not because of his godly powers, but because all he wants is his father's love, respect, and admiration. These are relatable motives that let the audience empathise with him, giving him more dimensions than a mere pantomime villain, but also making him more realistic. Understand: In real life, people's motivations are rarely black or white—while some of us hate to admit it, we usually prioritise our own incentives, which form our motives. That is why we connect with villains with believable motives—we can imagine them in reality.

Keys to Storytelling

A writer who chooses to base their story in a fantasy world musters an even greater duty than normal to make their characters likeable, their struggles relatable, and the world recognisable from a realistic perspective. There is nothing wrong with a fantasy writer falling in love with the world they've created—there is a problem, however, when they prioritise their fictional worlds over basic storytelling principles.

The best fantasy stories inspire, energise, and entertain because their writers embrace storytelling archetypes and manage to avoid getting bogged down by world-building details. Quality fantasy storytelling is a matter of prioritising the questions you ask yourself during the writing process. Whenever you find yourself fretting over what name to give some side character, pause and reflect on whether that character works within the story—a better question is, "how do their motives clash with my protagonist, and how can I represent that conflict?"

We all imagine ourselves creating a stunning new world filled with endless possibilities, but that will never be why people read your work. The fantasy world's purpose is to set the context. Fantasy stories find success because the stories focus on the core elements of storytelling. When this success comes, it is all too easy to confuse the cause and effect. If you're still not convinced, then ask yourself how long you spend thinking about the main characters' names in your favourite stories. You don't at all, because although their names are indeed fantastical—we scarcely meet Aragorns, Thors, or Darth Vaders in real life—they're simple, pronounceable, and they reflect real names. Instead, we remember these characters' brave deeds in the battle of Helm's Deep, their friendship, and their mutual struggles in the War of the Ring.

People remember stories such as *The Hobbit* and forget stories such as *The Silmarillion* because the former embraces themes that are universally relatable: personal growth, courage in the face of fear, and spurning comfort for adventure and new experiences. The purpose of a story is to immerse the audience in an experience, and it is only rare gems that manage to avoid such perennial archetypes (see Law 18, Accord with Timeless Myths). But don't read this as a polemic against world-building, because fantasy gives you the opportunity to enhance the storytelling experience. Because your world is unlike anything your audience has experienced before, they can sit back and enjoy the surprises your world provides.

Starting in 2005, Christopher Nolan's *Dark Knight* series of Batman films had a profound effect on the genre of superhero films. The genre was by no means new, but at the time it was in dire need of revitalisation. A multitude of cinematic flops had made the genre into a laughing stock. Audiences found something refreshingly classic and satisfying in *Batman Begins*—a story set in a realistic city, following a young man as he conquers his fears and accepts the call to the Hero's Journey. The second entry, *The Dark Knight*, introduced a new incarnation of Batman's arch-nemesis, the Joker, as Heath Ledger gave audiences one of the best antagonist performances of all time. The Joker brings Batman's world crashing down around him, and through a series of impossible dilemmas he forces Batman to transcend his limits and become the Dark Knight.

Nolan's *Dark Knight* trilogy proved that accordance with simple yet principal storytelling transcends all genres. Audiences now expected more than just dazzling special effects from their movies—they demanded good writing. But most importantly, these films proved that successful superhero films were grounded in reality.

Since then, characters have become more likeable and have relatable personalities. Action scenes featured in-camera cinematography, putting the audience right in the moment. The computer-generated effects are there, but minimal, and breakthroughs in technology mean that they blend seamlessly into the environment. The characters' everyday surroundings reflect modern-day society with the Internet and widespread smartphones. Any powers the characters have are indeed fantastical, but only pushed the limits of the technology that audiences can already see at their fingertips in their real lives.

When film director Sam Mendes worked on *Skyfall*, the next entry in the James Bond franchise, he took Nolan's work on the *Dark Knight* trilogy as inspiration. Mendes knew that directors could no longer rely on special effects and that audiences now expected good stories. The latest entry, *Casino Royale*, had achieved great success as a simple origin story, with Daniel Craig earning wide acclaim for his first performance as James Bond.

Prior to *Casino Royale*, James Bond films had strayed too far into the fantastical, with cheesy tongue-in-cheek plot lines leaving a poor impression on loyal fans of the franchise. The runaway commercial success and resounding praise from contemporary films had proven that any piece of superhero lore could be revived if the story was good enough, no matter how many past flops it might have suffered. At that time, darker, grittier, more realistic tales were just what audiences craved, and both *Casino Royale* and *Skyfall* delivered.

Good storytelling is, of course, not confined to the fantasy or science-fiction genres, but the crucial factor is their extreme commercial success—*Iron Man* grossed more than half a billion dollars at the box office, and the *Lord of the Rings* film franchise almost reached three billion dollars and 17 Academy Award wins from 30 nominations. Accordingly, Hollywood has taken notes and given audiences more of the same—they have overwhelmingly voted for these experiences with their wallets. To immerse the audience is to put them in a world that accurately reflects and stretches reality, rather than distorting it into an unrecognisable mess. Give the reader details that the character cares about rather than details that you the author care about. That is true world-building.

Reversal

Fantasy stories let us escape to exciting new worlds. We can picture ourselves in beautiful surroundings, perhaps with abilities far from the possibilities of our everyday lives. There's nothing wrong at all with providing this escapism.

The best approach is to draw inspiration from character archetypes and twist them in some way. Add a little spice to the soup. Give them an unexpected flaw that surprises your audience and hooks them in. This subversion of expectations is most potent when you lace those expectations with subtext. Two big, intimidating goons lumber up a hallway, only to carry on talking about foot massages. The stark contrast not only creates humour as the two men stumble awkwardly around the traditionally feminine topic—such unexpected delights are the stuff of real life. "You couldn't have written it," say people as they delight in watching some unanticipated real-life event unfold in front of their eyes.

Your story's alternate universe can only help to make it great, so long as you don't place it in the foreground and it correctly matches the tone you want to set. A dark dystopian future matches a story filled with cynicism and bleak prospects. An exciting, fantastical experience in space sets the perfect backdrop for a space opera adventure filled with loveable characters. Don't obsess over the details of the world you build, and certainly don't change aspects of your exciting story to fit the world. The story and its context form as one, and must fit together perfectly as pieces in the larger puzzle.

However, a talented fantasy writer knows that world-building is nothing more than a garnish to more critical aspects of storytelling like conflict and character development. If your story is like *The Silmarillion*, describing unrelatable characters with godlike powers in a vague and meandering tome that more resembles an encyclopaedia than a novel, no one will want to read it outside of your die-hard core of fans, because there's no reason for mass audiences to enjoy it. It can only serve as advanced material for those die-hards after they've been introduced to your work by a great first story.

> *Many world-builders know better than to contort their plot to loop through every country. They're aware that three countries max is the limit. To fit their 30 countries into the story, they'll need ten plots! Each plot opens with a hero in their own corner of the globe, dealing with their own problems. Since the heroes are barely interacting with each other (if at all), the narration can only follow one hero at a time. In any given scene, nine out of ten storylines are suspended so just one can inch forward. Of course, the heroes will slowly come together, forming an epic finish—someday, maybe.*
>
> —Chris Winkle, founder of Mythcreants

Law 6

Make Your Villain the Hero of Their Own Story

Everyone sees themselves as the hero of their own story, even if they are the villain of someone else's. One-dimensional villains may suit simple minds, but to add deep nuance and rich emotional experiences to your story, write a complicated, relatable villain. Don't pull any punches—clearly justify their motivations with an impactful opening scene. The worst villains are negative, power-hungry, and one-dimensional—avoid these traits like the plague. No matter how you've written the antagonistic force in your story, it must be understandable and strongly argued.

Observance of the Law

Black Panther came near the end of a ten-year cycle of superhero films in the Marvel Cinematic Universe, filled to the brim with loveable characters that drew audiences to superhero stories in a new yet undeniably successful way.

The film's first scene has two young men entering an apartment, checking behind their backs, and opening up secret compartments that contain weapons and maps. Outside the apartment building, a group of children play basketball. One child stops and looks up at the same apartment's window as a flash of light reveals a cloaked body of metal hovering outside it, almost like a spaceship.

Two women dressed in traditional African dress, armed with razor-tipped spears entered the apartment from the futuristic spaceship. The men stand, ostensibly confused at these bizarrely dressed women with shaved heads. With a further shimmer of light, a man comes into view, covered head to toe in matte black armour, and the women immediately bow. His helmet retracts to reveal a face resembling the taller of the two men. This is T'Chaka, King of Wakanda.

The two men kneel at the sight of the king, who smiles and brushes aside their deference, giving the taller man—named N'Jobu, a prince of Wakanda—a hug. Prince N'Jobu excitedly tells his brother news of their progress in America. The king smiles but seems distant. Unfortunately, this isn't just a meeting of brotherly friendship—T'Chaka reveals that N'Jobu's companion is a Wakandan spy who he's sent to observe and report on him. N'Jobu has acted against his original mission to the outside world—he has facilitated the theft of precious Wakandan vibranium, the element giving the Wakandans their superior technology, to arm oppressed black people around the world. In blind anger at this seeming betrayal from his own brother, N'Jobu attacks the spy. T'Chaka, in an attempt to break up the fight, kills N'Jobu. The king cries over his brother's dead body.

The shot cuts to focus on the same young boy outside, still looking up at the apartment window, as the same body of metal flies away into the distance. This young boy is N'Jobu's son, Erik. Orphaned and alone in a cruel world, the boy grows up to become known as Killmonger, a ruthless black-ops soldier with a talent for killing, hell-bent on avenging his father's death. Killmonger has known all along about his father's true status as a Wakandan prince, and the royal pretensions this gives him by right.

Meanwhile, the story's main character, T'Chaka's son T'Challa, has reluctantly inherited the Wakandan kingdom after his father's death in the events of the previous film *Captain America: Civil War*. T'Challa gains the right to be king by defending himself in ritual combat against a challenger, even after being weakened by the formula used to make such rites a challenge for potential new kings.

After winning the duel and claiming the throne, there is one last step. T'Challa must lay down in a bed of sand, and through a special ritual transported to the Ancestral Plane, where all dead kings go to rest. In a heartwarming scene T'Challa is reunited with his father's spirit. The two make a tearful embrace and the former king gives his son some words of wisdom and encouragement. T'Challa wakes up and resumes an action-filled plot as they hunt down Ulysses Klaue, who is threatening to steal precious vibranium.

But Killmonger, the true antagonist of the story, gains passage into Wakanda after ruthlessly killing and bringing the dead body of Ulysses Klaue to country's border. Boldly emerging in T'Challa's throne room, he criticises the king and his advisors for hiding their technology and not sharing it, arguing for oppressed black people around the world. Killmonger challenges the incumbent king to ritual combat to gain the throne for himself. Normally such challenges are not allowed, but Killmonger reveals the lower lip piercing that proves his Wakandan heritage, and the royal pretensions granting him the rights to challenge the sitting king under Wakandan law.

The fight proceeds, and Killmonger, with bared teeth and a mad glint in his eye, easily defeats a weakened T'Challa. In his moment of victory, he picks the defeated king up, throwing him off the waterfall, ostensibly to his death. Though met with cries of sadness from the beloved king's family and his subjects, Killmonger has lawfully claimed the throne of Wakanda for himself, and is thus rushed to perform the same Ancestral Plane ceremony. But his rush to the ceremony is not due to any greed for power.

Killmonger doesn't wake up in the same place that T'Challa meets his father earlier in the film. He wakes up in the same small apartment he and his father had lived in all those years ago. Seeing his dead father at last, he becomes the same young boy he once was. N'-Jobu looks back at him. Father and son have missed each other. Killmonger tells his father of his victory, just as any young boy would try to earn his father's pride, promising to continue his father's goal to help oppressed black people around the world. As the ritual comes to an end, Killmonger once again takes the form of a man. He wipes away a tear with his hand as he struggles to breathe in, resisting the urge to cry. He has had to kill hundreds of souls to meet the father he has missed so terribly, and struggled through years of poverty and loneliness. Though the film's conclusion is far from complete, Killmonger has closed a chapter in his own life.

Interpretation

Ostensibly just another one-dimensional villain, Killmonger is relegated to the background for a long portion of the story, as the film focuses more on the development of the main character. T'Challa has to struggle through doubts and challenges from his own people, and struggles to fulfil his kingly duties. The black market mercenary Ulysses Klaue is set up as a red herring, whose only purpose is to funnel as much valuable vibranium as possible. This lulls the audience into believing that this is little more than a simple tale of heroic realisation, with the new king defeating a one-dimensional enemy.

But when Killmonger kills Klaue and reveals his true goal to take the throne of Wakanda by ritual combat, the story takes a new turn. Killmonger argues strongly for his black kin and the struggles that they've had to suffer with slavery and civil oppression, making us doubt the rightness of T'Challa's predecessors. When he defeats T'Challa we think all is lost for the hero we've watched develop for most of the story up to this point. But in Killmonger's meeting with his deceased father, the audience is hit in the gut with a scene of enormous emotional resonance.

This return to their apartment instead of the grand plains from the earlier Ancestral Plane scene upsets the audience's expectations, and gives us the appropriate alternate perspective. Killmonger's motivation all along is to avenge his father's death. As all young boys do, he just wants to make his father proud. All of his ferocity is really a manifestation of these powerful and relatable motives. In the reunion scene with his father, the choice to show him as a young boy again connects the audience with his core motivation—no-one wants to imagine a young boy losing his father, and seeing the stunned relief on Killmonger's face makes us choke up and struggle to hold back the tears.

Seeing events from the villain's perspective is an effective way of connecting the audience with his motivations, and one you should study and practise. A strong technique is to show the villain's perspective first, almost in the same way one introduces a protagonist. But *Black Panther*'s initial accordance with the more familiar story route of sticking with the protagonist for most of the film, only to present a scene from the villain's perspective filled with emotional resonance, increases the effect tenfold. The character is primed throughout the story to be a ruthless killer, but then reveals to us a set of a strongly argued motives, partly through dialogue with the protagonist, but also through an emotional scene filled with explanatory subtext.

> *Most men are much too concerned with themselves to be malicious.*
> —Friedrich Nietzsche, 1844-1900

Keys to Storytelling

A story is only as good as its villain. The villain provides the main threat to your hero, directly working against their goals, creating conflicts, and motivating both individuals to move forward on their respective paths. Apart from providing movement to the plot, the real power behind a villain's impact on your story lies in the emotional footprint they leave.

That is why the best stories usually have the most relatable and empathetic villains. While we often say otherwise, life is grey and subjective. Good and evil are points of view, and no one ever thinks they are the evil villain in someone else's story. As a general rule, you can expect people to follow the line of greatest self-incentive—this isn't ruthless pragmatism; it's empowering. Life is full of "opponents" who directly threaten us or merely compete for the same goal as us. They're not evil; they're trying to improve their lot, just as are we. Competition is a sign of progress.

Conversely, a villain with little discernible motivation often makes for a boring story. A static, power-hungry villain that offers a mere physical threat to the hero is par for the course in average plots, and you must accept that your story can only ever be great if its villain brings sufficient emotional weight to the table. Understand: Adult stories embrace the shades of grey in humanity. Fail to accept this, and your story is nothing more than a childish fantasy.

You must, therefore, write your story with a deliberate focus on making your villain relatable and his motivations crystal clear. You will surprise yourself by how reliably you can captivate audiences by focusing *more* on developing the villain than the protagonist. History has proven that the best stories play host to the most strongly developed villains, and so you should make it one of your primary writing goals. Fewer stories achieve this than you might think, even though there are many tried-and-true methods of making this happen.

Show the Villain's Perspective in a Backstory

Instead of starting your story from your hero's perspective, start it from your villain's perspective. Show the scene that first motivated him to a life of crime, which made him swear revenge on your hero. Don't hold back; this scene must strike a resonant tone for it to have the desired effect. By showing this to your audience first, you establish the villain's motivation front and centre and give him the proper attention he deserves.

> *Whenever you take on playing a villain, he has to cease to be a villain to you. If you judge this man by his time, he's doing very little wrong.*
> —Colin Firth, actor

The villain in *Fahrenheit 451* is Captain Beatty, the book-burning fire station chief. Beatty grew up educated and well-read but shows a calculating, miserable nature. He has wearily concluded that people are happier without being exposed to written ideas. This backstory is palpable to the audience, who grow to see that his flawed actions at least come from a rational place—we don't agree with his opinions, but we can see how they came to be.

In Tolkien's *The Lord of the Rings*, the opening exposition explains the united armies of Middle-earth defeating the Dark Lord Sauron. We don't empathise with this one-dimensional villain by any means, but he loses his treasured magical ring, killing his bodily form. This establishes Sauron's singular motive: to regain his lost power by finding the ring. While exposition is a risky device, it works well in this case because it combines telling with ample showing—we not only understand Sauron's motivations, but we also feel inspired by the brotherhood between men and elves.

Conversely, in Shakespeare's *Othello*, the villain Iago's motivations are vague—he implies a resentment of Othello because he passed him over for a valued promotion. These events are never seen but instead merely told. While this conflict makes Iago a famed villain, the problem in *Othello* is that these events are implied and cannot have the same resonance. While they add context, a villain's empathy must be shown to have the desired impact.

The 1995 film *Heat* builds at a slow pace, with equal time to develop the two main characters, professional thief Neil McCauley and LAPD robbery-homicide detective Vincent Hanna. While their roles give the audience a strong clue as to their roles within the story, neither character is inherently good or evil. Both are middle-aged men, each with their own set of relatable problems. At the film's midpoint, when the tension seems highest, Hanna pulls over McCauley on the freeway and, recognising him, invites him to coffee. Face-to-face, the experienced yet weary men bond over their problems: Hanna's concern for his depressed stepdaughter Lauren and his string of failed marriages due to work, and McCauley's solitary life of a career criminal which, forbidding attachment and requiring mobility, makes his romantic relationships tenuous. Both characters reaffirm their commitment to their work and to using lethal force if necessary to stop the other.

These problems resonate because the audience sees them play out in the first act. We see McCauley become romantically involved with a young woman and the personal friction produced by his criminal life. We see Hanna argue with his wife and family over his unhealthy dedication to his work. There are parallels in these two men's struggles, and their mutual respect shown in their confrontational dialogue at the story's midpoint makes the confrontation all the more powerful. Take *Heat* as the model of a story that embraces the law of empathetic antagonists by making neither character the clear hero or villain.

Nobody is a villain in their own story. We're all the heroes of our own story.

—George R. R. Martin, author

Give the Villain a Vulnerability

Like all good heroes, your villain must have a vulnerability to set up the right amount of conflict in your story. Most importantly, the vulnerability must be believable. Even a cold, narcissistic villain can have many weaknesses—he grew up with the sharks in a life of crime, while hiding a deep longing to one day live a peaceful life.

The obvious reasoning behind this is that if your villain lacks a weakness, your hero has no way to defeat him. Tying your villain's life-force to a physical object gives your hero a clear route to victory: destroy the object. It provides your villain a counter-motivation of the most transparent and most understandable kind, and there's nothing wrong with writing motivations as simple as these. They're obvious and therefore accessible to all.

A villain must be a thing of power, handled with delicacy and grace. He must be wicked enough to excite our aversion, strong enough to arouse our fear, human enough to awaken some transi-

ent gleam of sympathy. We must triumph in his downfall, yet not barbarously nor with contempt, and the close of his career must be in harmony with all its previous development.

—Agnes Repplier, 1855-1950

In the *Harry Potter* series of books, Voldemort's weakness comes from the fact that his power and vitality lie in the Horcruxes, a series of magical items extrinsic to himself. Voldemort also carries a palpable insecurity from his failure to kill Harry in the saga's establishing act—this forms a deep personal wound at his failure to meet his own demands of grandeur that manifests in more cruelty and ruthlessness.

In *The Lord of the Rings*, while Sauron is the centre for all evil in the story, he isn't actually Frodo's opponent. Frodo's struggle is with the burden he has to carry. Think about it—we never see him fight Sauron, but we do see him carry the One Ring for most of the trilogy. We see multiple moments where Frodo gives into the power of the ring. Its weight is strong, and Frodo is a humble hobbit. His strength, and thus the ring's vulnerability, is in his determination, discipline, and purity of soul.

While we understand Sauron's life-preservation motivation, it's too one-dimensional to make him a resonant character. By making the true antagonism between Frodo and the ring, we make the story about Frodo's self-discipline and power over his desires. We can all understand fighting some temptation or addiction, and how it can be a villainous force in our own lives. In general if you enjoy a story, but its villain seems one-dimensional or weakly developed, then they're not the true antagonist—look a bit harder.

> *Every story needs its hero. And its villain. And its monster.*
> —*Obsidio* by Amie Kaufman and Jay Kristoff

Reversal

Stories lacking a well-developed antagonistic force backed by plenty of showtime are forgotten. Fail to create a strong antagonist and you deny your story the vital conflict and tension required to make it entertaining. On the other hand, the villain character does not have to be a tangible character in their own right—they can instead represent some relatable challenge for the protagonist to overcome. Life is about the grey areas, after all, and you don't always need a clearly defined enemy for your hero. Take a broader view and show your main character—and your audience—that life isn't as black and white as it might seem.

Law 7

Weave Foreshadowing Seamlessly into the Plot

Among their many traits, the best stories are unpredictable. Your audience wants to be led along a path with subtle breadcrumbs. In this regard, assume your reader is intelligent enough to recognise your clues. On the other hand, a twist ending will not be appreciated if it lacks any forewarning. You must learn the art of controlling potential energy— like a bow drawn fully taut, your plot must prepare its twist ending with a graduated series of clues.

Observance of the Law, Part I

Charles Dickens's book *Great Expectations* tells the story of the orphan Pip by taking readers on a first-person perspective through his arduous journey of self-realisation. Set in Kent and London in the first half of the 19th century, *Great Expectations* uses memorable contemporary scenes to establish strong themes, such as poverty, violence, and virtual enslavement. The story also creates a colourful cast of characters, all of whom have become timeless icons in literature. The following passage occurs just before Pip's fateful meeting with the convict Abel Magwitch in the churchyard:

> *Stormy and wet, stormy and wet; and mud, mud, mud, deep in all the streets. Day after day, a vast heavy veil had been driving over London from the East, and it drove still, as if in the East there were an Eternity of cloud and wind. So furious had been the gusts, that high buildings in town had had the lead stripped off their roofs; and in the country, trees had been torn up, and sails of windmills carried away; and gloomy accounts had come in from the coast, of shipwreck and death. Violent blasts of rain had accompanied these rages of wind, and the day just*

closed as I sat down to read had been the worst of all.

—*Great Expectations* by Charles Dickens

Interpretation

The passage above details Pip's observations on the weather, just before Magwitch's arrival, with particular emphasis on the sticky wet mud and the harsh, unrelenting rain. Just as the violent bursts of wind left a trail of chaos and destruction, his partnership with Magwitch will also leave a path of similar chaos and destruction in Pip's life. Dickens creates this dark omen by drawing parallels between the grim British weather and Magwitch's chaotic influence.

Great Expectations is a story of personal growth, and at every stage of the novel, Charles Dickens reflects this growth with a vibrant, ever-changing backdrop of movement and colour. These details are on the surface and keep the reader engaged, but the more astute students of his works know that each detail is meant to reflect some development in the plot. Dickens is a master at foreshadowing and can make even the smallest details blossom into satisfying plot developments when they finally come to turn.

When Pip takes what he later realises is Magwitch's dirty money, Dickens describes the bank notes in disgusting detail: "Two fat sweltering one-pound notes that seemed to have been on terms of the warmest intimacy with all the cattle market in the country." Even the money he gives to Pip smells of sweat, the notes ugly, greasy, and crumpled up. Its unflattering comparison with the "cattle market" also leaves little to the imagination. This rich bit of detail is one of many points at which Dickens lets the audience in on the secret that Magwitch is bad news. It also sets up one of the plot's strongest themes—that money's pursuit alone brings no good to anyone.

Visceral imagery will instantly conjure up the sensations you want your audience to feel, and thus the lessons you want to convey. Describe physical appearances like Magwitch's dirty crumpled bills to project the feelings of deep disgust and shame to come later in your story. Your audience will instinctively feel that your Magwitch character is bad news.

This is the power of material foreshadowing. The audience sees something that associates with an important character or event that will come into frame at a later stage of the story. Crucially, material foreshadowing hides essential plot developments in plain sight. This is the essence of foreshadowing—make the clue obvious without obviously giving away the plot.

Observance of the Law, Part II

Christopher Nolan's *The Dark Knight* tells the story of Batman and the Joker, each battling for the soul of Gotham City. Batman on one side, certain that the people can believe in good again, and the Joker on the other side, determined to show that even the best people can be made to do evil things.

The story begins with Batman and Harvey Dent, Gotham's new district attorney, capturing and arresting an accountant working for the Gotham mob. This coup gives them the evidence they needed to arrest hundreds of Gotham's worst criminals in one fell swoop. Dent's determination and ambition, even in the face of clear threats from the mob, leave an invigorating effect on Bruce Wayne. Wayne sees people like Dent as the real heroes of the city, and that only legitimate efforts can create a stable future for Gotham. Batman's own silent vigilantism can only go so far.

Wanting to learn more about Dent, Wayne joins him and his girlfriend at dinner one evening, asking him questions about his background and motives against the mob. Jokingly speculating that Dent is Batman, they hold up a menu to hide the top half of his face, splitting it in two. Perhaps seeing Dent as the pure and good saviour that he can't hope to be, Wayne says, "Look at this face. This is the face of Gotham's bright future." Dent hesitates to respond, revealing a smile as he says, "You either die a hero or live long enough to see yourself become a villain."

But Dent's darker side emerges as the story develops. Pushed to the limit after Commissioner Gordon's apparent assassination, Dent captures Shiff, one the Joker's henchmen. He ties Shiff to a chair in an abandoned warehouse, and threatens him with a loaded gun. Offering a flip of his same-faced coin to leave it "up to chance," Dent struggles to keep his composure, the studio lighting leaving half of his face in shadow. Batman interrupts Dent just as he is about to shoot Shiff, berating him for his rash act of aggression. He explains to Dent that if word got out about this—the upright district attorney threatening a criminal with a deadly weapon—then all the hard work they have done to put away Gotham's criminals would be for nothing.

The Joker manages to turn Dent by killing his girlfriend Rachel and burning half of his face off in the process. Dent wakes up in hospital to find his double-headed coin burnt on one side. Having lost everything, he goes on a murderous rampage, killing all the people he sees as responsible for Rachel's death, confirming the Joker's hypothesis that anyone can be brought down to his level.

Interpretation

The Dark Knight is a masterclass in foreshadowing, particularly with the tragic arc of Harvey Dent. Dent is set up as a virtuous hero who can bring Gotham out of the mire of crime, including the restaurant scene outlined above. But each of the main foreshadowing scenes does this while giving a subtle hint into Dent's darker potential.

The essence of Dent's character is the duality of using any means for the greater good—on the one hand, he is a shining example of the virtue that Gotham can aspire to; on the other hand, he is willing to expend a moral cost to achieve these same publicly espoused virtues. The film's use of foreshadowing makes this duality clear to the viewer.

Throughout the Shiff interrogation scene, the lighting leaves half of Dent's face in the dark. As Harvey Dent uses violence for what he perceives as the greater good of the city, the cinematography of the scene emphasises the public and private aspects of his personality. This thematic foreshadowing might seem simple, but it sends the right message in *The Dark Knight* because it sets up an idealistic character for a tragic fall from grace, while hinting at the doom on the horizon.

Keys to Storytelling

Foreshadowing is a time-tested way of providing a glimpse at future plot points. It makes critical plot points later in the story seem obvious and feel all the more satisfying. Foreshadowing needs to have the dualistic properties of not spoiling the surprise, while also being a clear hint when viewed in hindsight. Foreshadowing needs to stare the audience in the face without obviously giving away the plot—clearly showing the direction that the story is taking, without giving away any details of the key plot points to come.

People are better than you might think at picking up on hints and will enjoy trying to infer what they mean. By giving them these hints, your audience will develop expectations of how the plot will progress, creating an atmosphere of suspense. The audience becomes curious of whether the theories you've influenced them to develop are indeed true. Is she the murderer? Was it him this whole time? Is he going to give up on his dreams? When you need to add foreshadowing to a scene, your goal is to make the audience ask these questions. Practise this technique and you'll create curiosity, add to the suspense, and make the later plot developments feel all the more satisfying.

Foreshadowing doesn't have to be complicated, but it does need to fit into the scene you're writing. In

Romeo and Juliet's iconic balcony scene, Juliet is concerned about Romeo's safety as she fears her kin may catch him in his act of indiscretion. Romeo responds to her warnings by making it clear he would rather have her love and die sooner than not obtain her love and die later:

> *Life were better ended by their hate, / Than death prorogued, wanting of thy love.*
> —*Romeo and Juliet* by William Shakespeare

This beautiful piece of Shakespearean dialogue is an excellent piece of foreshadowing because it fits into the situation. It's not awkwardly shoehorned in for the sole purpose of hinting at the ending. Juliet clearly warns Romeo about the potential dangers of him pursuing her, and he responds in an iconically romantic fashion. Hearts flutter in the audience, but the more astute among them realise it's a hint at a tragic end for the two lovers. Eventually, he does get her love and dies for it.

The great military strategist Sun Tzu (541-482 BC) put great emphasis on defeating one's enemies through a state of *shih* (pronounced "sher"), not reliance on the size of their armies or the extent of their military technology. The concept of shih is best explained by example—picture the firm bow and arrow stretched tautly, the well-trained race car driver awaiting the green light at the starting line, or the well-rehearsed public speaker ready to take the stage and knock the audience flat. Shih is the state where potential energy is maximised, preparedness is at its peak, and you can defeat the enemy with the least amount of effort.

In storytelling terms, the best foreshadowing aligns with shih. Foreshadowing's role is to lay down the pieces of the puzzle before the audience—gradually, piece by piece, the final result becomes clearer, and the dramatic tension rises. Then, at the story's climax, the dramatic tension has reached its peak. The audience has seen all the pieces, and you can deliver the ending with maximum impact. You can only "defeat" the audience with such minimal effort at the ending through the continuous use of foreshadowing. Study this concept, and use clues to build the tension up to a maximal state of shih. It is the height of strategic storytelling.

See that good foreshadowing isn't telegraphed, nor is it injected into a scene for its own sake—to do so is to misunderstand its purpose. When writing foreshadowing into a scene, don't aim to give some telegraphed omen of future events, but intend to provide an interpretation of your story's thesis statement appropriate to that situation. The opening line of Ernest Hemingway's *A Farewell to Arms* is, after all, "The leaves fell early that year."

The Red Herring

The other side of foreshadowing is the red herring. A red herring's purpose is to dangle a tempting morsel of false truth in front of the audience, with the ostensible purpose of foreshadowing later parts of the story. It is, in fact, a ruse to distract the audience. This classic technique is prevalent in crime fiction, where the audience are subtly directed to suspect a character of a crime through bad manners or a rude tone.

Sir Arthur Conan Doyle's *The Hound of the Baskervilles* contains the quintessential red herring: he throws the audience off the scent of the real murderer, leading them to suspect both the escaped convict and Baskerville's butler, Mr Barrymore. By rudely refusing to answer Watson's questions, Barrymore becomes the prime focus of suspicion. We naturally suspect characters we don't like, so use this technique to divert attention from the real perpetrator of your mystery story.

In both *Star Wars: The Force Awakens* and *Star Wars: The Last Jedi*, Supreme Leader Snoke controls the First Order from a mysterious unknown location, manipulating Kylo Ren into carrying out his evil deeds. His military power and Force abilities make audiences ponder his origins. Is he the former Emperor Palpatine resurrected? Is he the Darth Plagueis that Palpatine refers to in previous films? Audiences are sure that he had to have some link to the older *Star Wars* stories.

The Force Awakens does indeed draw strong parallels between Snoke and Emperor Palpatine from the original *Star Wars* films—he is depicted as a mysterious figure appearing via hologram, manipulating events from behind the scenes, and is a powerful user of the Force with apparent prescience for future events. Nothing concrete is given for the audience to latch onto though, and audiences can only guess at his origins. These tidbits act as the false foreshadowing required for the events of the following film. After Ren kills his father, Han Solo, he shows great conflict; contrary to his goals, the act weakens him. At the time of the film's release, many saw this as a hint that Ren would turn away from the dark side in future films.

At the end of *The Last Jedi*'s second act, Kylo Ren indeed surprises all by murdering his master. By unceremoniously cutting Snoke in half and dumping his body on the floor, Ren has boldly unshackled himself from his cruel master and retaken his birth name, Ben Solo. In one quick action the film reveals that Snoke was nothing more than a clever red herring, and Solo assumes his former master's position as Supreme

Leader of the First Order. Subverting all expectations that he might turn to the light side, the unhinged young man takes the reins by force, leaving events open for the final film in the trilogy.

You too can use your audience's expectations against them. Play with these expectations by using a red herring to create initial suspense through the techniques described above, only to violently dispel them in one swift stroke. The louder your red herring thumps its chest, the more of a jolt you'll give your audience when you reveal the truth. Don't worry about betraying your audience's trust—they will love the surprise.

Reversal

Your audience will roll their eyes at a telegraphed omen which either gives away crucial details of the plot or attempts to set up a sequel before the story is even over. Any different kind of attempt to manipulate the audience's expectations of the future plot is, in itself, also a form of foreshadowing. There can be no reversal to this critical law.

Law 8

Structure Your Story around Change

Whenever you think a story is boring, it's almost always because it lacks structure. An amorphous collection of scenes invariably feels unnatural—like one long, drawn-out scene rather than a complete story. Writers of these stories have failed to think properly about their characters and how they change with the plot. Story structure is, at its most distilled, the illustration of a character's single defining attribute. Plan your story out into a finite number of acts, marking each with an irreversible action that shows an evolution in character.

Observance of the Law

The 1977 film *Star Wars* proved to be one of the first true blockbuster films. It broke many ticket sales records for the time, proving to Hollywood and the world that science fiction films had come of age. *Star Wars* was by no means the first science fiction or fantasy film—*Flash Gordon* and others like it had been relegated to the fringes of cinema. What separated *Star Wars* from its genre brethren were its groundbreaking special effects for the time, superior musical score, the loveable cast of active characters, and a simple story structure that moves relentlessly in a forward direction, that culminates in an immensely satisfying ending.

In *Star Wars*, the main character Luke Skywalker begins the story as a whiny teenager, who despairs in feeling that he is trapped on his uncle's farm on a backwater planet. Luke has little to no direction or control over his life. But one day he stumbles upon R2-D2, a droid carrying an emergency message from a princess of the planet Alderaan, also a member of the Imperial Senate. Following the message's instructions, Luke takes the droid to Ben Kenobi, a wise and mysterious hermit—Ben's presence alone appears to unlock remaining parts of Princess Leia's message. Ben explained to Luke that his father was a great Jedi Knight and that he has no choice but to fulfil that destiny by following him to Alderaan to deliver R2-D2's message to Leia's father.

Luke rejects Ben's offer, overwhelmed by the amount of new information he has consumed that day. Ben does not challenge this and they returned to Luke's farm, only to find his home and family burned. This horrific sight upsets Luke, but he forces himself to look at his aunt and uncle's charred bodies—in this moment he realises that he no longer has any ties to Tatooine. His family and livelihood gone, Luke agrees to join Ben, resolving to become a Jedi like his father before him.

From this point onwards, Luke Skywalker embarks on a series of daring adventures that awake character traits he never knew he had. He shows great resourcefulness in helping Leia escape the Death Star, and mental fortitude after seeing his mentor Ben's death at the hands of Darth Vader. Luke's personal development reaches a peak during his final attack on the Death Star. He chooses to ignore his targeting computer and trust the Force, the natural power within him. Luke's trust is rewarded as his friend Han Solo returns at a crucial moment, clearing the path for him to fire the proton torpedoes into the exhaust vent to destroy the Death Star and give the Rebel Alliance a new hope.

Interpretation

Star Wars is a masterclass in story structure. Luke Skywalker's rise from teenager to brave Rebel Alliance hero is a realisation of Joseph Campbell's "monomyth," better known in storytelling circles as the Hero's Journey. Luke begins the story as a naive teenager, almost dislikeable due to his whining and passivity. It takes a call to adventure followed by the severing of his ties to home that set him against the evil Empire. This provides the fuel to make him evolve into the brave hero that the Rebel Alliance needs to destroy the Death Star and save the galaxy from tyranny.

The story attracted such widespread positive acclaim, and an entire franchise to follow, because of its simple three-act structure. The most important key for you to notice is how easy the film is to follow—study this and emulate it in your own stories. Each act is marked by an irreversible action, designed to take Luke from conflict to catharsis, each testing an important aspect of his character. The shape of this movement is as follows:

1. Luke feels directionless as a young man and stumbles upon Princess Leia's emergency message inside R2-D2. He finds Ben Kenobi, who explains his Jedi heritage. The pair return to Luke's home,

only to find his family, and thus all ties to Tatooine, destroyed. Ben resolves to deliver R2-D2's message and teach Luke the ways of the Force, giving the young boy a new purpose in his life.

2. Ben and Luke recruit the dashing smuggler Han Solo to take them to Alderaan. They make it to the planet's marked location, but the Empire's Death Star superweapon has just destroyed it, and the station's tractor beam draws in and captures their ship. The unlikely trio rescue the princess in a daring raid, but Ben Kenobi dies in a duel with his fallen apprentice Darth Vader.

3. Luke, determined to avenge his dead mentor, joins the Rebel Alliance. They have come up with a plan to use the stolen Death Star plans stored in R2-D2 to destroy the station. The battle seems hopeless as Darth Vader and his TIE fighters pick off Rebel Alliance pilots one by one. At the point of greatest despair, Luke hears Ben's voice, telling him to use the Force. He switches off his fighter's targeting computer. Han Solo returns and clears the path for Luke, who uses his Force powers to fire proton torpedoes into the Death Star's weak point, destroying the station before it can blow up the Rebel base.

The director and writer, George Lucas, admitted to being inspired to create *Star Wars* by two main influences: Akira Kurosawa's adventure story *The Hidden Fortress*, and Joseph's Campbell's concept of the Hero's Journey. Both of these influences are characterised by a central hero, who, starting from humble beginnings, undertakes an epic journey that exposes and tests every one of his flaws. The hero, following a great mentor, gains a higher awareness of himself and learns the lessons that he needs to gain self-actualisation.

Other factors make *Star Wars* a great story, such as the lovable cast of characters and the exciting world of the *Star Wars* galaxy. But each of these factors cannot survive without the pacing and character growth that the simple three-act structure allows. Most of all, you should take encouragement that a simple structure can create such a high-quality story.

Keys to Storytelling

Great stories cannot have bad structure. Neglecting to consider your story's acts and what punctuates them can only lead to obscurity or disaster. It's counter-intuitive, but the best stories don't require big, complex turning points to entertain audiences; instead, they tend to rely on simple structures, because they are the easiest to follow. In its most distilled form, story structure consists of a series of build-ups and intense action sequences that build to the climax, which resolves the all of the plot threads, thus releasing the dramatic tension.

That is not to say that a formulaic structure is the panacea to good storytelling. Instead, the key is in the structure's definition—you must divide your story into defined sections, each with its own build-up of tension, and each ending with an intense action of great meaning to the character. An action can be done *by* a character or *to* the character, though the former is generally preferable (see Law 23, Write Proactive Characters). History has shown us that the three-act structure produces the most consistently satisfying interpretation of the above pattern.

> *I was amused many years ago when a writing teacher of some repute shouted in front of an auditorium that there was no such thing as structure. He went on and on about this. Later, looking at his materials and the terms he had made up for various story beats, guess how they unfolded? Yep, in a perfect, three-act structure.*
> —Write Your Novel from the Middle by James Scott Bell

In *Star Wars*, when Luke returns home with Ben Kenobi and finds his aunt and uncle executed, he realises he has nothing on Tatooine any more, thus ending the first act. He is free to start his Hero's Journey, and from this one action, the real story begins. Getting the story going is the first act's chief role. The second act sees the unlikely trio rescue Leia in a daring raid. Ben Kenobi's death and Luke's subsequent decision to join the Rebel Alliance marked the end of the second act, and so on.

Notice that none of these marking acts are pleasant— always make your act-defining move as cruel as possible (see Law 1, Be Cruel to Your Characters). When constructing your acts, take a step back from your story and draw out each section of the plot, marking each point where the action culminates in a release of tension. If you're struggling to find these points of high activity, or they're spaced too far apart, it's likely that you'll lose your audience's valuable attention. We need clearly defined points of change to punctuate the acts, where the characters or the plot take a clear and deliberate step forward. Design these movements around the characters—they have to mean something *to them*. Make your arrogant character see his true reflection, make your lazy character see the potential he's wasting, and make your rude character see the effect she has on people around her.

At the root of every boring story is a failure to create a deliberate, purposeful, and cohesive structure. Every individual element of the story must work together to form this single entity that we keep calling the story's structure. That is why we have consumed, and learned from, fables for thousands of years—they consist of a moral tightly wrapped into a short story. That is the height of structure in storytelling.

> *Structure is required in all of art. Dancing, painting, singing, you name it—all art forms require structure. Writing is no different. To bring a story to its full potential, authors must understand the form's limitations, as well as how to put its many parts into the proper order to achieve the maximum effect... There's a simple reason story structure is so important, and that reason is the simple fact that structure is what shapes character and conflict into an intellectually and emotionally resonant journey.*
> —*Structuring Your Novel* by K. M. Weiland

Reread or rewatch any one of your favourite stories, and upon inspection, you will notice that it conforms to a shape resembling the three-act structure. It is no accident. The three-act structure resembles the same pattern told in stories across a thousand cultures. The mythologist Joseph Campbell famously called this three-stage linear structure the Hero's Journey. By studying the myths of a thousand different cultures, Campbell saw the same universal patterns in their coming-of-age stories. Since these same story patterns occur so consistently across different cultures, he argued that they must come from deep within the human psyche. In other words, inspiring heroic stories are a natural product of human nature.

The writer John Yorke analysed how stories work in this way, and gave his own descriptive names to each of these three stages in his book *Into the Woods*. Each stage's name is descriptive of how they affect the main character, as follows:

1. Establish a flawed character—"Thesis" or "Love"

2. Confront them with their opposite—"Antithesis" or "Hate"

3. Synthesise the two to achieve balance—"Synthesis" or "Understanding"

In the beginning, introduce the main characters by showing how they do things in their normal lives. Try to hook the audience in with an opening scene that shows them a brief yet telling thesis statement of the hero's situation. Let your viewers invest in them and the normality of their home world. Your goal is to show them exercising their main flaw (the "lie your character needs to believe" as K. M. Weiland calls it) that holds their fragile world together. For Luke Skywalker, it is that he can't leave his boring life on his uncle's farm. For Thor, it is his perceived infallibility, the unconditionality of his place on the throne, and the primacy of military glory above peace and mutual prosperity.

The beginning transitions into the middle when an incident occurs which irreversibly forces your characters out of their normal life. For Luke Skywalker, it is the Empire destroying his home and family. He no longer has any ties to his home world and can finally leave it to create some influence over his own life. For Thor, it is his father Odin taking away his godly powers and banishing him to live as a mortal on Midgard (Earth in Norse mythology). By this point in the story, the characters have made their motivations clear, and the audience should know what threatens the protagonists.

The middle portion shows the characters attempting to solve the problem, only to find themselves in even worse situations. Think of this as the "out of the frying pan, into the fire" moment. Do not hesitate when you escalate the tension—err on the side of cruelty by threatening what your characters treasure most. The purpose of these challenges is to bring out the best in the characters, because, as in real life, how they act in the face of such obstacles says everything about their true character.

The middle transitions into the ending when the characters can act on the lessons they have learned from their trials. For Luke Skywalker, witnessing Obi-Wan's defeat at Darth Vader's hands makes him realise that his wise mentor is gone and that he can only rely on himself. For Thor, it is being knocked flat on his face, coming to the realisation he will not regain his divine hammer Mjolnir until he proves himself worthy, by saving others before rushing headlong into battle.

If you have correctly shown what the character values at the beginning of the story, then you will know what to threaten in the middle—and you must threaten it hard. The impact of this threat is proportional to how well you have developed the character's motivations and investments in the beginning. Thor's loss of his powers and his hammer hit him hard only because so much time has been spent showing how tied he is to his destiny as rightful king of Asgard. It is the harshest —and therefore the best—test a storyteller could have given him. Study this tenet and see that it applies to real life just as well as to great stories.

> *If the movie is written well, the audience will be fooled into thinking that at least one of the second-act problems is really the big third-act problem.*
>
> —*Win Bigly* by Scott Adams

In the end, all the central tensions of the plot are brought to their highest points and resolved in a moment of satisfying catharsis. The finale begins at your character's lowest point, and ends at his highest point, as the stakes rise to their highest level. Your ending must complete every thread of the specific story (the situation is different for series of multiple stories, see Law 13, Series Are a Right, Not a Privilege). Every delicate piece of foreshadowing you have laid down comes to fruition, and you must resolve the conflict between the protagonist and the antagonist. The worst sin that an ending can commit is to make the audience look back on the main plot and ask, "Why did any of that matter?" An unfaithful and inconsistent ending leaves us with a feeling of disgust like our time has been wasted. Avoid this by planning right to the end.

In his book *Thus Spoke Zarathustra*, Friedrich Nietzsche describes the transformation of the soul as a series of three stages, each punctuated by a metamorphosis of the soul. The metaphor that Nietzsche describes is as follows. At the beginning of life, a person is a camel—they bend down and accept the rules of society. They become civilised by learning and obeying all the rules put upon them by society. In the period of youth, the camel rises to its feet and makes its way to the desert where it becomes the lion. The mission of the lion is to defeat and kill the dragon. This dragon's name is "Thou shalt," and under each scale of this dragon "Thou shalt" is imprinted. The metaphor of the dragon is that the camel's rules become obstacles as the dragon works to exterminate the lion's "I will." The lion fights bravely, overcoming the fearsome dragon's commands. He tears off each "thou shalt," representing his power over his own decisions. Once the dragon is dead, the soul becomes a child—it follows its nature, beholden to no one.

Nietzsche's metaphor might seem odd to modern audiences, but it beautifully captures the spiritual growth of a hero overcoming the oppressive antagonistic force. He begins the story as the beholden camel, weighed down by the onerous duties that society places upon it, even though it longs to leave its safe home and experience some danger and excitement. The home represents the safe yet oppressive reality that the hero must leave in order to grow. Motivated by the trials of the harsh desert, the camel becomes the lion—a potent creature capable of brave deeds. The hero thus decides to extinguish all limitations by slaying the dragon. The dragon's name "Thou shalt," represents the oppression that the hero must overcome. The lion's essence is "I will," and he shouts "No!" as he refuses the dragon's imposition. As the lion slays the dragon, so the hero defeats the antagonistic force, gaining the freedom to follow his own will in the final child stage.

> *The way of the carpenter is to become proficient in the use of his tools, first to lay his plans with a true measure and then to perform his work according to plan. Thus he passes through life.*
> —*The Book of Five Rings* by Miyamoto Musashi

Do not discount structure for your story just because it seems cliché to the narrow-sighted community of critics and other writers. See these people for what they are: a vocal minority. The three-act structure has been used to great effect in many timeless stories that have proved themselves as perennial sellers. Study history and the consistency of these successes, not the fleeting and self-gratifying words of contemporary critics. Understand: Your focus must be your audience and providing a satisfying experience for them—you do not serve critics nor other writers.

Do not worry about following this structure to the letter either. The critical part of this is not necessarily the number of acts, nor their content, but the deliberation of your plan and the strategy behind a specific structure based around character actions—the pattern of the lie, conflict, rising tension, truth, and catharsis. You don't have to choose the linear three-act structure for your stories. You can profit from taking the core story pattern and extending it to whatever type of structure you choose.

Finally, do not fret that your story's length impedes its structure. For a tale of epic proportions, it simply requires more detailed subdivisions—divide it into the three sections, and further divide each of those into a miniature beginning, middle, and end. There are reasonable limits, and you must never ramble. Fyodor Dostoyevsky's novels are famously long, but have met with everlasting acclaim by following this rule. Understand: A story's worth lies in the clarity of its movements and the immersive capability of the experience it conveys—not in any arbitrary measure of length.

A visitor to the factory of the Ford Motor Company happened to meet Henry Ford himself.

Pointing to a finished car, Ford proudly declared, "There are exactly four thousand, seven hundred and nineteen parts in that model." Impressed that the president should have such details at his fingertips, the visitor subsequently asked a company engineer if the statement were true. The engineer shrugged his shoulders. "I'm sure I don't know," he replied. "I can't think of a more useless piece of information."

—The Little, Brown Book of Anecdotes

Akira Kurosawa's epic samurai film *Seven Samurai* is almost three and a half hours long with an intermission, yet it feels shorter because it moves so deliberately. Beginning in sixteenth-century Japan, a weak shogun oversees a land filled with power-hungry lords, masterless rōnin samurai desperate for work, and criminals preying on the weak and hungry. Under the guidance of their town leader Kambei Shimada, the peasants of a town leave in search of six samurais desperate enough for food to help protect them. One of them, Kikuchiyo, who is secretly the orphaned son of a farmer, sees the perfect opportunity to get some food by passing as a samurai.

Together, the samurai and the peasants journey back to the town and, although they're met with scorn, they gain many opportunities to prove their worth to their new hosts by defending the town from cruel marauders. In this detailed first act, Kurosawa sets up the conflict by identifying the antagonists through their deeds, and brings together the ensemble of protagonists through a logical sequence of events.

The example of *Seven Samurai* shows that the only caveat to story length is a great burden to make the cuts in structure clear. Do not let your story meander, and ensure that every beat is deliberate.

Your story structure does not have to be linear in terms of time either. Quentin Tarantino's 1994 film *Pulp Fiction* has a non-linear plot, told end-to-beginning-to-middle-to-beginning-to-middle-to-end. The film starts with the first half of the end scene, and then shows how Jules and Vincent started that same day without explaining this sequence. The film has three different plot threads that all work together towards the climax. This structure may seem insane after all we've just discussed—but it in fact proves the opposite, that clarity of movement and a deliberate structure transcends time itself. It is widely considered among the best films of all time, and all who have seen the film come away feeling satisfied.

Pulp Fiction works because the individual scenes are self-contained and do not require much context, and each successive scene succeeds in building on the previous one. The beginning is a light-hearted introduction to Jules and Vincent by watching how they work, with some memorable dialogue. The middle of the story develops the conflicts further, as Mia Wallace overdoses on Vincent's heroin, and Butch Coolidge reneges on his boxing match-fixing deal by defeating and killing his opponent in the ring. If the story was told on a linear timeline, the rise in tension might not be as congruent.

The point to these examples is to show that while structure is infallible, it is flexible, and you should not follow it like a strict set of instructions. When Napoleon Bonaparte was asked what principles of war he followed, he replied that he followed none. He conquered the rigid Prussians, and most of Europe, by using his genius-like ability to respond to and capitalise upon circumstances. The essence of this law is not that you rigidly follow a past expert's structure, but that you create *a* structure that works for your story.

History has indeed shown us that the three-act structure most often works best, but in truth, it is the stories that move in the clearest way that succeed and last the longest. As long as your story has some semblance of a defined beginning, middle, and end, you'll form a suitable structure for keeping your audience's attention.

Few write as an architect builds, drawing up a plan beforehand and thinking it out down to the smallest details. Most write as they play dominoes: their sentences are linked together as dominoes are, one by one, in part deliberately, in part by chance.

—Arthur Schopenhauer, 1788-1860

Reversal

It is a romantic idea to think of the tortured writer relying on successive bursts of genius, but it is rarely practical. Over enough time, far more writers will find success by outlining and working on the structure of their stories. Not only does it produce a better end product, but this conscious act of outlining and structuring makes your job more manageable in the long run. No possible good can come from ignoring this critical law.

Law 9

Subvert Expectations

Audiences are good at recognising genre tropes. The only times you truly shock your audience will be in the moments your story subverts the expectations they have formed about the story's genre. Use this fact to your advantage. Pick a story trope, hint at it a little, only to completely subvert it— you can repeat this trick endlessly. Lead your reader down a road they think they know. As they recognise the ostensible ending in the distance and walk towards it, they don't see the unexpected hidden trap you've laid at their feet.

Observance of the Law

In Jordan Peele's *Get Out*, we meet a young black man named Chris and his white girlfriend Rose as they make their way to Rose's parents' country estate. Rose reassures Chris after he jokes that her family won't "chase him off the front yard," revealing his nervousness at meeting her wealthy white parents.

On the way, they hit a deer, and the police come to investigate the incident. The policeman asks for Chris's identification, but not Rose's. Chris, familiar with this situation, complies, but Rose reacts with anger, bothered at what seems like racial profiling. The officer backs down and doesn't report the deer incident.

The couple reach the Armitage house and we meet Rose's parents, neurosurgeon Dean and hypnotherapist Missy. The encounter becomes awkward after a few racially insensitive non-sequiturs by Dean, such as "You know, I'd have voted for Obama for a third term," with no referential context. Chris, once again used to such situations, smiles and plays it off as benign nervousness on Dean's part. But several more events like this occur. Rose's brother Jeremy expresses some assumptions about Chris's natural athleticism in an uncomfortable way—espousing his love of Mixed Martial Arts, he drunkenly tries to put Chris in a chokehold. Rose has had enough and vents her frustrations in front of Chris, who begins to feel more uneasy as these events pass. Further creepy encounters with the workers on the Armitage estate, whom he notices are all black, make strange noises in his presence, bursting into tears for no apparent reason.

The Armitages host a party at their estate, where more of these weird situations happen, but more insidious than before. Women walk straight up to Chris and feel his muscles, and other guests come out with non-sequiturs describing their admiration for black public figures such as Tiger Woods. He meets another black man, Logan King, whom Chris recognises. He decides to take a photo of Logan, but leaves the flash on by accident—Logan wakes up from his trance and begins screaming at Chris to "get out." The family try to pass off Logan's erratic behaviour as an epileptic seizure. However, Chris's friend Rod, an agent in the TSA confirms his suspicions that Logan closely resembles a young man who has been missing for months. The situation, growing weirder and more discomforting with every scene, comes to a head as he finds some old photos of Rose in prior relationships with black men, revealing that Rose had lied when she told him he was her first black partner.

Interpretation

Many great writers have profited from exploiting the myriad of tropes in the horror genre. *Get Out*'s subversion of so many of these firmly established horror tropes makes it stand out among the pack. Plot twists and subversions of tropes do not require a single moment of great surprise; all they require is a deep study into the genre's most established patterns, an establishing sequence that appears to accord with them, and then a subtextual disruption of those patterns by achieving the same ends in a new way.

Horror stories typically succeed by building tension through discomforting situations. 1979's *Alien* builds tension by accompanying the unsuited crew of the *Nostromo* through a mysterious alien craft. This storytelling technique works well because the *Nostromo*'s crew aren't specialists in exploration or science, they are effectively space truckers. They are unfamiliar with seeing structures so different to their own, and their simultaneous awe and unease reflects onto the audience. We relate to the crew's experience because we imagine ourselves having similar reactions to the film's horrific events.

Get Out accords with this expectation but in a different way—by building tension through what the film's director Jordan Peele called "racially clumsy" moments. The main character Chris is black, visiting his white girlfriend's rich parents on their country estate. The racially clumsy dialogue is there but it isn't seen in an evil light—race aside, the awkwardness of Chris's first meeting with his in-laws is something we can all relate to.

The discomfort grows as Rose's brother makes some strange and insensitive comments about black people's athleticism. These comments seem to infuriate Rose, who seems more affected by all of these incidents than Chris. He isn't thrilled about them either but isn't as upset as she is, because the racial clumsiness isn't a new thing for him. Rose's rants are a subtle way of building trust with the audience because it's yet another relatable situation. This step is important, because it acts as a red herring in the face of the film's indirect disruption of that same hint—it makes the successive shocks even greater.

Get Out manages to stand out as a unique gem in the horror genre by subverting many of its long-established tropes. Though there is plenty of violence at the end, it does not require any of that to build the discomfort—it is amply supplied by the social awkwardness created by a racially clumsy series of events that strike a deeply resonant chord with the audience. Audiences had not seen this done before in a horror film, generating the great surprise and joy that won Jordan Peele critical acclaim and many awards on his directorial debut.

> *In other words, the story does not trick the player, it is the player that tricks himself.*
> —Hideo Kojima, video game designer

Keys to Storytelling

The simplest way to subvert expectations is as follows: establish a trope, reinforce it to build the audience's trust, and then show the twist. It's bait and switch in its most basic form. The most important thing to remember with this law is that the expectation lives in the audience's mind—there must be no explicit confirmation that their expectations are correct, only a couple of misleading clues. You give them multiple chances to wake up and realise what's about to happen, but cast doubt at the same time, and when you deliver the twist, they realise the trust was obvious all along.

In *The Hound of the Baskervilles*, Sir Arthur Conan Doyle creates the quintessential red herring—he tricks the audience into believing that the family's butler and the convict are the perpetrators of the story's crime. Sir Arthur's master stroke was in playing to human nature—namely in the way he shows the butler's defensiveness at Watson's questioning and in the suspicious way he goes about his work. The butler's refusal to answer Watson's questions sets off our alarm bells: isn't that what all criminals do? Second, his snootiness sets off further alarm bells, because we take an instant disliking to characters like this in real life.

Of course, *The Hound of the Baskervilles* was a trailblazer on this front, and in the centuries after its release, the defensive and rude red herring character became a trope in itself. You must study your genre, learning the tropes and expectations of the current times. These tropes change and shift over time, so keep your ear to the ground and make note of the patterns in plots and characters. If the subversion tactics of *Get Out* end up becoming common in the horror genre, you must do a 180-degree turn and subvert *those* expectations. This is the height of creativity.

No matter the genre, and whatever the trope, the timeless quality of the subversion of expectations is in the pattern as described above. First, establish the trope in some superficial way. Second, reinforce the trope with some obvious action—show this to the audience to build their trust. Third, subvert the trope. This three-step process is repeatable and straightforward—the only variables are the genre, the audience's mind, and the trope itself. These are the elements you must monitor to ensure your subversion will work. Awareness of them is critical for the serial subverter, so if you develop a reputation for doing this, then subvert *that* and write more plainly to keep your audience guessing.

In Zack Snyder's film adaptation of *Watchmen*, Adrian Veidt is set up as a preening and effeminate executive, more concerned with his wealth and status than anything heroic. But upon being cornered by a shooter, he uses his supernatural strength to rip a tall floor lamp out of the ground and beat the assassin senseless with it and finally choke him to death. Snyder further subverts the audience's stereotypical expectations of Veidt's effeminate character when it transpires that he hired the assassin himself as a distraction from his nefarious long-term plan. In a similar way to *Get Out*, *Watchmen* subverts cultural stereotypes to shock the audience and make them beg for more.

Reversal

As with foreshadowing, any attempt to resist a subversion of a trope is itself an attempt to subvert. This is a risky manoeuvre since it may only satisfy the savviest of audiences. You should subvert expectations in a way that's congruent to the main story, and not take it as an opportunity to show how talented you think you are—don't make a deus ex machina. The key to any subver-

sion of plot is not in the degree of the twist, but the in-
directness in its formation—there is no explicit reason
for your audience to expect a given trope, it's a matter
of playing with their expectations.

> *Don't be surprised at Fortune's turns and*
> *twists: That wheel has spun a thousand yarns*
> *before.*
>
> —Hafez, poet, fourteenth century

Law 10

Conflict Is Everything—Guard It at All Costs

Stories don't require a lot of material to work well. Do not underestimate the simple power of playing host to a cast of likeable characters all in conflict with one another. Most of us feel timid in our daily lives, afraid to rock the boat—this may work in real life, but in storytelling it is suicide. The most reliable way to improve any story is to dial up the conflict between its characters. No one wants to read a story about sweet characters on the same wavelength who agree on everything. Create sparks and don't be afraid to start a fire.

Observance of the Law

In 1947, a playwright named Arthur Miller was at his wit's end. His first play, *The Man Who Had All the Luck*, had been a flop, lasting only four performances on Broadway. Miller had previously written some radio plays and even the screenplay for a film, but the world of Broadway theatre was proving to be a tougher pro-position. He could not let his next play, *All My Sons*, suffer the same fate. Miller had based this play on the true story of the Wright Aeronautical Corporation's conspiracy to knowingly supply defective aircraft parts during the Second World War. A real-life tale full of hypocrisy, selfishness, and intrigue would surely have rich potential for a good play.

In *All My Sons*, the main character Joe Keller is a wealthy factory owner. His wife Kate lives in the hope that their son Larry, who went missing in action in the Second World War, is still alive. After three years of waiting on Larry's fate, the Kellers' son Chris wants them to move on and finally accept Larry's death, which would allow him to marry Larry's former fiancée Ann. The audience learns that Ann's father is in prison for patching and sending out defective aircraft engine parts while working in Joe's factory—Joe was also been charged and convicted of this same crime as the business owner, but exonerated on appeal. While

Ann's father suffers in prison, Joe has returned home to his family and grown his business further.

As each character's façade of politeness thins, the plot thickens. It becomes clear that each character has their own strong motivations. Deep down, Kate is distraught at the likely death of their son Larry, and Chris's plan to marry Ann would make Larry's death real. Joe acts defensively about his past conviction for fraud and the criminal negligence that mired his aircraft engine business, but it becomes apparent that he is in denial over his role in the crimes that cost the lives of his countrymen and those close to him. Ann's suffering from her father's imprisonment and the unfairness surrounding it further succeed in firming Joe's denial into steel.

These combined tensions all rise over the course of the story. There is an uncomfortable undertone of resentment between all the characters. The reasons for the Kellers' mutual denial of the true events crystallises in the story's final act as they stop holding back, arguments break out, and everyone's desperation is made clear as Joe reveals the truth about his role in the engine part scandal. Each character has multiple mixed motives, whose contradictions cause further frustration and conflict. The contending values in each character over the protection of their family, versus the importance of objective moral integrity, show the power of corruption and its effects.

After an hour or so of tense and subtext-filled dialogue between the play's characters, audiences clutched at their seats, gasping at the story's final resolution. Miller had succeeded in taking a small cast of characters in a simple setting and turning that into a drama filled with resonant themes such as flawed ambitions and burning resentments. It all demonstrates conflicts that provided endless movement and emotion. *All My Sons* was an immediate success.

Interpretation

The perennial success of *All My Sons* proves that a great story doesn't need a large all-star cast or a wondrous setting. Above all, a story needs *conflict* like a human needs oxygen. The crucial application of this principle in *All My Sons* is that each of the play's characters has clearly defined motivations going into the story: Joe is defensive and in denial of his crimes; Kate is in denial over the death of her son, and her husband's complicity in it; Chris is torn apart by loyalty to his family and the prospect of a new life with Ann, who in turn wants Chris to shed his dependency on his family. None of these motives are ambiguous because they're on display throughout the course of the play, in scenes that pit each of these conflicting motives against each other.

All My Sons will continue to enjoy countless Broadway revivals and paperback reprints due to its raw, distilled accordance with this time-tested law of storytelling. Had the characters all treated each other with reasonable politeness and reached a mutually satisfying conclusion, the story would have bored its audience to tears. There's no need for complicated subplots and a massive cast of varied characters, just a cast of characters designed from the start to have understandable conflicting motives. Understand: Conflict is the engine of life. If you take a story and distil it a dozen times, you're left with its conflict. In any given scene, raise the stakes, get everyone's passions high, and stoke that fire. There will always be the possibility of great conflict and tension.

> *Conflict is what story is all about. Without it, the character would achieve his goal in minutes, all the loose ends would be tied off, and the story would be happily ever over. That may be nice for the folks in your story, but it's going to bore readers into rigor mortis... Don't be afraid of creating characters who spark against each other. Arguments should abound, even among*

friends. In life, we often think of likeable people as nice people. But, in fiction, that's not quite how it works. In fiction, nice characters are conflict-sucking vampires out to sap your book's lifeblood and leave the story pale and limp in your readers' hands.

—*Structuring Your Novel* by K. M. Weiland

Keys to Storytelling

In the realm of storytelling, there is no higher priority than the creation of conflict: clashing motives, exposed flaws, and obstacles to people's dreams. A story without conflict is little more than a news report—and even the news reporters are doing better at storytelling these days than we like to admit. The trouble is that most storytellers spend too much attention on things that are not related to the interpersonal conflict between their characters, or the obstacles blocking the protagonist's path. They focus on world-building, they fret over how to optimise their writing schedules. If the protagonist meets all of her goals in act one without any challenges, while getting on politely with all of the other friendly characters, then there isn't much there in the way of exciting drama.

Conflict drives a story forward, creating new events, and pushes characters to act, providing struggles for them to overcome. If you're struggling for a concrete understand of what conflict actually is, then replace it with the term "chaotic friction." An obstacle causes character A to act, which further causes them to argue with character B, which further alienates character A into even more action, and so on. In other words, a small amount of change at the beginning leads to a larger unpredictable effect later on. Audiences delight at stories that unfold in such a way, and you need to use the notion of chaotic friction to your advantage to achieve the same ends.

Stephen King once explained how he would often start his novels: He would begin by placing a cast of characters in a difficult situation and let them work their way out of it in as intuitive a way as possible. This approach meant that the audience didn't have to look too hard to find the primary conflict, and it forced him into writing proactive characters that bump up against each other (often in bloody ways). Baking conflict right into the story's setting is a powerful approach because it optimises the writing process.

However, King also claimed that even he didn't know what would happen next as he was working on his novels. Such an idea is romantic but rarely practical. Most of us do not possess King's innate descriptive talents and, accordingly, we must not rely on such streams of intuition or bursts of inspiration to write our stories. In most cases, to neglect a long-term story outline will result in the author suffering through countless rewrites as they blunder back and forth from scene to scene.

To get serious about our writing, we must think deeply about the protagonist's obstacles and the conflicting character motives before we write the first line. The types of conflict we need to strategise are two-fold. The first type acts as thematic conflict. This addresses the underlying subtextual problems and resentments bubbling up from the characters over the course of the entire plot. The second type serves as the primary driver of the interpersonal character chemistry. This addresses the clashing motives and distinct personality traits that create the chaotic friction in front of our eyes. After watching a performance of *All My Sons*, we can walk out of the theatre with crystal clear pictures of these two sides to dramatic conflict—that is the benchmark.

We may roll our eyes when the media tries to dramatise a cheesy news piece with tenuous obstacles, but they're really trying to tap into this timeless axiom of storytelling, and more often than not it succeeds in capturing their audience's attention. Let's be pragmatic about this—in general, you can improve any given scene by finding where its core conflict is and ramping it up a notch. This approach produces more arguments, more underlying tension, and more suffering—the meat and potatoes of storytelling. Cast any sweetness aside and, at every point in the story, ask yourself "How can I hurt this character more?" (See Law 1, Be Cruel to Your Characters.) We are not doing this to be sadists; we are doing this to maximise chaotic friction. It's sandpaper, not Teflon, that sparks great character chemistry.

> *Try this: Select a scene in your manuscript that doesn't seem as strong as it should be. Take each character in the scene and bump up the conflict between them by 25%. Find a way to do it. Add an annoying quirk, or interruptions, or a more scathing remark. Get the fire going then stoke the flames. Dialogue full of conflict and tension is also the fastest way to improve your scenes.*
> —*How to Write Dazzling Dialogue* by James Scott Bell

Do not be put off by the moral ambiguity in stoking drama—these techniques work in stories because real life is full of niceties, and we feel we have to stifle our words precisely to avoid conflict. But chaotic friction makes our lives interesting, and interpersonal friction helps us to express our thoughts and resentments. The ability to face down conflict without fear or apology gives us a great deal more satisfaction and success in life, because most of the time everyone else lives in that state of constant repressed anxiety. To repress ourselves and be sweet to everyone all the time for the sake of peace is unhealthy because it stokes the fires of repressed resentment, giving us ulcers and taking over our lives.

The most common way of showing conflict is through dialogue, as Arthur Miller did in his plays. Don't make your characters merely interact; let them argue and scheme against each other. A friendly conversation over coffee can be made more interesting by adding a dose of intrigue. One of the coffee-sipping friends wants to nudge the other into some action that may be counter to their interests. The audience sees this unfolding and wants to know more. Or perhaps your leading love interests spar from the moment they meet. They know how to push each other's buttons, and can't help but argue in earnest. That is how Jane Eyre and Edward Rochester topped the list of fictional lovers, perhaps only rivalled by Leia Organa and Han Solo. In either case, the pair of characters sparred from the moment they met due to their distinct personality traits. They each laid bare their true selves in a vulnerable way. That, by the way, builds the trust that is necessary for intimacy. Why can't love ever be simple? Because then it wouldn't be so exciting.

What's really behind this technique is the effective planning of your characters. Give each character an agenda, and make sure that your cast's agendas conflict in some way. In each scene, ask yourself what each character is after, and how it conflicts with the other characters' motives. Doing this should set them up for some exciting dialogue permeated with conflict. Lay their motives bare through the subtext of the argument. Set up your characters to cross swords as soon as the words hit the page—this not only makes your job more comfortable as a storyteller but it provides the optimal conditions for an exciting scene.

As stated, story conflict is not just about verbal sparring. You must see it in broader terms—monitor each character's underlying motives, and the ongoing opposition they face in pushing forward with their goals. What is the internal struggle that a character faces over the course of a series? How does that cause them to rub against their companions? How does that lead to further plot developments? To fully embrace the concept of chaotic friction is to stand back and plot every character trajectory, every permutation of events, and produce a satisfying product for your audience. That is truly the height of strategic storytelling.

Reversal

If you neglect conflict or purposely tone it down out of cowardice, then you'll bore your readers to tears. The key to this law is the degree of control you have over your story's conflict. Place your hand on the dial and make the tension rise and fall. As with all aspects of storytelling, each instance of conflict must serve the story as a whole. To take this advice and merely conclude "Ah, all I need then is to make this argument more furious here and add some more verbal jabs there," then your lazy attitude will shine through to your bored readers.

To work, chaotic friction needs to contribute to a story's central themes. Think of it in terms of answering broad story-spanning questions, not just something you can tweak here and there. It is whatever pushes the characters to achieve their goals, and it is whatever allows them to express their feelings and motives in an unfettered, vulnerable manner. Neglect this fundamental law of storytelling at your peril.

Law 11

Characters Must Learn from Their Mistakes

No one likes people who bumble carelessly through life, never learning from the variety of mistakes they make. Such people are lost causes, and we instinctively know to stay clear of them. In contrast, we admire people who learn from their mistakes and strive to improve themselves. People—and readers—are forgiving of flawed people making mistakes, but only so long as they see what they did wrong and never repeat it. Show your characters shaking off their old selves and stepping into new shoes. This personal metamorphosis can be the biggest source of the education that your story provides.

Transgression of the Law

The *Fifty Shades* film series were adaptations of E. L. James's self-published erotic fan-fiction novels. Their place on the cinema screen was inevitable after the book series had sold millions of copies worldwide. The success was completely unexpected, as erotic novels usually don't experience such a widespread readership.

The three books in the series follow Anastasia Steele, a literature student, and Christian Grey, a wealthy business magnate. After Steele's journalist roommate becomes sick, she reluctantly agrees to interview Grey at his company headquarters. Not sure what to expect of Grey, she is surprised to meet a dashing, charming young man. Though Steele finds the encounter intimidating, she also finds herself captivated and desperate to see him again. Though enigmatic and claiming to be above such things, Grey admits he wants her too.

They begin to date. But as the couple grow closer, and the relationship becomes sexual, Steele learns about Grey's controlling nature. Though Grey enjoys massive wealth and a great deal of respect in his life, he is hopelessly insecure. Before they sleep together for the first time, Grey describes his "boundaries" in excruciating detail—particularly his rule that he takes absolute control over their intercourse, and that she submits to his every demand.

This strange need to be in full control of every aspect of their sex life soon extends to Steele's life outside of their relationship. Grey demands absolute compliance in the bedroom, yet keeps emotionally distant from Steele. While she plays along with the BDSM sex while it is novel and exciting, she realises she does not want a long-term relationship with a man who has such dire emotional issues and breaks off the relationship, thus concluding the first story.

In the second story of the series, Steele takes a job at a publishing company, despite knowing that three people in the position have quit within the last 18 months. Steele resumes the relationship with Grey, only on the condition that it be on her terms. At no surprise to the audience at all, his controlling issues rise back to the surface worse than ever. When she declines to work for him instead due to the clear conflicts of interest, Grey buys out her current employer and starts exerting his will over the company.

A past girlfriend from Grey's past, still obsessed with the billionaire, stalks the pair and intimidates Steele on multiple occasions, even pointing a loaded gun at her towards the end. After this conflict seems to bizarrely disappear of its own accord, Grey dramatically falls at his knees before Steele, crying out over his shame that his sadistic tendencies have manifested in the need to control everything in his life, including the need to physically harm anyone who looks like his crack-addict birth mother. He follows up this emotional tirade by proposing marriage to her, which she accepts.

The third story covers the couple's early married life. But a break-in attempt at Grey's company headquarters is enough to persuade him to hire a security detail for his new wife and build her a house all to herself. Much of the conflict once again arises out of Grey's monstrous insecurity—in one scene, he has a completely unprovoked dramatic outburst at Anastasia for not changing her email address to her new married surname, which he'd assumed she'd take.

While the pervasive online marketing efforts and the success of the book series ensured the film series' commercial success at the box office, it did not gain much critical acclaim.

Interpretation

There is no character development at all throughout the entire *Fifty Shades* series, and every single character in the series remains unchanged, learning nothing from their experiences. At the end of the third book, Christian Grey still exhibits the same insecure, controlling behaviour over Anastasia, who outwardly begrudges these negative traits, only to return to him expecting different results. They're both equally guilty of cultivating a mutually abusive relationship.

To be fair, *Fifty Shades*'s premise does not allow for much personal growth for either character. Anastasia, a weak and passive student, meets the rich yet one-dimensional Christian Grey, who pursues her until she agrees to marry him. She makes token protests but then, over again, submits to his will. The character development that the stories attempt to portray are only skin-deep, since their actions and choices reveal a lack of personal development.

Even with their relationship out of the picture, Anastasia lacks proactivity—what the literary critic Rose Fox has identified as the need for protagonists to "protag." Anastasia's first interview with Grey is set up by her roommate, and she only goes reluctantly after much cajoling. She is set up to be a passive character, not inciting any new plot threads. At no point is she in control of her life; it's all controlled by Grey. She's superficially represented as a strong character, while in reality she's just blown about by the demands of those around her.

Grey buys the company that Anastasia works at after she refuses to work for him, then he fires her boss when he starts making passes at Anastasia, even though the story has telegraphed this her boss's attractions right from the start. It's Grey who proposes to Anastasia, and in spite of his pathetic begging, she accepts. Grey emotionally blackmails her into using her new marital name at work. He tries to stop her from going out for drinks with her friends. He follows Anastasia across the country even after she expressly tells him that she needs space. The list of abusive behaviours that Anastasia responds to with damp protests is long and consistent throughout the story.

This abusive behaviour would work from a storytelling perspective if it set up the initial conflict of the series, but Anastasia's typical reaction to all of these attempts at control is token resistance, followed by inevitable submission. She claims to want a "hearts and flowers" relationship but does nothing of significance to try to achieve this goal.

Anastasia's decision to break up with Grey shows some resolve and is the best choice for her character, but it isn't satisfying as an ending because nothing has changed deep down in either character. Anastasia learns that Grey, while charming and dominant, is in fact monstrously insecure and, as a result, ashamedly manipulative of people around him. She's had her fun on his helicopter and learnt all about BDSM sex, but she realises this can't work in the long term, so she comes to her senses and dumps him. We can't imagine either Anastasia or Grey making different choices from the start of the story.

A more interesting route would have been to subvert this entirely and flip the Dom-Sub script on its head. Make Anastasia dive headlong into the world of BDSM, going down a career-threatening route of debauched kinky sex, bringing her new boyfriend out of his shell and snapping him out of his emotional issues. In this alternate script, characters would evolve in a way that audiences could see just by watching their choices change over time. *Fifty Shades* completely failed to create anything new, meeting superficial needs and showing that hype can drive more sales than it rightfully should. It sits firmly in the "guilty pleasure" category.

Keys to Storytelling

Character evolution can only occur under load. If there is no real challenge to the characters' deeply-held beliefs, or if they don't express their motives at any point, no character evolution can occur—and this rarely results in an exciting story.

Imagine a story where a character faces repeated problems. The character learns nothing from these obstacles, continuing to show the same personality from start to finish, making the same mistakes over and over again. That character is unrelatable and their story is bland. In real life, we find such people insufferable, because they either whine about their circumstances or lurch from one avoidable disaster to another, often guilting others into taking the fall for them.

A story has meaning when we can relate to the people in it and watch them change by seeing how they behave in new situations. We live alongside them as they suffer through trials, watch as they become wiser and stronger, and become invested in them. We learn the same lessons they do. We grow as they grow. We want to see them face the bully down who picked on them in the first act.

Without character evolution, Neville Longbottom would remain a shy and unconfident young wizard, getting pushed around by Slytherin bullies. Luke Skywalker would remain the whiny teenager stuck on his uncle's farm, doing nothing with his great Jedi heritage and potential. Thor would remain the headstrong knucklehead who recklessly puts others in danger. Nick Carraway would remain hypnotised by Jay Gatsby's world of superficial glitter, frittering his time and money away on shiny objects lacking any true worth. These characters would either meekly accept

their circumstances or arrogantly bluster past any critical feedback.

Too many writers fail to develop their characters
only to miraculously solve their problems at the end,
thinking that they can solve a story like an algebraic
equation. This common misstep fails to see the point of
storytelling—to immerse the audience and give them a
good time. We find the deus ex machina so exasperat-
ing because a story's purpose is not to get the character
what he wants at the end of the journey, but the journey of discovery he needs to take to get there. The
story "He wanted to slay the dragon, and so he did.
The end," isn't going anywhere near the best seller
lists. The story "He wanted to slay the dragon and had
to go through many trials, growing in both wisdom
and strength to do it. The end," hits closer to the mark.

The Hero's Journey

Joseph Campbell noticed through his extensive research into the myths created by a thousand different
cultures that the same patterns occurred in each of
these myths. Each legend followed some interpretation
of the coming-of-age story: A young person leaves their
safe home, and is placed through challenges that make
them transcend their limits to gain honour and
strength. Such myths often centre around a boy's trans-

ition into manhood—a metaphor for the character's evolution from weak to strong, from coddled to virtuous.

Due to its reflected similarity across so many different cultures, Campbell distilled these legends into the concept he called the "monomyth." Today, we more often call it the Hero's Journey. The main idea is that the hero goes through massive transformations, both internal and external, which force him to lay aside his underdeveloped traits and, through a series of epiphanies and development, grows into a higher version of himself.

Campbell realised in his research that this pattern of the Hero's Journey repeats in so many different cultures due to a fundamental part of the human psyche. Humans are spiritual creatures, and at every point in our history we have always tried to find meaning in our existence. The inspiration provided by the Hero's Journey lies in the revelation of the immense amount of potential that's hidden within all of us.

That is why the first book in a multi-part series usually follows the Hero's Journey pattern—it establishes the hero by showing the growth of a person into the hero we know and love in later parts of the series. The hero's status must be earned, and this early investment in their development gives the later stories far more potential.

Human societies never seem to grow tired of Hero's Journey stories—repeated iterations on essentially the same theme continue to enjoy consistent acclaim. *Star Wars* is just the *Iliad* in space, after all. Understand that history has repeatedly proven to us the universality of the Hero's Journey, and you should not feel shy about using it for your own story. The positive change arc is a widely recognised and loved story structure with infinite applications, and society will never tire of it—use that to your advantage.

The Stages of Evolution

At the beginning of the story, your character holds onto a false premise about their reality that holds them back in a tangible way. Luke Skywalker believes that he'll never leave his uncle's farm, and that has become a self-fulfilling prophecy. Nick Carraway is left spellbound by Gatsby's luxurious world of parties, quite unlike his home town, and this leaves him in danger of searching for wealth and social status over genuine human connection. The storytelling expert K. M. Weiland coined the concept "the lie your character believes."

Character development is the process of identifying their lie, showing it to the audience through a series of errors, and challenging the character to instead realise the truth—this is unique to each character and each story. The character holds value in their lie, and when they're challenged, they're forced to let go of the negative aspects of their character, but this needs to be framed in a way that seems threatening to the character's wants. The goal of character evolution is create wounds and heal them; sometimes you get scars, but they have meaning. In storytelling, we need to make our characters learn the hard way.

> *A Cup of Tea*
>
> *Nan-in, a Japanese master during the Meiji era (1868-1912), received a university professor who came to inquire about Zen. Nan-in served tea. He poured his visitor's cup full, and then kept on pouring. The professor watched the overflow until he no longer could restrain himself. "It is overfull. No more will go in!" "Like this cup," Nan-in said, "you are full of your own opinions and speculations. How can I show you Zen unless you first empty your cup?"*
>
> —A Zen koan

In your story's first act, you need to answer the question, "What does your character ostensibly *want*?" Their lie should define this—they *think* they need something because of some misguided set of beliefs. Then, ask yourself "What does your character *need*?" The truth should define this—it's their medicine. Think of this comparison like a child who asks for more ice cream at dinner—they think they want more sweet treats, but you know it'll only make them feel sick, so you encourage them to eat an apple or an orange instead. Let us also take an example in cinema: In *Star Wars: The Force Awakens*, Kylo Ren wants to kill his father because Snoke has convinced him that this will make him stronger in the dark side of the Force. In reality, Ren feels enormous conflict and resentment at his family—what he *needs* is to resolve his anger, reconcile with his father, and realise that Snoke has been manipulating him into becoming a pawn in his evil plans.

In that same story, Rey wants to stay on Jakku because she believes her family will come back for her. What she *needs* is to focus on her own future. Rey experiences some warnings about the truth, through the vision she has when she touches the Skywalker lightsaber, followed by Maz Kanata's prophetic encouragement that she stop looking to the past. But this only scares her, threatening everything she holds dear —this outburst reflects the investment in her lie. Character evolution can't come about in any one realisation of the truth—it needs to be a compound process to have meaning, the character has to initially reject the red pill and double down on their lie. Rey does reach her evolution point in her final encounter with Kylo Ren, which reveals her naturally strong Force abilities and opens up a new world for her.

Though deep down Rey hates her lonely existence on Jakku, she knows it well and accepts her life of effectively forced labour. She is terrified of missing an opportunity to see her family again. But it's only by leaving the planet to take on a heroic quest that Rey can realise her potential. At the beginning she makes choices that indicate her fear and need to stay behind, refusing the Hero's Journey. But by the end of *The Force Awakens*, Rey has learned that she can help others by facing her fears and going out into the world to experience new things. Her character evolution for this story is tangible and shown to the audience.

Rey realises that she can stop wasting her life working in a junkyard and do something positive for downtrodden people like her former self. Unlike Kylo Ren, she achieves synthesis with the truth in *The Force Awakens*. Rey is no longer the same person holding onto her past. The audience sees this metamorphosis when she defeats Kylo in their lightsaber duel and chooses not to return to Jakku, but to stay and help General Leia Organa's Resistance. Understand: The most important piece of character evolution is having a lie to desperately cling onto—the more desperately they need to cling, the more satisfying their eventual revelation. Challenge them, make them only cling tighter at first, and then let them unravel until they can let go of the lie and embrace the truth.

Force your character to choose responsibility and heroism over the known world and oppressive safety to give meaning to their Hero's Journey. Making this a *choice* is far more effective at showing your audience the sacrifices that the hero has had to endure to complete her character evolution.

In the 19th century, Friedrich Nietzsche described a three-stage metaphor for the evolution of the soul in his book *Thus Spoke Zarathustra*. At the beginning of their life, a person is the camel; they bow down and accept the loads that society bears on them. This represents the character's safe but oppressive home life. The camel goes into the desert and becomes a brave lion. This stage is an analogy for the character leaving home to begin his quest. The lion's name is "I will," and his goal is to slay the dragon. The dragon's name is "Thou shalt," and underneath every one of its scales is written "Thou shalt." The fearless lion tears off every one of these scales with his sharp fangs, and through determination the dragon "Thou shalt" is slain. The lion's mission is complete. The lion evolves into the child, not representing immaturity, but the freedom to do as his soul desires. Understanding the meaning behind Nietzsche's metaphor requires an open mind, but it represents the movement of a person from oppression to self-realisation, and each metamorphosis requires letting go of some aspect of the past self. Campbell's later work on heroic legends reflected Nietzsche's metamorphosis metaphor.

In the 1999 film *The Matrix*, the hero Neo's character evolution closely accords with Nietzsche's three-stage metaphor. He starts as a quiet, unassuming man with a job that forces him to obey the demands of his authoritarian boss. In this first stage, he represents Nietzsche's camel. An opportunity opens up for him to leave the virtual world for the real world by choosing the red pill. This choice accords with the camel leaving his home world to journey into the desert. In the real world, humanity's cutting-edge immersion technology allows him to instantly learn martial arts and gain the sharp teeth and claws of Nietzsche's lion.

The oppressive world-spanning regime of the machines and the Agents represents the dragon that Neo, now the lion, must slay. The machines control the actions of all of humanity, while giving them a false illusion of free will through the Matrix system. Through great trials, Neo defeats the Agents and rescues his friends. In the end he can read the Matrix code, and uses his newfound abilities to defeat Agent Smith with ease. He has slain the dragon, and through his new godlike powers, achieves complete free will. He can come and go as he pleases, literally able to fly and bend reality to whatever he can imagine. Neo has completed Nietzsche's final metamorphosis, from the lion into the child. Observe the immense satisfaction created and the groundbreaking success that *The Matrix* was able to achieve with such a simple, unfettered retelling of a classical metaphor (see Law 18, Accord with Timeless Myths).

The Tragic Downfall Arc

Not every character arc needs to be positive—far from it. Some of the most compelling character arcs are tragic falls from grace. Harvey Dent begins Christopher Nolan's *The Dark Knight* as a virtuous, brave hero for justice, but ends the story as a deranged murderer. Batman is forced to make an impossible choice for the greater good of Gotham City—to take the fall for Dent's string of revenge murders, keeping his earlier mob convictions intact. Unlike the positive evolutions described above, the tragic downfall represents the loss of some great potential and the pain arising from that loss. The character can't just start bad and stay that way—the pain of lost potential makes this arc meaningful.

Both of these characters start the story with a lot going for them. The previous film, *Batman Begins*, has established Batman as the vigilante protector of Gotham City, striking fear into the hearts of criminals. Harvey Dent is the city's promising new district attorney, securing convictions for many dangerous criminals in the Gotham City mob. The Joker corrupts Dent by murdering his fiancée, and he goes on a murderous rampage that only Batman can stop, who in turn has to sacrifice his heroic identity to save Gotham. Harvey Dent loses everything; so does Batman, but by choosing his moral virtues over glory and fame, he becomes the hero Gotham deserves.

Understand: The power and value in the tragic downfall arc is in the great potential you show in your characters from the beginning. Make your characters full of promise, and then destroy it all through corruption or disillusionment. Meanwhile, use the ensuing conflict as an opportunity for one of your other characters to show their virtue through good, conscious choices. Following this simple pattern will give your story the makings of the perfect tragic downfall arc.

Reversal

Not every character in your story has to evolve. Some can sit in the background. But all your major characters must leave the story different to how they found it. Maybe they already knew the truth at the start of the story. But it hurt them, so they kept it hidden and pushed it back.

Major characters can go along a character arc that is flat, while still providing an engaging story. How is this possible? K. M. Weiland explains in *Creating Character Arcs* that "[readers] enjoy it because it is still a story of change. The difference is that the protagonist is the one changing the world around him, rather than the world changing the character, as we find in Change Arcs." Our character enters the beginning of Weiland's Flat Arc just as strong as ever, but has to face monumental challenges to his belief system—usually manifesting in the breaking down of systems he once believed in.

This system often works well as the second story of a three-part series, occurring after we've watched the hero rise to prominence and let us invest in his abilities and his belief system. Take the following analogy: In our own lives, we finish school and feel unstoppable, but this is due to our limited perspective. The education system has been our longest-running foe, and we're not aware of the even greater challenges facing us after graduation. When we join the work world, we learn that there are unforgiving deadlines to meet, scheming colleagues, and myriad sacrifices. Look back on your past self and notice how naive, callow, or big-minded they seem. All the growing challenges in our lives and the experiences that meet us challenge our established beliefs and force us to grow stronger still.

> *So continually remind yourself, Lucilius, of the many things you have achieved. When you look at all the people out in front of you, think of all the ones behind you. If you want to feel appreciative where the gods and your life are concerned, just think how many people you've outdone. Why be concerned about others, come to that, when you've outdone your own self? Set yourself a limit which you couldn't even exceed if you wanted to, and say good-bye at last to those deceptive prizes more precious to those who hope for them than to those who have won*

164

them. If there were anything substantial in them they would sooner or later bring a sense of fullness; as it is they simply aggravate the thirst of those who swallow them.

—Seneca, first century AD

Law 12

The Hero and Villain Must Share the Same Goal

For your story to have tension, you must create a legitimate threat to something that the characters care about. If your villain's motives don't spark any kind of real resistance from your hero, then there's no threat. To create real emotional resonance in your audience's hearts, your hero and villain must seek the same thing—this can be a literal object, or your villain can threaten something less tangible that your hero nevertheless deeply identifies with. Giving your hero and villain the same goal with opposing motives and alternate methods is a recipe for a great contest.

Observance of the Law, Part I

In the 2005 film *Batman Begins*, a young Bruce Wayne is at a low point. Voluntarily placing himself in an Asian prison, he fights—and easily defeats—his fellow inmates for sport. After one such fight, he is visited by the mysterious Ducard, who encourages him to join his League of Shadows to learn the ways of the ninja. Ducard, a senior member of the League, becomes his mentor in combat and philosophy, and the wise yet pragmatic father figure that Bruce needs at this juncture in his life.

Bruce excels at his ninja training, developing strength and speed that allows him to beat his fellow trainees. His final test before his induction into the League of Shadows is to execute a criminal. Bruce refuses, deciding this is not how he wants to achieve his goals. Ducard berates Bruce, telling him that the greater good is more important than any individual life: the man is a murderer and must himself pay the price for his crimes. Bruce is unmoved and confirms his choice. He will never kill anyone, regardless of their actions— everyone is redeemable.

Bruce burns the League's headquarters and returns to Gotham. He uses his company's tech to fight the criminal underworld, seeking to exact revenge on those representing the criminals who killed his parents. With childhood friend Rachel Dawes' help, Bruce redoubles his vow never to kill while he fulfils his mission to make Gotham safe. Through a series of investigations, he finds clues to a mass drug smuggling operation supported by corrupt police officers.

As the story transitions into the final act, the League of Shadows return. They're led by Ducard who reveals himself as their real leader, Ra's al Ghul, and the group as the real orchestrator of the drug smuggling operation. Ra's al Ghul reveals to Bruce that they plan to "cleanse" Gotham of its corruption and chaos by destroying it from within. Ostensibly dealing in illicit drugs, Ra's al Ghul and the League plan to release nerve gas into Gotham, creating a mass panic that destroys the city.

Interpretation

Bruce Wayne and Ra's al Ghul aim to clean up Gotham City in diametrically opposed ways. Bruce Wayne chooses to become a symbol of hope for everyday people, while discouraging organised crime through intimidation and fear. Ra's al Ghul and the League of Shadows' goal is a more literal interpretation, as they aim to destroy Gotham in a blaze of cleansing fire.

The story's core conflict is this contrast in the two men's approaches to the same goal. When Bruce is given his final challenge at the League of Shadows, this split is made clear as he's forced to choose his path—it's in this choice that Bruce Wayne first becomes Batman. Although we side with Batman's virtuous approach to solving the chaos in Gotham, there is a clearly reasoned pragmatic argument for Ra's al Ghul's methodology. More importantly, forcing Bruce to make a moral choice between two means to the same end gives him an opportunity to prove his moral rectitude.

Give your hero and villain the same goal with opposing interpretations. Make either character pursue the same goal but each in their own way. In both cases, you must state and clearly argue their motives in the first act. Treat your hero and villain equally—the best villains always have at least the same amount of relatable motivation as the hero. Giving both of them a strong motivation ensures that your story moves forward in a deliberate direction. To do otherwise, to fail to force either of your characters into a choice, is to meekly ramble from one plot point to another.

Observance of the Law, Part II

The 2018 film *Avengers: Infinity War* was the culmination of ten years' worth of plot and character development within the Marvel Cinematic Universe. All the conflicts from each of the Avengers' own films were leading up to their confrontation with Thanos, the true villain of the shared Marvel universe.

Thanos's goal is to achieve balance in the universe, motivated by his own species' decline through starvation and scarce resources. He reasons that by forcefully halving the population of every planet he and his vast army come across, he will help the remaining people of that culture from starving themselves out of existence. Thanos has spent many years doing this the old-fashioned way, going from planet to planet, separating the population in half at random, and having his army slaughter the unlucky half—a fair solution in his mind, since he does not discriminate by wealth, status, or any other determinant.

Thanos's original plan with humanity was to manipulate cat's paws such as a possessed Loki, and Tony Stark's destructive artificial intelligence Ultron, to conquer Earth on his behalf. But as the events of the *Avengers* films show, the team of talented heroes prove too strong for the indirect strategy. So, Thanos resolve to find all six of the Infinity Stones, each one filled with mystical powers, created at the birth of the universe itself. When he gathers all six and harnesses their power with the use of his Infinity Gauntlet, he can kill half of all living beings in the universe with the mere snap of his fingers.

The Avengers' goal is clear: find and protect the Infinity Stones that Thanos needs for his plan, the price of failure being universal mass slaughter. Throughout the story, each one of the Avengers is forced to make an impossible choice—sacrifice their friends, or give Thanos what he wants. They are all pushed to their limits as they fight desperately to stop their strongest foe yet.

Interpretation

A decade of exciting films, each building the suspense, primed the Marvel Cinematic Universe for a high-stakes showdown. Sufficient time was taken to develop each of the Avengers, and Thanos was well-established as the real orchestrator of all the evil that they'd had to face. The audience had lived through the same struggles as each one of the Avengers, and there had been speculation over when they would meet their ultimate foe. This meant that the film needed little time to establish its conflict.

The film starts right after Thanos's forces have captured the Asgardian refugee vessel and slaughtered half the people on board. This scene alone is an excellent example of Show, Don't Tell, as the threat level is clear. People are better at understanding subtext than you might think—seeing the ravaged death and destruction wrought by Thanos communicates clearer than any clever explanatory dialogue. Thanos is a cruel villain, but his morality is not the key here—the key is the clarity with which that's communicated, and starting your story right in the action is always the best way to achieve that.

In spite of his brutality, the audience can just as easily think that Thanos is the story's protagonist. He's the most active character in the story, and the Avengers spend most of it reacting to his moves and rising to challenge him. Thanos's motivations are clearly demonstrated and thus understandable through his actions, and that he repeatedly states his reasons for his self-appointed mission in a strongly argued way.

Understand: When writing your story's protagonist and antagonist, you must write each side's motivations keeping in mind that both believe they are the hero of their own story. The morality behind their choices is irrelevant, though the convention is to make your "real" hero more virtuous; they only need to be two different and strongly argued ways of achieving the same goal. To write a villain that could just as easily be the hero of the story is the height of storytelling; it's a strategy that will give your story's confrontation untold emotional power, and make it a more meaningful struggle for either side.

The contrast between hero and opponent is powerful only when both characters have strong similarities. Each then presents a slightly different approach to the same dilemma. And it is in the similarities that crucial and instructive differences become most clear.

—*The Anatomy of Story* by John Truby

Keys to Storytelling

A villain must be written with the hero in mind; the villain must challenge the hero's specific beliefs. The flat, one-dimensional antagonist is all too common nowadays because it takes real effort to write a meaningful opposition for a story's most important two characters. One tends to find that the harder something is, the less competition we have, so this leaves us with ample room to delight our audiences with our well-thought out rivalries.

There is one key to such rivalries: a villain that shares the same goal as the hero, but believes in a different way of achieving it. Your villain must have abundant opportunities to challenge everything that the hero believes, and thus you must create the hero and villain with symmetric focus. Heroes and villains are multipack goods, not to be sold separately.

In either character's case, express their motives as early as possible, and make their motives easy to understand. An opening scene right in the action can be the richest indictment of everything your villain stands against—both Marvel's *Black Panther* and Christopher Nolan's *The Dark Knight* use this technique to introduce their iconic villains.

In real life, good and evil are often subjective. People follow their line of greatest incentive, and this manifests in behaviour that either benefits or hurts others. We always see ourselves as the hero of our own story, and we inevitably come across opponents who challenge us or even threaten us. A hero from one person's perspective is someone else's villain. Opponents are, therefore, inevitable. There is always someone out there competing for the same goal as you.

In any career or sporting contest, it takes the right opponent to bring out the best in you. What better way to improve than to have your success under threat from a potent rival, just good enough to shock you into seeing the required progress still ahead of you? An opponent of equal ability, ready and eager to challenge you, is a better motivator than any speech or self-help book.

In 1964 when Cassius Clay faced Sonny Liston in the boxing ring for the first time, Clay had spent the months leading up to the bout taunting his older opponent, calling Liston an old man past his prime. As the reigning champion, Liston could not allow this young man's disrespect and irritating behaviour to continue. Before the fight, when it was Liston's turn at the weigh-in, Clay stood at the back of the audience, acting like a man possessed. He jumped up and down, laughing maniacally and shouting, "I fooled you, chump! I fooled you! I'm gonna whoop you so bad!"

When the opening bell rang, Liston charged at Clay with a hook that missed by a mile. This pattern repeated itself throughout the fight. Clay would taunt Liston, holding his hands down as if to bait him in. Liston would fall for the bait, coming in closer to Clay with some wild strike, only to suffer a devilishly quick yet powerful jab that sent him reeling. By the eighth round, Liston was so exhausted by Clay's dancing footwork and repeated unexpected blows that he refused to get up. The fight was over.

Soon after the fight, now heavyweight champion, Clay converted to Islam and changed his name to Muhammad Ali. He would beat Liston again in a year's time, though in this second fight he managed a win by a knockout. Ali's winning punch came so fast, and so out of the blue, that many watching claimed that no punch had landed. They claimed that Liston had thrown the match. Liston knew differently—and failed to get up in time. Ali had won again. Liston would go on fighting for another five years, but neither man's career was ever the same again.

Though Muhammad Ali went on to reach new heights of stardom, it was his first rivalry with Sonny Liston that started him on this path. If he had not sparked this rivalry with the former heavyweight champion, he would not have become a star.

In your stories, create strong opponents for your characters who are capable of matching them in the right ways. Liston was both proud and arrogant, and Ali exploited these traits by provoking him into forgetting his fighting style. Your characters will have different opposing personality traits, and you'll need to use those accordingly. Rivalries work best when the opponent is at or above your main character's level of competency. Give the hero a realistic chance of winning in a way that forces him to make meaningful improvements to his skills and strategies—there is little point in writing a cold and ruthless opponent to a similarly Machiavellian character. Only the right opponent can pull the hero upwards.

Scaling up the conflict, a truly mighty foe can be a good fit for a team of characters who have to put aside their differences and learn to work together. The villain is far too strong for any one of your heroes alone, and you must explicitly show this to the audience. A tactic used in *Avengers: Infinity War* was to show Thanos beating the Hulk. We expect the Hulk to win his fist fights, and seeing Thanos suplex him on the deck catches us off guard.

Villainy in Threat and Opposition

Without the dual threats of direct opposition or meaningful competition, a character is not a villain. The blandest villains in stories are one-dimensional and offer no direct opposition to any of the hero's stated beliefs. Conversely, if you have failed to show that the hero has a goal, then there is nothing for the audience to latch onto when the villain acts within the story.

In *Star Wars: The Force Awakens*, we know that Rey desperately longs to have a family. We're shown that she lives alone and that she has been there for a long time. Rey tells BB-8 that she's waiting for her family, and upon meeting Finn and Han Solo, she feels like she has a family again—a father figure in Han and a brother in Finn.

Kylo Ren, on the other hand, grew up in privilege. He was surrounded by love from an early age, but he seems desperate to kill his family. This conflict is set up when Snoke tells Ren that passing the "test" of killing

Han will take him to new heights of dark side power. Ren does murder Han Solo at the end, and this flattens Rey—but interestingly, it also deflates Ren's fighting spirit, which completes the mirrored picture between the story's hero and villain. The opposition is straight-forward, and it's spelt out to us in the simplest language of all: action.

> *The Boys and the Frogs*
> *Some boys, playing near a pond, saw a number of frogs in the water and began to pelt them with stones. They killed several of them, when one of the frogs, lifting his head out of the water, cried out: "Pray stop, my boys: what is sport to you, is death to us."*
>
> —*Aesop's Fables*, sixth century BC

Virtuous Villainy

This "matched opposite" principle does not mean that your villain can't be just as virtuous and morally up-right as your hero. If both of them fight for a good cause, this can provide you with the opportunity to explore two different sides of morality.

Let us once again take an example from Marvel's work by looking at *Captain America: Civil War*. From previous films in the franchise, we know that both

Tony Stark and Steve Rogers are good people trying to do their best. But in this story, they have clearly opposed goals: Tony wants to make the Avengers more legitimate, while Steve is concerned that a forced political solution will limit their ability to help humanity. Tony is acting out of a place of shame and guilt after unleashing Ultron on the world, while Steve stands up for what he believes in, refusing to bow to political pressure.

Neither of these characters is wrong. Both have good moral reasons for doing what they do in the story, and it provides an alternative experience for audiences used to a singular antagonist. Understand: The labels "hero" and "villain" are optional. The obvious success of this configuration in *Civil War* should prove to you the merits of writing two equally virtuous characters sharing the same goals. The heartache as two former friends battle it out creates endlessly satisfying drama.

Their Shared Goal is the Conflict

Going back to our previous example in *Star Wars: The Force Awakens*, we can extend the hero and villain characters to a broader scope: the Resistance and the First Order, respectively. Both of these forces want to find Luke Skywalker. The First Order is at the height of its power, and Snoke's ultimate goal is to wipe out the remnants of the Jedi. The Resistance, led by Leia Organa, want to bring Leia's brother Luke back to help them in their desperate fight against the First Order.

They share the same goal: find Luke Skywalker. This mutual goal forms the backdrop of the entire film. The First Order is on Jakku to find a missing piece of their map to Luke Skywalker. The Resistance have beaten them to the punch, and their star pilot Poe Dameron has already arrived on the planet to collect the map piece from Lor San Tekka.

Luke Skywalker is the centre of all conflict in *The Force Awakens*. It's fitting that the story's protagonist, Rey, is the one to discover him on Ahch-To, because Luke's reveal is a dramatic moment emphasised both by dramatic music and Rey's look of shock. This end is perfect because it resolves the central conflict. The Resistance has found him, and the First Order has failed. This technique actually makes your job as a storyteller easier, because it self-generates endless juicy conflict. In your story, whether the hero and villain are large organisations or individuals, their shared goal will inevitably be the heart of the conflict's story, and it must therefore also be central to the climax of the story.

Reversal

You must always write your Caesar and Cassius as two sides of the same coin—one cannot exist without the other. Without a villain to oppose your hero, there cannot be any conflict and therefore no meaning to your story. Ignore this critical law at your peril, unless your goal is to write B-movies.

Law 13

Series Are a Right, Not a Privilege

A series of stories can only stand on strong foundations, built from the ground up. Boundless sums of money have been wasted attempting to create shared story universes where no such right has been earned. A multi-part series of stories can only exist when its constituent stories are entertaining, when they develop likeable characters, and most importantly, are self-contained. Build investment in your characters, then put them through hardship, and finally allow them to achieve catharsis. Once again, you must master the art of controlling potential energy—the longer the tension is drawn out, the more satisfying the feeling of catharsis upon its release.

Transgression of the Law

The 2015 iteration of *Fantastic Four* was the fourth attempt to bring this comic creation to the big screen. The ground-breaking success of the *Avengers* saga and more serious superhero stories such as Christopher Nolan's *Dark Knight* trilogy meant that other film studios wanted to capitalise on their comic book properties—the attraction of big box office hits was too strong to resist.

Critics and audiences alike had only moderately enjoyed the prior reboot attempt of *Fantastic Four* in 2005. The film had a tongue-in-cheek feel and suffered from the conflicts between its comedic and serious tones. But some fun dialogue and impressive computer-generated effects had been enough to entertain audiences for its two-hour runtime.

2005 had also seen the release of Christopher Nolan's *Batman Begins,* and darker, grittier interpretations of comic book heroes such as Batman seemed to enjoy great critical and commercial success. So it was not all surprising to see the *Fantastic Four*'s second reboot in 2015 attempt a similarly dark and gritty tone.

This reboot attempt did not pay off. At the box office on its opening weekend it only managing half of its $60 million target. Critics slammed the film for its cynical use of a dark tone, its glib and excessive exposition, and its lazy computer-generated effects. But most criticised of all was its clunky attempts at building a shared universe—it made constant references to unseen and irrelevant elements outside the scope of the film at the expense of the film's main narrative.

Most tellingly of all, its director Josh Trank appears to have disowned the film, explaining in a deleted Twitter post that there had been a "fantastic version" of this film before the studio had allegedly interfered and organised extensive reshoots.

Interpretation

2015's *Fantastic Four* was one of many failed attempts to capitalise on the success of the superhero film genre. Likely enticed by the potential for the box office blowouts enjoyed by film sagas such as the *Avengers* series or *The Dark Knight* trilogy, they made too overt an attempt to emulate the elements that made those films so successful, appearing not to learn from the storytelling strategies that were the actual cause of those films' success.

Fantastic Four tried hard to emulate *The Dark Knight*'s dark and gritty tone with little thought as to why it works so well for the Batman character. Because Batman has no special powers to speak of, it's entirely possible to create an entertaining story in a real-world setting. But fans of the comics will know that *Fantastic Four* does not lend itself well to a setting like this—traditionally it's a tongue-in-cheek plot line with fantastical magic-like abilities. You can only demand audiences take your material this seriously if you meet two conditions: first, you spend the time investing in your characters, and second, balance the dark tones with occasional humour and levity.

It also tried hard to reference outside characters and concepts from the comic books, probably because the *Avengers* saga has many characters all within the same shared universe. But this approach works for the Avengers because Marvel took the time to develop each character in their respective film adaptations. Each character has their own solid, self-contained origin story that makes the audience care about them. There is no such thing as the free lunch—do not expect a payoff without first letting your audience create an emotional investment in your characters.

Fantastic Four's writers appeared to want to treat these key factors in storytelling like items on a checklist, rather than the crucial moving parts of an entertaining and self-contained story. The film might have been a success if it had focused on telling its own self-contained story. It provides the quintessential example of how *not* to set up a robust series of stories—avoid weaving overt exposition into every stage of your story, avoid making glib references to a shared universe the audience has never seen and doesn't care about, and finally avoid demanding respect and payoff from viewers when it gives them a mediocre experience in return.

Observance of the Law, Part I

J. K. Rowling's *Harry Potter* series of books followed the title character through his seven academic years at Hogwarts School of Witchcraft and Wizardry. The character Harry Potter has his own mythos since surviving the evil Voldemort's attack as a baby, becoming "The Boy Who Lived." At age eleven, fortune plucks Harry out of the misery of his life with his adoptive family, the Dursleys, and thrusts him into the wizarding world. Harry is stunned to find that his great reputation precedes him.

Each new academic year sees a new *Harry Potter* adventure with new challenges, bringing Harry and his friends closer together. But a lingering and ever-present threat grows, lurking behind the scenes. That threat comes from Lord Voldemort, who rises in power as Harry's time at Hogwarts progresses. In the first book, *The Philosopher's Stone*, Voldemort has barely enough energy to manifest on the back of Professor

Quirrell's head. But by the time of the fourth book *The Goblet of Fire*, he has gathered enough strength to return to bodily form and murder the school's star pupil Cedric Diggory.

This underlying threat that gathers strength year-on-year provides Harry with plenty of motivation to develop his wizarding skills—not to mention the school exams he has to pass. As the books progressed closer to the end of the series, events take a far darker turn. Harry's motivations become all the stronger in the fifth book, *The Order of the Phoenix* when his godfather Sirius Black is cruelly murdered by Bellatrix Lestrange, Sirius's own cousin and one of Voldemort's cronies.

Harry finds and destroys the Horcruxes, a collection of magical items that Voldemort has imbued with his life essence. By this point, Harry has grown in both magic and personal power—all the suffering he has been through by this point has had made him far tougher and braver than before. The heartache has a cumulative effect on both Harry and the loyal audience who have followed his journey from the beginning. All the tension from Voldemort's rise and the years of hardship have built to an unbearable level, so when Harry rallies the school together and Voldemort is finally killed, it gives them the catharsis that they deserved.

Interpretation

The *Harry Potter* series of books took the world by storm. Lines of dedicated fans waited for days outside of bookshops before each book's release. The genius behind the *Harry Potter* phenomenon is the sustained level of cruelty and heartache that Harry and his friends are made to endure throughout the series of stories. Each successive book provides a brand new threat, more severe and deadlier than the last. J. K. Rowling manages to build the tension steadily until it is almost unbearable. Every jab from the Slytherin bullies, each dose of pain inflicted on Harry's close friends, it all raises the stakes higher and higher. Beating Harry down like this in each story, and seeing him rise to each new challenge with greater magical skill and mental fortitude, is precisely what is needed to build the book series with a growing snowball effect.

The underlying theme of the *Harry Potter* series is the importance of standing up for your friends and family when times are tough. Harry and his friends stand by each other when they needed it the most, and this camaraderie builds the audience's investment in the characters all the more—they in turn become the audience's friends through this shared adversity. Learn from how the *Harry Potter* series develops its characters and puts them through shared hardships that bring them closer together.

When you build up the tension like this over the course of a series, and refuse the audience any meaningful catharsis, you keep them hooked, and they take on a sort of ownership of the hero's struggles. They too have survived through all kinds of heartache, and that relates them to characters such as Harry Potter. Keep building the tension to as high a level as you can, then, and then in the final story give them the payoff that your audience desperately wants and deserves. That is the height of strategic storytelling.

Observance of the Law, Part II

The Marvel Cinematic Universe is perhaps best known for its *Avengers* ensemble films, which have captivated general audiences with its serious yet entertaining fantasy action themes. The MCU's series began in 2008 with John Favreau's *Iron Man*, which saw Robert Downey Jr catapulted from controversy to beloved stardom. His interpretation of the classic comic book character Tony Stark as a larger-than-life mechanical genius successfully won over audiences. This film's runaway success contrasted against superhero flops at the time that had left people wondering if the genre was dead for good. Any such doubters were proved wrong with the success of this fun, self-contained story.

But something unusual happened with *Iron Man* that people hadn't expected: it had a short post-credits scene. After all the film's action had finished, audiences saw Tony Stark approached by a mysterious character clothed in a large leather jacket and distinctive eye-patch. It was Samuel L. Jackson playing Nick Fury, inviting Stark to discuss the formation of an "Avengers Initiative." Each new film in the Marvel Cinematic Universe built on top of *Iron Man*'s success, giving audiences a beloved franchise that set a precedent for future shared universe stories.

Interpretation

Marvel Studios achieved new levels of success with its *Avengers* franchise by taking the time to build each one of its core characters. They built the series on firm foundations by making a series of fun yet dramatically hefty films, each one an entertaining self-contained story in its own right.

The earliest three origin stories—2008's *Iron Man* and 2011's *Captain America: The First Avenger* and *Thor*—took great care not to push the broader Marvel Cinematic Universe into the story overtly. Many shared-universe films had failed by prioritising this aspect over the quality of the storytelling. But Marvel's films succeeded by introducing and establishing an ensemble of likeable characters one by one, which meant that by the time audiences sat down in front of cinema screens to watch *The Avengers* in 2012, they were already invested in the characters. They knew who all these characters were, their personality quirks, the struggles they had endured, and loved them for it.

The later films in the Marvel Cinematic Universe took the ensemble to much darker places. 2016's *Captain America: Civil War* and 2018's *Avengers: Infinity War* enjoyed great acclaim because of a kind of compound multiplier effect. The heroes' individual stories develop their characters even deeper, and the struggles the ensemble films make them face gives their plights further meaning. That in turn makes their personal stories even more fun to watch, and so on—the effect compounded.

When building your own stories around a shared universe, use the Marvel Cinematic Universe's example as follows. First, focus on introducing your characters in robust and self-contained origin stories. Don't overtly shove your shared universe in the audience's face—instead, hint at it in the epilogues of these first stories. See which parts of this your audience likes and dislikes, before playing your hand too early.

Second, hint at an all-powerful behind-the-scenes antagonist who secretly pulls the strings behind each of these stories' villains. Bring your ensemble together to fight larger foes, but continue to hold back from confronting them with the series' behind-the-scenes antagonist for the time being—that can come later. Repeat this cycle of building more self-contained stories for each of your heroes, and feel free to introduce brand new characters. You can use more overt messages about your shared universe in these later stories.

Third, write an ensemble story that tears your team of heroes apart in an emotionally driven battle between friends. Just like 2016's *Civil War*, make this centre around the hero-hero dynamic as discussed in Law 12, The Hero and Villain Must Share the Same Goal—each opposing character needs a strong, character-defining motive for this conflict. Tailor each side's goals to the personality traits they've shown before in your series, such as the shame and guilt felt by Iron Man, and the mistrust of authority in Captain America. By threatening the team itself, you remind the audience of their deep investment in the series as a whole.

Finally, follow this with the long-awaited confrontation with your series' main antagonist. Your team of heroes reuniting once more after their prior breakup to face this ultimate threat will have more meaning. Most importantly, your audience gets the gratification of finally facing down the main villain. Start this story right in the action, with your Thanos character putting his cruelty and fighting prowess on clear display.

If there is one key lesson from this law, it's this: Take your time. You can't expect instant payoff from your ensemble in the first story of the saga. Build individual characters into strong icons through their own self-contained arcs. Build and then threaten the team dynamic. Use this proven template to create your own series of stories based around a shared universe.

The Hare and the Tortoise

The hare was once boasting of his speed before the other animals. "I have never yet been beaten," said he, "when I put forth my full speed. I challenge any one here to race with me." The tortoise said quietly, "I accept your challenge." "That is a good joke," said the hare; "I could dance round you all the way." "Keep your boasting till you've beaten," answered the tortoise. "Shall we race?" So a course was fixed and a start was made. The hare darted almost out of sight at once, but soon stopped and, to show his contempt for the tortoise, lay down to have a nap. The tortoise plodded on and plodded

on, and when the hare awoke from his nap, he
saw the tortoise just near the winning-post and
could not run up in time to save the race. Then
said the tortoise: "Plodding wins the race."

—*Aesop's Fables*, sixth century BC

Keys to Storytelling

Where a single story can have an impact, a series of interconnected stories provides an exponential compounding effect. The series enriches the mythology, and deepens the connection between the audience and your characters. For these reasons and more, a series of connected stories should have far more impact than the sum of each story by itself.

A well-written series of stories will bring untold benefits to your writing career. But to pull it off, you need a strategic mind and the ability to step back and work on the grand scale of three or more stories instead of a single one. It takes more work, but it comes with exponentially greater rewards.

Why three parts? History has shown us that the most emotionally satisfying, memorable, and validating series have contained three individual stories. But this isn't an iron rule—you can think in terms of a broader beginning, middle, and end. They play into a wider structure, with each story acting as its own part in the saga. This section will show you how to create the perfect series of stories, and how to avoid some of the most common pitfalls along the way.

Each Story Must Be Self-Contained

The most important part of a three-part series is that each story is entirely self-contained. You must resolve the specific conflict in each of the three stories. You cannot cut the ending of your first story early just because you're going to include extra details in the second story—audiences will see through your cynical attempt at the cliffhanger. Great stories conform to a rhythm of investment, then conflict, then truth. If you take hours of your audience's time only to give them unsatisfying ending cut off halfway, they will not return for your second story, because you wasted their time and interrupted the story's natural rhythm.

If your first story is a classic Hero's Journey where your plucky band of heroes has to defeat a superweapon owned by an overarching evil organisation, you must resolve that central tension in the story by destroying the superweapon, not the underlying enemy. Whatever the main tension of the specific story is, you must resolve it before the ending—you can't leave your audience hanging just because the true enemy of the series is still at large.

LAW 13

*As a general rule, plan to tie off everything re-
lating to the main arc's conflict. Whatever remains is fair game to be carried over to subsequent books.*

—*Structuring Your Novel* by K. M. Weiland

The benefits of having a more extensive series are that
you have far more space to extend each of your characters' arcs. Each part of your series must have a journey
that your character follows, even if it's not conclusive
to their development. A simple Hero's Journey story
can provide a beautifully simple arc for your hero, and
genuinely great character arcs extend way beyond the
first story.

Think of Luke Skywalker and how he evolves from
Star Wars to *Return of the Jedi*. He starts the first film as
a whiny teenager with no direction in his life, but ends
the last film as a wise and powerful Jedi Knight. That's
a titanic shift in character. You can't achieve that level
of character evolution in a single story—there aren't
enough hours of screen time, and a book with thousands of pages will scare off potential readers.

So step back, and gaze upon the vast space you have
in front of you—this is your canvas on which to develop fantastic new characters. Draw each story's conflict,
how it's going to shake your characters, how it's going

wake them up and show them the truth. Repeat this for each character in your ensemble.

Building your saga in this way with each story building its own conflict and resolution, character development and tragedy, as you determine to make each one a fantastic story in its own right, will ensure your trilogy will stick in people's minds forever and transcend the potential that each story has on its own merits.

Patience is Everything

History has shown us that the best series have a first story that has a simple structure, focussing on building investment in its core cast of characters. So start simple then, and create a linear plot with a limited cast of core characters.

In these beginnings, your characters are at the start of their respective journeys—they're at the point where they are most invested in the "lie they believe" as K. M. Weiland puts it. Show them in humble beginnings, both materially and morally. Your hero lives in a tiny room in a busy city, gazing out onto the city at night time, wishing they could go on an epic adventure.

As always, *show* this and don't merely *tell* it. In *Star Wars: The Force Awakens*, Rey reacts coldly to BB-8 and tells him to leave her alone and carry on back to town where he can find his owner, Poe Dameron. When BB-8 looks all sad, she softens and rolls her eyes, letting him stay the night. We observe much about Rey's original character because it's a crucial part of her wider character arc.

A poor writer would have had Rey overtly say, "I'm independent but also lonely. I push people away because my parents abandoned me when I was young and I'm terrified of the same thing happening again." It would have spoiled her character development because we would have had no visceral connection to her first situation. Thankfully we got something much better than this.

In the film's first scene, we see Finn at the moment that he decides to leave the First Order. Poe kills a stormtrooper, and Finn goes to try and save him. He reaches out, puts his hand on Finn's helmet, and dies. Finn stands up, in a daze, unsure of what he's doing, the bloody battle going on around him. Nothing is said, but it communicates volumes.

Finn knows that he's part of an evil organisation that does unspeakably evil things to innocent people on a mass scale. This is the foundation on which Finn builds for the remainder of the story, and the turning point is watching his friend die. He's not sure of himself, or where he needs to go, but he sure as hell knows that the First Order is a cause he can't be a part of any more.

The Force Awakens faced criticism for being too safe a story. These critics missed the point of creating the first story in the broader saga: it needs to be a solid, simple foundation for the rest of the series. Audiences need to be shown, in straightforward and understandable ways, visceral examples that display your characters' core traits.

Build up the first story to a confrontation with the main villain. If this main villain is to be the core of the series, you don't want to have some weak conflict just because you know it's evident that neither the hero or villain will die at this point. Surprise your audience by raising the stakes in some way. If your hero has a mentor, have the villain kill the mentor. This technique worked for the original *Star Wars*, *The Force Awakens*, and countless other Hero's Journey stories.

As discussed in Law 12, The Hero and Villain Must Share the Same Goal, the conflict between the hero and villain works best when it's focused on a shared goal. The shared goal in *The Force Awakens* is finding Luke Skywalker. Rey and Kylo's lightsaber duel is inconclusive because neither character is ready for that challenge to mean anything. Rey's discovery of Luke on Ahch-To, after all the conflict has subsided, brings the story to a satisfying close.

So do the same for your story. Bring your hero and villain together if you have to. If the villain is only within the confines of that story, have your hero defeat him. Otherwise, have some other shared goal that they're working towards, and aim squarely towards that as the goal of this first story. You don't want to bring things to a crescendo too early. The purpose of this story is to build investment in your characters in situations that show the start of their arcs, not to prematurely bring the series to a cathartic climax.

When faced with a difficult problem to resolve or a goal we wish to achieve, we often are tempted to take striking and energetic actions. Though it is possible to achieve temporary results in this fashion they tend to collapse when we cannot sustain the vigorous effort. More enduring accomplishments are won through gentle but ceaseless penetration, like that of a soft wind blowing steadily in the same direction.

—*The I Ching,* eighth century BC

Hit Them Where it Hurts

The middle portion of your series needs to feature the cruellest and darkest challenges to your protagonist. Threaten or take away what the characters most value —whatever it is, you need to have developed this earlier on. Lay bare every single one of your characters' flaws, and push the envelope of cruelty to make their arcs more meaningful.

We laid the groundwork in our first story to build investment in our characters. We used the Show, Don't Tell principle to show the audience our characters' main personality traits through the way they act and approach moral choices. The first story had some basic level of conflict—its purpose was to give our characters a leg-up out of their initial situation. They took a deliberate step in the right direction, toward the truth they need to believe to become genuinely great people.

At this point, we need to poke those weaknesses in the cruellest way. The purpose of this is to show that the real world is harsh and that whatever gains they might have made in the first story are only the beginning.

Your first story ended on a high note. The characters felt comfortable; they thought it was all over. So start the second story with a frightening crisis that wakes them up out of their happy daze. Did they spend the end of the first story celebrating at their base? Start the second story with the enemy swooping in and obliterating that base as your heroes barely escape—*Star Wars: The Last Jedi* pulled this off with an exciting opening sequence that grabbed the audience's attention.

This shock is necessary to set the harsh tone for the rest of the second story. Your characters aren't out of the woods by any means, and this is how things are going to go for the time being. The conflict is just getting started. Things have to get progressively worse and worse for your protagonists.

In *The Empire Strikes Back*, the Millennium Falcon breaks down over and over again. The heroes get captured and turned over to the Empire. Luke tries and fails in his Jedi training with Yoda.

In Sam Raimi's *Spider-Man 2*, Peter Parker loses his job, he faces romantic rejection, and the main villain beats the daylights out of him not just once but several times.

Don't see these examples and think they're excessively negative. In both of these examples, these hardships show the heroes' flaws to the audience. Raimi perfectly designed the struggles for this purpose. In the first story, we showed character traits, in the second story we show character flaws.

In each scene progression in the second story, we continue building up this tension to the story's self-contained natural climax, where it reaches its peak. You can't be soft at this stage. The ending must be cataclysmic—something that brings down their world and means something to everyone involved.

The Empire Strikes Back, once again, proves itself a masterclass where this principle is concerned. Luke rushes to fight Darth Vader before he's ready. He gets his hand cut off, and Vader reveals himself as his father. Han Solo is finally caught and frozen in carbonite right before Leia Organa's eyes, after they have both given in to their love for each other. When Leia says "I love you" to Han as he is lowered into the freezing chamber, we know it's real. We know these strong emotions mean something because of all the conflict we've put them through in this story.

We lay bare all our protagonists' most fundamental flaws in the second story to make them into the heroes they need to be for the final conflict in the third story. In *The Empire Strikes Back*, Luke learns that he needs to be less headstrong before rushing into conflict. He realises that he needs to yield to the Force and to let events transpire around him, rather than trying to control them all the time. It's because of the wisdom, the strength, and the patience that he gains in the second story, that he can face his father and the Emperor in *Return of the Jedi*.

Reach the Apex with Catharsis and Truth

The final part of your saga should provide the audience with a resolution to its over-arching conflicts. It's the ending of the series, and you need to treat it like the ending of any great story. All loose ends are tied up, and the main characters complete their arcs.

As stated, any story in a series must have a definitive outcome in its climax, and at least some partial victory for the main characters. But the third and final entry in your series has a weighty responsibility: it must create and provide resolution to its own story threads, while also doing the same for the series as a whole.

Where your saga's midpoint offered the cruellest challenges to your main characters, this final part must faithfully use whatever concepts you developed there. Don't discard them, or your audience will feel like all the heartache your heroes suffered was for nothing— it's tantamount to a betrayal. Not only that, it misses the point of the midpoint's conflict: to set up your hero with the tools he needs to slay the big villain.

In *Return of the Jedi*, Luke Skywalker uses all the lessons he learned in *The Empire Strikes Back* to defeat the Emperor. He shows restraint at Jabba's Palace, preferring to subtly manipulate events until pulling out his lightsaber is absolutely necessary. Luke shows patience by waiting to confront his father Darth Vader and the Emperor. He shows that he has come to terms with Vader being his father by calmly playing on his emotions, drawing him away from the dark side indirectly. Luke fighting Darth Vader is just what the Emperor wants—it'd be fighting on *their* terms, not Luke's.

Staying faithful to the midpoint's conflicts will also keep your audience engaged in your characters' development and instil a feeling of hope among the rising tension that your saga should provide. Whatever your main characters were like in the first story, they should have developed into much stronger versions of themselves by this point. Your hero who started off as a humble teenager should now be a wise and strong leader. Your maverick rascal sidekick should now show maturity and patience with others.

> *If you make a trilogy, the whole point is to get to that third chapter, and the third chapter is what justifies what's come before.*
>
> —Peter Jackson, film director

You must *show* these series-spanning character developments early in the saga's ending to set the context of the more meaningful battle to come. Show your hero's maverick side-kick being patient with the hero's leadership, in a situation where she would have previously rebelled. Don't fall into the common trap of overtly verbalising this growth, like having her say "I've grown up since then." Character development can never be explained—just like a scientific idea, you need to prove it. Your audience won't internalise character growth until it's shown to them through the choices the character makes.

In *The Dark Knight Rises*, Bruce Wayne realises that he can't fight all of his battles alone. He enlists the reluctant help of Selina Kyle as Catwoman. Returning as Batman he fights his strongest enemy yet, Bane, who easily defeats him, though not without a brave fight. This defeat shows audiences that Batman isn't a match for this villain, and must begin to use his friends to help him out. His recovery in the pit and daring escape from it also shows the audience his determination and bravery. *The Dark Knight Rises* is more of a war than a personal battle, and Batman enlists an army of police officers and friends to rise to Bane's challenge.

In *The Return of the King*, Aragorn is no longer the reclusive outlaw we saw in *The Fellowship of the Ring*. He's witnessed the breakup of the fellowship, he made it through the Battle of Helm's Deep, and he's seen loyal allies killed at the hands of Sauron's evil armies.

Aragorn has matured into the brave leader of men worthy of the crown of Gondor—we are shown this as he takes the sword Andúril, forged from the wrecked remains of his forefather's defeat, and commanding the armies of the undead. At the ending, we see him leading an army of men up to the gates of Mordor. While this is a ruse to distract Sauron, the importance of this act is in its symbolism: No one before Aragorn has dared raise an army at Mordor's gates, which in turn distracts the Dark Lord's notice from Frodo and Sam. The audience knows this is bravery fit for a king, and the team effort that this shows in helping Frodo and Sam destroy the One Ring is a far cry from the reclusive Strider they were introduced to at the start of the series.

In *Return of the Jedi*, Luke stands over his defeated father, seeing his severed hand, and looking back at his own, covered in a matching sleek black glove. He faces the all-powerful Emperor, and casts aside his lightsaber, refusing to play into his games. At this moment, Luke shows he has cast off all his immaturity and impatience. The Emperor scowls; he has failed. Luke will not be turned to the dark side. Understand: The picture of a simple act of bravery tells what thousands of lines of dialogue never can. Let your audience experience the crescendo of your hero's arc. Experience is always preferable to a verbose explication.

Think of this final section of your saga as the coda of a long orchestral piece—the realisation of character growth, the resolution of all tensions, and the moment your audience can finally breathe. Whatever cruelty you doled out on your main characters in the second story must have positive consequences here—the lack your characters showed in the first story is long gone, replaced with the strength they need to face their ultimate enemy.

Reversal

You should only employ the model of the multipart saga for stories of epic scale, where a single standalone story cannot deliver the same amount of content. Do not extend stories to multiple parts for its own sake. Your audience will recognise this as milking out your plot.

Each part in the series must have a meaningful conclusion to its own specific plot, so use this as a simple test: If your story can't be split out into three parts, each showing a meaningful progression on the previous one, then don't write it as a series just yet. Save it for a bigger story with a more epic setting.

Law 14

Make Bold Choices

Do not tread lightly when writing your plot's twists and turns. Your readers want to be grabbed roughly by the arm and hurled headlong into a good story—be the one storyteller out of a hundred to give them that pleasure. Too many authors make timid decisions that end up ruining their work. Timidity betrays weakness of thought and a lack of planning. Avoid this fate by firmly pushing your story in a definite direction. Your best work will polarise your audience. Accept this fate, and never fear being disliked for the fallout of your bold narrative choices—usually the opposite is true.

Observance of the Law

George R. R. Martin set his *Game of Thrones* saga in a medieval-themed fantasy world of kings, each king vying for ultimate power and using Machiavellian tactics to reach their goals. The series creates a fantastical world of dragons and magic, filled with gritty scenes and down-to-earth characters.

The first book in the series, *A Song of Ice and Fire*, follows Eddard "Ned" Stark, a salt-of-the-earth leader who rules his people with wisdom and justice. The king, an old friend of Ned's, recognises his qualities and makes him the King's Hand, a lofty promotion. But master deceivers lead Stark, a virtuous, down-to-earth family man, on a journey of political intrigue and manipulation throughout the story; the tension rises as multiple plots gradually come to bear against the king's successor, the teenaged Joffrey, and Ned is framed for the king's murder.

Most audiences at first see Ned Stark as the main character of the series, and therefore untouchable. But his surprise execution in the final act of the story shocks audiences, as this cruel act by Joffrey makes them wonder who will die next. However, this pattern has become a common theme to the point of cliché within Martin's works, since he's ended up killing off most of his major characters. Audiences have come to expect this pattern from all future *Game of Thrones* stories.

> *The Boy and the Nettles*
>
> *A boy was stung by a nettle. He ran home and told his mother, saying, "Although it hurts me very much, I only touched it gently." "That was just why it stung you," said his mother. "The next time you touch a nettle, grasp it boldly, and it will be soft as silk to your hand, and not in the least hurt you."*
>
> —*Aesop's Fables*, sixth century BC

Interpretation

The investment built up throughout the first story in the popularly-known *Game of Thrones* series makes it all the greater a surprise for Ned to be executed at the end for no good reason at all. Martin's renown for killing off his main characters has become a known trope in itself, but at the time, audiences marvelled at his boldness. The political intrigue and manipulation that causes Ned's death and the cruelty of Joffrey invests readers and viewers more than a bland, happy ending ever could have.

Audiences realise that no character in *Game of Thrones* is safe, creating a highly-strung tension that grows as the series continues. Due to the well-known storytelling trope called "plot armour," audiences can't imagine that so many of the main characters can get killed off at any moment.

Learn from Martin's example, then, and subvert established tropes with boldness. Never apologise for upsetting the status quo in your storytelling—audiences delight at such strong plot twists. Revenge is a dish best served cold, and you should take the same approach with your bold narrative choices—deliver shocking blows quickly and with little fanfare.

This twist at the end of *A Song of Ice and Fire* also opens up a realm of new possibilities within the story's world—the main character is dead, who can take his place at the centre of the story? Thematically this fit in well with the *Game of Thrones* series itself, since it is a series of stories about ruthless leaders all fighting for the Iron Throne, the centre of royal power. The constant death and jostling for power compliments the saga's underlying theme perfectly.

Audiences love Ned Stark, and Martin's choice to unceremoniously kill him off certainly upsets more people than it pleases. But the measure of a twist's popularity is beside the point—the key measure is its shock factor. Knock back an audience, and they'll always return for more, because they enjoy the ride and wonder what other surprises you have in store. Compare it with the "shock and awe" tactic in military strategy—the "enemy," or the audience in our case, is left shocked, mouth gaping wide, unable to react or speak. Understand: Your best plot choices will split your audience down the middle, and they'll leave your story with experiences they'll never forget.

The problem with this technique arises once it becomes a predictable pattern—major *Game of Thrones* characters would routinely kill each other in increasingly gruesome and undignified ways. What was once painful, shocking, and attention-grabbing turned into a kind of predictable game.

The reversal of the bold move is to avoid losing sight of why it works. Shocking the audience with one unexpected twist after another is a seductive rabbit hole that's all too easy to stray further into. The point of a shockingly bold choice is that it's carried out at the moment the audience least expects it—making it into its own trope gives it the opposite effect. Avoid this fate by closely monitoring your audience's expectations and using it as your barometer—when you find the next trope, undermine it one bold stroke.

Keys to Storytelling

The best image for the bold narrative choice is the underdog boxer delivering a knockout punch right when his opponent least expects it. The audience—and no doubt the opponent—are knocked flat by the speed and boldness of the attack.

Any hesitation in your plot movements will come off as lulls in the drama and inconsistencies in your characters' actions. As you hem and haw, dancing on the edges of some bold choice, it becomes unclear what your story is really trying to say because it never commits to any one course. Look at it this way: By continuing to play it safe, you actually guarantee obscurity, not the fury you're so afraid of, since wrath implies a certain level of respect.

The goal is to make your audience's jaws drop, turn to each other and ask, "Did they really just do that?" The obvious way to set this up is to embrace established storytelling tropes and character archetypes. Spend lots of time setting up a character as your main villain, only to kill him off in the second act. Or establish a wise mentor for the hero, showing him as a beloved character and trusted friend, only to have him turn evil at the last step.

It's easy to conflate this tactic with Law 9, Subvert Expectations, due to the inherent need to embrace the unexpected in our storytelling. But this is not about mere plot twists, this is about making a choice with your story structure swiftly and unapologetically— grasp the nettle with all your might.

Try this experiment: Think of the most controversial action you could take in your next story. Which character does your audience like the most? In your sequel, kill them off, giving your main protagonist all the more motivation for their noble quest. Never fret about upsetting your audience, because that's the point—such twists give your audience the emotional experience they're looking for. Immerse your audience in an emotional experience then, don't dither around trying to pander to their vaporous wants.

Stephen King famously told writers to "kill your darlings." This advice applies both to writing concisely, and in reference to the power of killing off a beloved character. The exact character you choose to kill off matters little, but take King's command as a kind of metaphor for your most daring narrative choices. Let us examine the three main positive effects of pulling off the bold manoeuvre.

> *Writing is selection. Just to start a piece of writing you have to choose one word and only one from more than a million in the language. Now*

> *keep going. What is your next word? Your next*
> *sentence, paragraph, section, chapter? Your*
> *next ball of fact. You select what goes in and*
> *you decide what stays out. At base you have*
> *only one criterion: If something interests you, it*
> *goes in—if not, it stays out. That's a crude way*
> *to assess things, but it's all you've got. Forget*
> *market research. Never market-research your*
> *writing. Write on subjects in which you have*
> *enough interest on your own to see you through*
> *all the stops, starts, hesitations, and other im-*
> *pediments along the way.*
>
> —John McPhee, journalist and author

First, it creates a constant under-the-surface threat. The majority of stories don't involve the death of the hero, so by brutally executing your hero, you create tension among your audience as they realise that no character is safe. Take Ned Stark from *Game of Thrones* or Dumbledore in *Harry Potter*. Your bold, unapologetic twist does away with the "plot armour" trope and your audience anxiously wonders who you'll kill off next.

Second, a character sacrifice adds great meaning to other characters' arcs. As stated in Law 1, Be Cruel to Your Characters, stories are about failure and conflict; characters have to earn their happy successes. A final fight that ends in victory has more meaning if it follows a devastating loss. In some cases, such as *Avengers: Infinity War* or *The Great Escape*, a disastrous failure can be a more poignant ending—it creates abundant opportunities for your characters to show virtue. Let the dying character show dignity and goodness in his final moments, and his friends rally to his side in vain.

Third, terrible dilemmas bring out the most vulnerable exposures to your characters' personality traits—give them a choice with no positive outcome and everything at stake. In *Sophie's Choice*, the title character Sophie is a Holocaust survivor. On the night that she arrived at the Auschwitz internment camp, a camp doctor made her choose which of her two children would die immediately by gassing and which would continue to live in the concentration camp. Of her two children, Sophie decided to sacrifice her seven-year-old daughter, Eva, in a heart-wrenching decision that has left her filled with an unconscionable guilt that she never overcomes. *Sophie's Choice* would not have left people with as much of a heart-wrenching shock if it had dithered with this bold decision. Learn from its example and give your characters impossible dilemmas that challenge their virtues right to the breaking point—this is the only way to show the audience who they are.

Force your main character to make an impossible choice between the death of a loved one and his guiding principles. The choice you go with doesn't matter as much as the boldness with which you take it in the story. When a character dies for his principles, it demonstrates their heroism better than if they beat great odds in a final fight.

Remember that your best storytelling decisions will split your audience down the middle. The more vocally your audience react to killing off this character or that, the more you can be certain that you've pulled off this technique. The master storyteller acts just like the classical seducer: they take their audience on a journey of their choosing, unafraid to move from one scene to another—any pandering or dithering and the magic is lost.

Reversal

Manage your boldness and know when it's not needed. Killing off characters for its own sake sets a predictable pattern, producing the opposite effect to your original boldness. To become predictable as a writer is to court disinterest. Interpersonal relationships tend to die first of indigestion, not hunger, and too much predictability will ruin your mystique as a storyteller. Keep your audience guessing, and they'll get addicted to your works.

Fans need to care about characters. Don't kill so many principal characters that you need to continually replenish them. If your audience thinks all the characters you introduce will die, they'll avoid becoming attached. Once a bold choice is made, never go back on it —never bring a dead character back to life. The deus ex machina that brings the hero back to life is an unforgivable sin usually committed for financial reasons over story quality. How can a publisher make money if they've alienated half their readership?

If your story is intended for a broad audience, then bold, controversial choices may produce a sour taste or create a reputation that puts investors off your future work. There are many people who want to passively consume a story—the choice of whether to give them that is all yours.

> *Like Alexander the Great, Philip had the reputation of being a heavy drinker. Once when drunk he gave an unjust verdict in the case of a woman who was being tried before him. "I appeal!" cried the unfortunate litigant. "To whom?" asked the monarch, who was also the highest*

tribunal in the land. "From Philip drunk to Philip sober," was the bold reply. The king, somewhat taken back, gave the case further consideration.

—*The Little, Brown Book of Anecdotes*

Law 15

Tighten with Relentless Rigour

Cut anything from your story that does not serve it. Any unnecessary parts will distract the audience from the important parts of your story. The best way to avoid fluff is to plan well and have a definite goal in mind before you start drafting. When editing your drafts, your goal is to get to a point where to remove any single paragraph, sentence, or word would cause the story to not make sense. Be concise both in your writing and the plot itself. Create an elegant flow from scene to scene by tightening down on every necessary detail.

Concise Writing—A Clarification

In February 1854, Fyodor Dostoyevsky was finally free. After four years of exile with hard labour in Siberia followed by a term of compulsory military service, his time was now his own. He had spent these years of freezing, back-breaking labour planning novels in his head, and he could often be found mumbling his characters' dialogues. Now he was free, and Dostoyevsky was determined to use his precious time to write as much as he could. Out of this fruitful period came *Crime and Punishment*, his book about a young man named Raskolnikov who planned to murder a pawnbroker for her money. The care and attention to detail with which Dostoyevsky created his works shines through the pages, as readers explored Raskolnikov's psychology in times of desperation and hatred. Dostoyevsky's later works correctly predicted the rise of totalitarian regimes in his own country and abroad, and modern psychologists praise his uncanny descriptions of torturous mental illnesses.

Crime and Punishment is over five hundred pages long. It is an unfortunate fact of life that even with such a richly detailed story of greed and the human psyche, the average reader feels put off by the story's vast length. Novels written by Russian authors of the mid-nineteenth century such as Dostoyevsky, Tolstoy, and

Chekhov typically have narrative tension that takes time to get going, and modern readers often find them hard to get into. *Crime and Punishment,* with its five-page mumbling monologues from Raskolnikov, can be dull for the reader desperate for some action. Patient readers are rewarded, however, as one chapter features some horrifying event that, like Pandora's box, lets loose all the story's conflicts. The plot flies from that moment on. Reading a long, building novel is a bit like pushing a heavy vehicle up a large hill in order to catch a fast, accelerating ride back down. It's hard to get started, but the thrill and rush of the return journey are worth it.

The lesson from *Crime and Punishment* is not to avoid writing long stories, but to make you aware of the unfortunate fact that people will make unfair snap judgements of your work from its length. If your stories take time to build into the action, then the few weaker readers who pick up your book will give up before your plot starts moving in earnest. However, Dostoyevsky's work has not been lost in obscurity by any means—it is more popular than ever. All of this boils down to a choice the storyteller must make when it comes to length: On one hand, to embrace your story's gradual rise in tension and make it enjoyable to the kind of advanced readers who appreciate literature like a long, drawn-out meal. On the other hand, to make a snappier, action-rich story that engages readers of all levels. The 2017 film *Blade Runner 2049* chose the former route, and while it suffered at the box office, it is widely considered to be one of the best sequels ever made. Conversely, the original 1977 film *Star Wars* moves at a relentless pace right from the beginning and the results speak for themselves. The choice between these routes is yours alone, and neither option is inherently right.

There is, however, a series of time-tested techniques critical for all storytellers. None of these techniques are about story length in an isolated sense, but instead about tightness. Tightness is the degree to which your story avoids meandering, sticks to its themes, and moves in a deliberate direction from start to end. Failure to avoid narrative wandering and vague prose shows a lack of clarity in your planning and vision, sending your audience to sleep.

Ego is the Enemy—Stop Focusing on Yourself

You are writing a story to be consumed by an audience. Every rambling, overlong story is a failure in the control of ego indulgence. Put yourself in your audience's shoes, and ask yourself if your story wanders. Does it contain unnecessary details that you put in just because you like them? Did you fail to cut that scene even though it serves no purpose? Your story is not a chalkboard for you to scribble on aimlessly—no one in the audience can read it, you end up with chalk all over your hands, and you make a horrendous screeching sound.

Tell a story and immerse the reader in an experience outside their normal reality. To tell a tight, concise story is to direct them along the natural, seamless flow of a river—no diversions allowed. Think of that image whenever you feel stuck on what to cut, and in your drafts ask yourself what you can remove while still retaining a clear and logical flow of events.

> *A friend was recounting to [Franklin Pierce] Adams an apparently interminable tale. He finally said: "Well, to cut a long story short—"* *"Too late," interrupted Adams.*
>
> —The Little, Brown Book of Anecdotes

Get Clear on Your Structure Before You Start Drafting

Clear writing is the result of a conscious effort to write towards a well mapped-out narrative goal, where sufficient time has been spent in the outlining and planning phases. A clear goal created by relentless planning gives you purpose and a precise direction for your writing. It's much easier to sit down and write when you have an accompanying chart for all the character arcs and plot details. Failure to plan will cause endless meandering in the writing process, and interminable boredom and confusion for your readers.

> *Obscurity and vagueness of expression is always and everywhere a very bad sign: for in ninety-nine cases out of a hundred it derives from vagueness of thought, which in turn comes from an original incongruity and inconsistency in the thought itself, and thus from its falsity. If a true thought arises in a head it will immediately strive after clarity and will soon achieve it: what is clearly thought, however, easily finds the expression appropriate to it. The thoughts a man is capable of always express themselves in clear, comprehensible and unambiguous words. Those who put together difficult, obscure, involved, ambiguous discourses do not really know what they want to say: they have no more than a vague consciousness of it which is only struggling towards a thought: often, however, they also want to conceal from themselves and others that they actually have nothing to say.*
>
> —Arthur Schopenhauer, 1788-1860

Clear, Concise Writing Will Benefit All Areas of Your Life

The results of having a clear goal in your head will shine through in a concise writing style that gets straight to the point. Clunky sentences are obstructions, unrelated sub-plots interrupt the pacing, and clever yet unnecessary dialogue distracts from the rising tension in the scene. Writing with clarity ensures you avoid these pitfalls by keeping everything to the point. The following action points will help you to tighten your prose. Do not think you are exempt from studying prose style if your medium isn't literature—screenplays, film scripts, and every aspect of your daily life will all benefit from a clear, understandable, and deliberate writing style.

Writers who get to the point provide a pleasing, unfettered experience for their readers. It might sounds strange, but you don't ever want your audience to remember they're watching your movie or reading your book—instead they need to be immersed. Let them *bathe* in the world of your story and forget their troubles. A clear, flowing writing style is the only way to achieve that. This approach is not only required for professional storytellers, it also provides untold benefits to all areas of your life. This same writing style will improve your grades, make you more effective at your day job, and turn you into a more engaging conversationalist.

Aim for Shortness and Clarity

Pulling out the thesaurus to use some ten-dollar word reeks of adolescent insecurity. It's always obvious to the reader, distracting them from the story you're trying and failing to tell. Why write "conceptualisation" when "concept" will suffice? Why write "whilst" when "while" will suffice? In everyday life, we roll our eyes at the people who fluff their sentences in an attempt to impress others, and your audience will think the same way about your writing if you make the same mistake.

> *Hemingway won the Nobel Prize for literature in 1954. Five years earlier it had been awarded to another American novelist, William Faulkner. The two writers did not have a very high opinion of each other. Faulkner said of Hemingway that he had no courage, that "he had never been known to use a word that might send the reader to the dictionary." When Hemingway heard this, he said, "Poor Faulkner. Does he really think big emotions come from big words? He thinks I don't know the ten-dollar words. I know them all right. But there are older*

*and simpler and better words, and those are the
ones I use."*

—*The Little, Brown Book of Anecdotes*

One Sentence, One Concept

Don't mix multiple concepts into a single sentence.
Chained sentences may seem to flow well in terms of
trains of thought, but they actually confuse the reader.
Multi-tasking is often messy in everyday work, and in
writing it's usually a disaster. Long, meandering sentences dilute the points you're trying to make. In film,
there is the advantage that a visual image can show
multiple things at once. In writing, you must embrace
the medium's limitation and use it for your benefit by
using rich, descriptive imagery.

Remove Filler

Get rid of unnecessary adverbs and reduce your adjectives where possible. The reader does not need to be
told that your character "ran quickly," because running
is rarely done at walking pace! Your goal is to reduce
your prose down to the smallest number of words
while still conveying the same message. Every word,
every sentence, every paragraph, even every *chapter* is
a candidate for cutting. Each of these parts is either
working for or against your story's goals—leave too

many unnecessary parts, and you'll leave your reader confused and disinterested.

Avoid Unnecessary Telling

Your role as a storyteller is not to explain, but to show. Don't worry that a lack of adverbs or adjectives will make your story fail to express itself correctly, because telling the reader that the hero felt nervous with various adjectives misses the point. Instead, show it like this: "He held his shaking hands together, the warm sweat greasing his clenched fingers. He inhaled, and peered around the corner into the darkness ahead."

> *The road to hell is paved with adverbs.*
> —Stephen King

Write in a Subject-First, Action-Oriented Style

Try to start each sentence with the subject and the action they carry out. The subject is the noun that "does" the verb, and should introduce the sentence. Structure your sentences with the picture of "X did Y to Z," not "Z was Y'd by X." Our human minds find it easier to digest the first sentence because it clearly describes what's happening.

We favour the action-oriented style because it allows for a much more concise style of writing. Writing in a passive-oriented style forces verbosity, because you're chasing the action, rather than starting with it. It forces a roundabout and cluttered mess of words. The action is the most critical part of the sentence, and thus the verb should be given its proper place.

Compare the following two examples:

1. After being walked by his owner, the comfy bed warmed around the dog's tired legs.

2. The dog lay in the warm, comfy bed after his owner took him on a walk.

Not only is the second, more active-oriented example shorter, what's going on is much more transparent. When you want to identify who the story's main character is, this technique can be useful for your wider story. Using the first example would make it ambiguous. Is the owner the main character? The second example removes any doubt.

> *I went from being a bad writer to a good writer after taking a one-day course in business writing. I couldn't believe how simple it was. I'll tell you the main tricks here so you don't have to waste a day in class. Business writing is about clarity and persuasion. The main technique is keeping things simple. Simple writing is per-*

suasive. A good argument in five sentences will sway more people than a brilliant argument in a hundred sentences. Don't fight it. Simple means getting rid of extra words. Don't write, "He was very happy" when you can write "He was happy." You think the word "very" adds something. It doesn't. Prune your sentences.

—Scott Adams, cartoonist and writer

Cut Anything Not Required for Your Story to Make Sense

Everything in your story should lead seamlessly from the start, to middle, to end. There shouldn't be any content that distracts or diverts attention anyway for even a moment. If even a single paragraph doesn't relate to the core message, the main character's development, or the overarching conflict, cut it from your story.

Side plots are a common culprit. You may find one of your characters interesting, and want to develop that character more. But does it serve the broader plot? The way to answer that question is to look at whether the pacing shifts feel unnatural when you skip from one chapter to another. Does this character serve a key purpose in the climax? If not, you may find that the painful process of cutting his side of the story serves a higher goal.

Having multiple plot threads can only work if they build the tension and conflict at equal rates. Cutting out of a tension-filled confrontation scene to a lighter scene with nothing at stake will cause endless frustration, and grind the pacing to a halt. There's nothing more satisfying than to ride the wave of rising tension, and you achieve this in your story by focusing on the main thread and not deviating until it reaches the climax.

Not Sure What to Cut? Return to Your Plan

Aside from obvious examples such as the ones above, less obvious candidates for cutting come in the form of unnecessary bits of dialogue and scene descriptions. It's easy to say "cut it if it's unnecessary," but how do you identify these subtle but damaging parts? The answer is simple: You should always write scenes with a set purpose in mind first. At the start of the writing process, step back and draw out the story's overarching plan. Plot out each character's arc, and a general overview of how the character gets there. Creating clear goals for yourself makes the writing process much easier.

Constant Rigour

During the Renaissance, artists were expected to create new works at a relatively high rate. Leonardo da Vinci (1452-1519) would often face ridicule from his peers for the time he took to finish his pieces. To these critics he would repeat his motto, "Ostinato rigore," or "Constant rigour." Da Vinci had a relentless work ethic focused on the details, and the results speak for themselves in both his lasting legend and the value of his artworks. By refusing to rush out unchecked work and embracing da Vinci's motto of "Ostinato rigore," we make our stories more enjoyable and increase their chances of everlasting success.

> *First drafts are slow and develop clumsily because every sentence affects not only those before it but also those that follow. The first draft of my book on California geology took two gloomy years; the second, third, and fourth drafts took about six months altogether. That four-to-one ratio in writing time—first draft versus the other drafts combined—has for me been consistent in projects of any length, even if the first draft takes only a few days or weeks. There are psychological differences from phase to phase, and the first is the phase of the pit and*

*the pendulum. After that, it seems as if a differ-
ent person is taking over. Dread largely disappears. Problems become less threatening, more
interesting. Experience is more helpful, as if an
amateur is being replaced by a professional.
Days go by quickly and not a few could be
called pleasant, I'll admit.*

—John McPhee, journalist and author

Enlist Trusted Friends and Hire an Independent Editor

Seek advice from colleagues, friends, and family—or, better, an independent third party. Seek objective, honest feedback. Their stated reasons for whether they like it or not are always correct, but their gut feeling about whether they like it is always correct. Ask them if they can tell you who the hero is, who the villain is, and how they change throughout the story. Can they give you a precise answer? If not, work on making these aspects of your story more concise and clear. Taking this external perspective is one of the most effective ways to deliver the best story to your audience.

Don't Take Criticism Personally—Be Open to Every Edit

Every good story has gone through a rigorous review stage, and finding things to pick out and cut is always the easiest part. We may feel resentful when someone finds holes in our work, but this feeling is counterproductive. Think of it this way: It's much better for our editors to spot problems at this stage before our story goes into production.

Professional vs Unprofessional Publishing

There is an unfair stigma against writers who self-publish their work—that somehow a work is not "really" published until a twenty-something intern at a publishing company arbitrarily picks it out of a ten-foot high pile of submissions. Do not be ashamed to self-publish your story—it gives you the freedom to put in as many rounds of edits as you want. Where a publishing house would pressure you to get your book to an acceptable level and release it quickly, you can instead take as much time as necessary to tighten your story with the relentless rigour that makes a classic. The battle isn't between self-publishing and traditional publishing, it's between professional publishing and unprofessional publishing. More edits, more fine-tuning, more work, equals a more professional product.

Read Your Work Aloud

Print out a written copy of your story, and read it aloud to yourself. Bring a pen and a highlighter, because you *will* notice any sentences that don't read well. If a sentence is overlong or doesn't read well, then adjust it and rewrite as necessary. You'll surprise yourself with how good your instincts are in this exercise.

Structural Issues? Don't Panic

A big problem to watch out for in this editing stage is a whole host of structural issues baked into your story, with much of the content mired in side-plots that go nowhere, and excessive development of side characters. These errors beg some serious questions about how you let it get to this stage. The most important thing is not to panic; it just means you'll have a harder job separating the good parts to keep from the bad parts to cut. Keep a clear head and don't throw out months of work—there's something valuable in there.

> *The difference between a common writer and an improviser on a stage (or any performing artist) is that writing can be revised. Actually, the essence of the process is revision. The adulating portrait of the perfect writer who never blots a line comes Express Mail from fairyland.*

—John McPhee, journalist and author

A Warning

Don't lose sight of the optimal path of story creation. Start with a plan. Take this early step seriously, and design a strong structural frame. Then, do your drafting. In this stage, optimise for volume, and focus more on getting your story on paper than on getting your prose perfect. There's no point in agonising over a paragraph you might well remove a month later. Once you're certain you've finished your first draft, close your laptop and don't look at your story for at least a week. After months of writing, you've earned a break. But the true purpose of this time away from your story is to grow a fresh perspective—when you return to create your second draft, you'll notice problems that you glazed over in your first draft. Your first revisions make your second draft acceptably readable to your fans. Then your next revisions make your third draft acceptable to your critics. This process is iterative and can go on for as long as you like. With time on your side, there isn't any excuse for not publishing a near-perfect work of art. Perfect may be the enemy of done, but at least striving for perfection will yield far more satisfying results than rushing out a sloppy, unfinished story for some quick money.

In general, your audience will appreciate punchy candour over excess verbosity, so favour the rubber end of the pencil over the lead. However, this law doesn't concern length in isolation, but instead the degree of clarity and tightness. Indeed, the more die-hard among your fans will enjoy more detail, especially in story genres such as fantasy or science fiction, so be judicious in how you serve these people.

The length of J. R. R. Tolkien's *The Lord of the Rings* can make it difficult for new or rusty readers. Tolkien was a linguist and world-builder first, and this reflects in the rich details of his characters and locations. In spite of its vast length, *The Lord of the Rings*'s success comes through in the classic heroic themes that it touches upon—Frodo's dedication, Sam's bravery, and the friendship formed through mutual struggles. See that longer-form prose does not limit a story from serving an audience well.

The main reversal to this law is that writers often conflate "concise" with "short," a fallacy that can destroy critical character development scenes for the sake of brevity. Stories desperately need this kind of content to make sense. Tightening your story means cutting out the waste by removing unnecessary parts that do not serve the story. Instead of saying, "This story is too long," say "This story is too directionless." For example, an uncomfortably long and drawn-out tension can do wonders for your scenes. In such cases, worry less about the word count, and worry more about stretching the elastic band of discomfort as far it'll go. Turn the screw as gradually as you can, and you'll create an unforgettably tension-filled scene that will become an unforgettable defining moment for your story.

> *Gradually [Oliver Wendell Holmes Jr] assumed the privileges of the manor. Things he had not dared to touch he began now to use as his own. Grandfather Jackson's high desk stood in a corner of the library. Wendell had always been proud of Judge Jackson, pleased when in court he had to refer to his opinions. Now he stood at the desk to write his opinions. "Doesn't it tire you?" Fanny asked, watching him write, one knee propped against the desk. "Yes," Wendell replied. "But it's salutary. Nothing conduces to brevity like a caving in of the knees."*
>
> —The Little, Brown Book of Anecdotes

Law 16

Humour Is Always Welcome

Regardless of genre, humour is always welcome. But a moment of levity is especially welcome when it distracts the reader away from a serious backdrop. A single, short, well-delivered line can make your audience forgive ten chapters of demure tragedy. Humour that pokes fun at your characters or some element of your story can be an indirect way of exposing some truth. It also reminds the audience they're here to enjoy themselves, and shows them that you don't take yourself too seriously.

A Child's Perspective on Serious Events

Our first example is Harper Lee's book *To Kill a Mockingbird*. This classic piece of literature gives many great examples of the humour of youthful perspectives on serious situations. The primary source is the contrast between Scout's perspective as a young girl with our perspective as adults.

To Kill a Mockingbird's status as a cultural icon is partly because of the gravely severe subject matter that forms the story's backdrop. A black man is falsely accused of sexual assault and graphic examples of racism abound in every chapter. But for a story with such grave seriousness woven into its pages, Harper Lee knew when to grant the audience a reprieve. Scout brings us to a point of humane perspective as she recalls these horrible events during tense criminal trials from a child's perspective. Her innocence doesn't cheapen the issues raised in *To Kill a Mockingbird*, it brings humanity to it.

> *I suppose I should include Uncle Jimmy, Aunt Alexandra's husband, but as he never spoke a word to me in my life except to say, "Get off the fence," once, I never saw any reason to take notice of him. Neither did Aunt Alexandra. Long ago, in a burst of friendliness, Aunty and Uncle*

> *Jimmy produced a son named Henry, who left home as soon as was humanly possible.*
>
> —*To Kill a Mockingbird* by Harper Lee

Scout's observations make light of the unhappy marriage between Uncle Jimmy and Aunt Alexandra. The word "burst" is comical because it makes us imagine something sudden and quick that quickly fizzles into nothing. While we might allude "burst" to something more adult, Scout's description of it as "friendliness" highlights her innocence.

> *I said if he wanted to take a broad view of the thing, it really began with Andrew Jackson. If General Jackson hadn't run the Creels up the creek, Simon Finch would never have paddled up the Alabama, and where would we be if he hadn't?*
>
> —*To Kill a Mockingbird* by Harper Lee

When Jem breaks his arm, he places the blame on Dill. This is clearly a lie since they have not seen Dill for over two years, so Scout responds to this accusation with the above remarks. The humour lies in Scout taking Jem's ridiculous allegation and exaggerating it to the point of absurdity.

These wonderful pieces of innocent humour give us a break of levity from the deeply charged themes in *To Kill a Mockingbird*'s plot. The story has its sad moments in spades, and moments of happiness such as these take our minds back to Scout's innocence, even if it's only temporary—it keeps our spirits up.

Using Humour to Build a Character

Our second example is the 1942 film *Casablanca*. The humour in this film centres around the main character Rick Blaine, whose displays of dry wit both establish his personality and provide some much needed moments of levity. The film came out during the Second World War, and many of the actors were actual European war refugees. Watch the famous *"La Marseillaise"* scene again—the emotions on their faces are not a product of acting.

To depict stomach-churning characters such as Major Strasser during the time of the actual war against Nazi Germany might seem like propaganda, or at least an unwise move. But the genius of *Casablanca* is that it carefully balances the seriousness of the story's backdrop with a series of some of the most famous comedic quips in cinema history.

Here are some of these quips. Firstly, when the desperate smuggler Ugarte begs Rick to give him protection from the occupying Germans, the audience is shown Rick's cool, aloof attitude at the beginning of the story. It's building up his character:

> *Ugarte: You despise me, don't you?*
> *Rick Blaine: Well if I gave you any thought I probably would.*
>
> —*Casablanca*, 1942

Next, Rick's head waiter Carl denies a young patron and her chaperone an audience with Rick, proving his aloofness and rule-breaking nature:

> *Customer: Um, waiter? Will you ask Rick if he will have a drink with us?*
>
> *Carl: Madame he never drinks with customers. Never. I have never seen it.*
>
> *Customer: What makes saloon keepers so snobbish?*
>
> *German Banker: Perhaps if you tell him I run the second largest banking house in Amsterdam?*
>
> *Carl: Second largest? It wouldn't impress Rick. The leading banker in Amsterdam is the pastry chef in our kitchen.*
>
> *German Banker: We have something to look forward to.*

Carl: And his father's the bellboy.

—*Casablanca*, 1942

And lastly, when Major Strasser finally commands Captain Renault to close Rick's café, his grey moral virtues are laid bare:

Captain Renault: I'm shocked that there is gambling in this establishment!
Waiter: Sir, here are your winnings.
Captain Renault: Thank you.

—*Casablanca*, 1942

These examples show that dialogue can be one of the most efficient ways to convey humour—telling joke is easier than developing an elaborate physical prank. Little comedic quips here and there keep the tone from going too dark. The jokes come so quick and fast that every scene, no matter how severe it may seem, is one beat away from a laugh.

Casablanca is a devastatingly funny film. Its humour is vital given the severe backdrop of its setting—amplified by the literal war going on at the time. Its purpose wasn't to bring any serious issues to light; it was to gives its audience two hours of fun, and raise their spirits during a time of war.

Learn from *Casablanca*'s example and contrast your story's dangerous setting against occasional one-liners that keep up your audience's spirits. So long as your story's humour is well-timed and balanced, it will provide a contrast and thus add to its moments of seriousness.

Using Well-Timed Quips to Lighten the Darkest Moments

Our third example is Christopher Nolan's 2005 film *Batman Begins*, notable at the time for being the first live-action retelling of the comic book character's origin story.

The film begins by investing time in showing the love and goodness of the protagonist's father. Young Bruce Wayne falls into an old watering hole, injuring his leg, and leaving him terrified at the hundreds of startled bats that emerge from the depths of the hole. His father climbs down saved him, teaching him a valuable lesson about strength in the face of fear.

After investing this time showing the love and goodness of his father, Joe Chill kills Wayne's parents in front of him, leaving them to die in the street. Wayne had only wanted to leave the theatre performance they were attending because of his fear at the bats in the show, and the horrible crime he witnesses leaves him feeling responsible and emotionally scarred.

Later in the story, as a young man, Wayne spurns his privileged lifestyle. He leaves his Ivy League college and chooses a journey of self-discovery, preferring to live in squalor in an Asian prison. One day, an inmate marches up to Wayne and throws what is left of his meagre broth onto the ground. Wayne immediately sparks a fight with the bully, making quick work of him and several other inmates, showing off his fighting abilities and aggression.

Armed prison guards intervened, pulling Wayne off the inmates he's beaten so easily. After Wayne demands to know why this was happening, one of the guards responds:

> *Prison guard: "For protection!"*
> *Wayne: "I don't need protection!"*
> *Prison guard: "Protection for them!"*
> —*Batman Begins*, 2005

The camera then pans to a dozen inmates struggling to stand up after the fight with the film's hero.

Christopher Nolan's *Dark Knight* trilogy of films takes a different turn to traditional and even contemporary superhero movies, by placing Batman in a realistic world without any fantastical superheroes or magic powers.

The example cited above is one of several examples of humorous levity in an otherwise dark story. Nolan shows the audience the love in Wayne's family, only to have this situation shattered in a random act of needless violence. It leaves the hero both feeling ashamed of his fear and with a cruel, aggressive streak that shows itself in the prison fight scene. Even then, the joke that t the prison guards are protecting the other prisoners and not Wayne lightens the load of the until-then grim story.

Later on, Wayne gives his expensive coat to a homeless man, on his way to confront one of the story's antagonists, the crime boss Falcone. Predictably, this goes poorly, and the crime boss's goons beat him and throw him onto the street. The naive Wayne saw judges and police officers helplessly watching their confrontation in Falcone's club, proof that fear and intimidation are preventing justice from being served in Gotham City. The mob *has* to be stopped.

After he's returned to Gotham City as Batman and successfully intimidated the once all-powerful Falcone, he spots the same homeless man, terrified for his life. Bruce locks eyes with the man and says, "Nice coat," before flying away. Not only does this lighten a particularly dark scene, but it also emphasises Bruce's evolution as a character—he's gained confidence and beaten his fears.

> *Make it dark, make it grim, make it tough, but then, for the love of God, tell a joke.*
>
> —Joss Whedon

Keys to Storytelling

An occasional dose of appropriate humour is the best way to relieve a story's seriousness. A quick piece of funny dialogue can remind your audience that they're experiencing a story about human beings with a sense of humour. Know when to deliver a joke at the right time, then, and your audience will forgive a hundred pages of grim drudgery.

Humour brings your story down to earth, reminding the audience that they're here to be entertained, not lectured at with unrelenting seriousness. To respond to crises with humour can be a healthy response to our real-life struggles. Those humourless individuals we come across tend to irritate us with their holier-than-thou temperaments, always making everything about some pressing issue.

This is why we love those who can make us laugh the most, be it a real-life friend or a character in a story.

This does not necessarily make them the comic relief, dedicated to making wisecracks, breaking the tension, and nothing more. A character who can display humour at the right moment is a mature character—it's a sign that they can see the funny side even when times are uncertain.

Psychotherapist Carl Jung was known for the humour with which he treated his patients. His warmth and laughter made it impossible for patients to see him as the stereotypical self-important therapist. To do so would have made his patients more defensive and less receptive to treatment. Upon greeting one patient, he grinned and said, "So you're in the soup, too!" To Jung, each appointment was an opportunity to be present in the moment with another human being. By remaining on the same level as the patient, and not aloof and analytical, the session was something to be enjoyed by the patient. This approach healed the patient's soul better than any cold seriousness.

> *I am the happiest creature in the world. Perhaps other people have said so before, but not one with such justice. I am happier even than Jane; she only smiles, I laugh.*
>
> —*Pride and Prejudice* by Jane Austen

Humour, however, cannot exist in a vacuum; it can only contrast against seriousness. Each of the listed observances has a serious backdrop, selectively using comedy to provide levity when it's required. Not once does the humour fall flat or seem out of place, because it's judiciously applied to relieve the audience of the tension at the right time. Think of humour as a kind of release valve for your story's dramatic tension.

In the fourth century BC, the royal family of Macedon split in two when King Philip married a young girl from the aristocracy. At dinner after the wedding, a general of Philip's drunkenly applauded him for marrying a girl who could finally provide him with a pure Macedonian heir. Philip's son, Alexander, threw a cup of wine at the man for implying that he was a bastard child. The other nobles in the wedding congregation watched in stunned silence as a boiling argument ensued. Finally, Philip had had enough. He stood up, drew his sword, and charged at Alexander, only to trip and fall on his face in his drunken stupor. The palpable tension broke and the entire congregation roared with laughter. Alexander shouted, "Here is the man who was making ready to cross from Europe to Asia. He cannot even cross from one table to another."

Later, in the third century BC, the great Carthaginian general Hannibal led an army through Spain, Gaul, and across the supposedly impassable Alps. Their goal was to discourage the Romans by fighting them on their own soil, and they mostly succeeded. Even though Hannibal lost three-quarters of his men in their desperate march across the Alps, they won a series of unlikely victories against the famed and numerically superior Roman legions.

Two years into their campaign across Rome, Hannibal's soldiers met again in Cannae. Exhausted, demoralised, and vastly outnumbered by the well-trained Romans in front of them, his men fell silent with fear. A Carthaginian general named Gisgo rode to Hannibal, who could feel the fear trembling in his voice. Hannibal turned to his officer and replied, "There is one thing, Gisgo, that you have not noticed. In all that great number of men opposite, there is not a single one whose name is Gisgo."

Both men burst into laughter, as did the rest of the Carthaginian army as the joke spread, and so all the tension disappeared. As the laughter subsided, the men relaxed and realised that a leader who could make a joke at a time like this must be truly confident in his chances—they had beaten the odds before, and they could do so again today. The Carthaginians, swept up in a tide of inspiration, won one of the most acclaimed military victories in history against the Roman army.

The Battle of Cannae is still hailed as one of the most strategically brilliant victories in history, and its lessons are taught in military classrooms to this day.

Just as Hannibal was able to break the tension in his army's ranks with a single one-line joke, you can do the same with any level of dramatic tension. In fact, the higher the level of pressure, the more fragile it is, and the easier it is to break. But the point is not the breaking of the tension itself; it is the effect that this breaking has on the audience. It inspires the audience with hope in the protagonist's chances of victory, and that if he doesn't succeed, at least they're going to enjoy the ride.

From our earlier example in *Batman Begins*, the nightmarish reality in which the young Wayne lives comes to the fore as he lets loose his aggression on the unsuspecting prison inmates who see him as a privileged westerner. The prison guard's joke dissolves this tension after he quickly dispatches them. Bruce shows his courage and ferocity as well as his fighting prowess, and the guard's quip brings this already funny moment back down to earth. Once Bruce has become Batman and exacts his revenge by intimidating the crime boss Falcone, he spots the old man he gave his coat to years before. The "nice coat" quip lightens the mood and emphasises his transformation from the scared, naive young man to the brave hero who uses fear to exact vigilante justice.

Use this technique to create a cyclic effect of tension-building as the story progresses to the final act. Build some tension, then release a little bit with some levity. Build the tension again, going further this time, and deliver some more levity. Then, as the film reaches its climax before your audience knows it, you've let the tension build to the story's ultimate climax, providing the perfect ending.

> *The idle business of show, plays on the stage, flocks of sheep, herds, exercises with spears, a bone cast to little dogs, a bit of bread into fishponds, labourings of ants and burden-carrying, runnings about of frightened little mice, puppets pulled by strings all alike. It is your duty then in the midst of such things to show good humour and not a proud air; to understand however that every man is worth just so much as the things are worth about which he busies himself.*
>
> —*Meditations* by Marcus Aurelius

Reversal

Mark Twain wrote that "Humour is only a fragrance, a decoration. Often it is merely an odd trick of speech and spelling." Just like a sweet fragrance can make us sick if overdone, a lack of balance in tension and humour can ruin a film's serious tone.

Consider the 2017 film *Pirates of the Caribbean: Dead Men Tell No Tales* as your cautionary tale on how not to execute humour in a story. The film is the fifth entry in a series that had originally amused audiences with great chemistry between the love interests and the enigmatic rogue Jack Sparrow. The characters in the first *Pirates of the Caribbean* film work because the humour is subordinate to an entertaining story that touches upon timeless themes such as forbidden love and adventure into the unknown.

But once the second and third films in the series have seen the love story of Will and Elizabeth come to a natural conclusion, the series begins to rely on slapstick comedy, forced jokes, and Jack Sparrow outdoing his own prior feats of bumbling drunkenness. An appearance by Paul McCartney as Sparrow's uncle, hyped before *Dead Men Tell No Tales*'s release, turned out to be an unfunny, overlong, out-of-place scene that makes little sense and contributes little to the overall story. In the midst of all the chaos, the story seems incoherent and bloated, failing to align with any discernible structure. Film critic Mick LaSalle of the *San Francisco Chronicle* called the film "a jumble of half-baked impulses" wedged into a played-out franchise.

Remember that humour's role is to provide levity against a serious backdrop. Overdo it and risk your audience not taking you as seriously as you might hope. A consistent tone is more important than giving your audience an occasional laugh. Misuse humour and mistake its purpose, and your audience won't be sure what your story is trying to say.

Also stay aware of humour's diffusing effect on dramatic tension—this is largely a matter of timing, so know the right time to apply the release valve. If you're trying to build tension in a scene, then avoid any poorly timed jokes. In this scenario, keep the tension rising. Prematurely relieving a pivotal scene's dramatic tension with a joke at the wrong moment might ruin any serious points you want to make.

> *Following a well-received after-dinner speech by George Ade, a noted lawyer rose to speak. His hands buried deep in the pockets of his trousers, he began: "Doesn't it strike the company as a little unusual that a professional humorist should be funny?" Ade waited for the laughter*

to die down before replying: "Doesn't it strike the company as a little unusual that a lawyer should have his hands in his own pockets?"

—*The Little, Brown Book of Anecdotes*

Law 17

Write along the Line of Greatest Intuition

Audiences are especially good at spotting when you try to force the plot. Realising that you need to place some artificial decision or event just to make your plot work is a bad sign. Nothing ruins an audience's immersion like an unrealistically idiotic decision by your character. Put yourself in the character's shoes. What is your first instinct? What would you do? Choose that action for your character.

Transgression of the Law, Part I

In 2000, the author Dan Brown wrote a novel titled *Angels and Demons* that would later prove the start of professor Robert Langdon's glittering career, particularly in the successful book *The Da Vinci Code*. *Angels and Demons*, however, had an unusually wide plot hole that none of the highly educated characters realised. The unstable antimatter canister, the central threat of the story, is monitored by a camera constantly, its threatening stillness broadcasted across the globe to international TV networks.

In their furious attempts to find this object, no one manages to see the obvious clue there: Since they are receiving video from the broadcast, the camera is emitting a signal, which can be triangulated and thus located. In spite of this glaring plot hole, great care is taken to explain how undetectable the antimatter is, and the characters even cut the electricity to entire city blocks to help them locate the antimatter.

Further to that, the bumbling police officers only serve to heighten the suspense as the time runs out for each successive cardinal in danger. Professor Robert Langdon is forced to think on his feet and rely on his in-depth knowledge of religious iconology. Each new clue forms a fascinating insight into this once-obscure academic field, and the race against time to save the cardinals—not to mention the city of Rome itself—rises to a crescendo as the antimatter canister's timer approaches zero.

Interpretation

While *Angels and Demons* met with great success in the form of wide readership, its glaring plot holes were not missed by the more astute among its audience. The 2009 film adaptation even went so far as to immediately lampshade these plot holes, as one of the main character Robert Langdon's first suggestions is to try triangulation, and, later on, he berates the police officers for their bumbling ineptitude as the assassin abducts cardinals in plain sight.

Had the story's highly educated characters noticed at any point that the anti-matter could easily be located using triangulation, a method dating back to the Roman republic, the story would be over and all threat extinguished. This fragile link is the usual problem with plot holes, and any time a writer leans too heavily on plot over intuition—if this piece of the plot fails to occur, then there's no story.

Angels and Demons is an incredibly fun and immersive book that opens insights into the fascinating world of Vatican Rome and its religious iconology. These qualities are arguably more important than the presence of any plot contrivances—if you as a storyteller are satisfied with that outcome, then, by all means follow in this book's footsteps. It is not an egregious example of plot contrivance by any means. But there is more often than not a feeling of dissatisfaction when a story treads into the territory of "Okay, we need this to happen to get this person over there." Your audience enjoys the thrill ride your book takes them on, but it sits firmly in the "guilty pleasure" category of their mind.

> *The moment fiction becomes dishonest is the moment it ceases to matter.*
> —*Structuring Your Novel* by K. M. Weiland

Transgression of the Law, Part II

In the 1990s, George Lucas's intentions with the *Star Wars* prequel trilogy were simple: Tell the tragic backstory of Anakin Skywalker, showing his descent into the evil Darth Vader from his original film saga. Loyal fans had waited over a decade for the return to their favourite film saga's return to the cinema screen. His production company Lucasfilm announced three new films offering terrific possibilities given the recent advancements in cinema technology, and the chance to expand the beloved *Star Wars* universe with new stories.

Sure enough, in 1999 *The Phantom Menace* brought millions of people out to see what Lucas had in store. In spite of the audience's excitement, the film found mixed reception. Filmgoers were glad to see modern special effects and especially grateful to finally get to enjoy a new addition to the *Star Wars* saga. But after the hysteria had died down, a few critics noted the distinct lack of character chemistry that had made audiences fall in love with the original films, not to mention a bizarre plot based mostly on intergalactic politics, and the film's over-reliance on computer-generated special effects.

The second entry in the prequel trilogy came in 2002, *The Attack of the Clones*, and Lucas claimed to have listened to the criticisms of *The Phantom Menace*, notably by reducing the role of the Jar Jar Binks character, whom many filmgoers and critics had found unbearable to watch. However, *Attack of the Clones* still suffered from similar problems: for starters, it relied even more on special effects than before. But more crucially, Lucas had intended this film to be the love story for Anakin and Padmé, but the neither of the characters show any chemistry with the other. Instead of developing characters through conflict, action, and tension, every other scene was filled with dull exposition against a blue screen saturated with computer-generated imagery. Nothing felt real.

The third and final entry in the prequel trilogy came three years later in 2005 and with greater anticipation than the prior two films. *The Revenge of the Sith* was, after all, supposed to show the crucial final step in Anakin Skywalker's fall to the dark side to become Darth Vader. This film was meant to act as the crescendo for the dark unrest rising inside Anakin, as all his frustrations with the Jedi come to a head. And that potential appeared to have paid off—the film received much more positive feedback than the previous two. The exciting opening scene shows some of the chemistry and friendship between Anakin and Obi-Wan Kenobi, establishing their characters with action and humour. The dark manipulations of Chancellor Palpatine are the highlight of the film, especially when he reveals himself to Anakin and the Jedi as Darth Sidious, the Sith Lord pulling the strings behind the scenes.

However, strange plot threads permeated the film that don't seem to make sense. Not one of the Jedi council notices—much less tries to intervene in—Anakin's personal struggles. In one scene, Anakin anxiously confesses his dreams of Padmé's death to Master Yoda, only to have the Order's grand master casually brush him off with a nebulous reminder of the fragility of life. In the final act, Obi-Wan suddenly appears to Anakin and Padmé in the middle of their reunion—his timing cannot worse, as it causes Anakin to instantly suspect his wife of betrayal, strangling her with the Force, harming the loved one he's fallen to the dark side to protect. Shortly after, Padmé dies giving birth to their twins, Luke and Leia. No reason is given for her death other than that she has lost the will to live after Anakin's turn to the dark side. And the ending seems a frantic race to tie all the plot threads into a neat bow resembling the start of the original Star Wars saga. The end scenes include Darth Vader in his suit, the Emperor in his cloak, and a young Grand Moff Tarkin standing proudly in front of the Death Star under construction, followed by Obi-Wan delivering the newborn baby Luke to his family on Tatooine.

Interpretation

When George Lucas announced the *Star Wars* prequel trilogy, and that it would follow Anakin Skywalker's fall to the dark side, there was eager anticipation among loyal fans of the franchise. After decades of waiting, these films had the potential to show a tragic fall-from-grace arc for the real man behind Darth Vader's mask. Also, fans would finally have the opportunity to see new *Star Wars* films with modern special effects and contemporary actors. Reportedly, Liam Neeson was so excited to star as Qui-Gon Jinn in *The Phantom Menace* that he didn't even read the script before agreeing to the role. It became clear after their release that the goal of the *Star Wars* prequels was merely to achieve plot ends and showcase the latest in computer-generated special effects, and that this came at the expense of anything resembling the original saga.

On release, in spite of the audience's delight at the new *Star Wars* material, film critics noted dull, lifeless performances from the key actors, and plots that relied heavily on constant expository dialogue rather than action and lively characters. Where the original saga succeeds through simple stories closely resembling timeless myths like the Hero's Journey, these new films have tensionless stories filled with unintelligible plots about trade disputes and underhanded politics.

Where there were once lovable characters interacting with great chemistry, the prequels portray stern, emotionless characters who barely interacted in a human way. They are not characters, then, but lifeless pawns on a board game meant to get the plot from A to B. Audiences need to emotionally connect with characters, and that is never possible when they're merely mouthpieces for glib exposition and placeholders for the plot.

The films are indeed full of computer-generated special effects, and their over-dependence on blue screens means the actors can't interact with real-life environments. Understand: Audiences are only superficially impressed by dazzling visuals, and only for a limited time. Such effects are like the pretty icing on a delicious cake, or the garnish on a thick steak. It is the cake or the steak we're after—the interpersonal conflicts and character arcs.

The *Star Wars* prequel trilogy achieves all the plot ends that Lucas desired, but it is the clearest modern example proving that good storytelling should never be subordinate to plot. Instead, start with a set of realistic characters in a situation, and let your plot follow the natural outward progression of events. That doesn't mean neglecting to structure or outline your story beforehand—in fact quite the opposite—you need to be thinking of whether your plot follows an intuitive path at the planning stage. You must think about how your characters will react to these plot developments and interact with each other. If they act like human beings with flaws and emotions, your audience will love them. If you let them all act like bland, emotionless pawns, your audience will forget them.

The Jay and the Peacock

A jay venturing into a yard where peacocks used to walk, found there a number of feathers which had fallen from the peacocks when they were moulting. He tied them all to his tail and strutted down towards the peacocks. When he came near them they soon discovered the cheat, and striding up to him pecked at him and plucked away his borrowed plumes. So the jay could do no better than go back to the other jays, who had watched his behaviour from a distance; but they were equally annoyed with him, and told him: "It is not only fine feathers that make fine birds."

—*Aesop's Fables*, sixth century BC

Keys to Storytelling

Plot contrivance is the most recognisable sin in storytelling, especially if it's some unforeshadowed event or a stupid decision by the main character. Audiences recognise it more often than any other storytelling error because it's so prevalent in the professional worlds of writing. Professional writers resort to it so often because it's a painless route to take—if you're 30,000 words into your novel and realise you have no logical way of getting your characters from A to B, then the expedient route of writing a spurious plot hole feels less painful than the frightening prospect of having to start from scratch.

Too many writers suffer from a sort of tactical hell of their own creation. Pushed into a corner by their own nonsensical plot devices, they have to patch up these plot holes with further contrivances. These writers are constantly reacting to circumstances, never feeling on the forward foot. It's a weak position that leaves the writer feeling bullied by their own work, having suffered a lot of unnecessary existential dread.

The solution is to know your goals and take a strategic approach to storytelling. Instead of resolving to determine every single beat of your story from the project's outset, you must decide to take a broader view. Design the outline of your character arcs, the beats leading to the ending, and the underlying message of your story. In her guide *Outlining Your Novel*, author and storytelling expert K. M. Weiland emphasises the importance of this step in the planning process. It gives you the shape of your story, while still allowing you the required latitude to fill in the details at a later stage.

This attitude has been used for centuries by history's greatest military leaders. Napoleon would sometimes issue orders to his Marshals in the form of general statements of purpose, instead of giving them rigid orders to follow to the letter. Young, agile, and quick of mind, his subordinates were able to use this latitude to come up with brilliant solutions to the problems passed onto them. You should aim to emulate this model in your storytelling. To attempt to detail every single event in your plot from the start is a Sisyphean task that can only yield the pain of repeated rewrites. Just as Sisyphus from Greek mythology exerted incredible physical effort to push his immense boulder up the hill only for it to fall right back down, by failing to take a broader view and pay attention to your story's structure, you'll plague your project with unnecessary work. Avoiding such pointless blustering will make writing a more streamlined and less painful process not just for yourself, but also your editors and readers.

Broad-minded planning and responding to circumstances according to a larger goal often relies on your intuition. When Napoleon faced unexpected setbacks to his military strategies he would calmly assess the situation and quickly come up with a response. We don't want to stay in "react mode," but we have to acknowledge that life is unpredictable—keeping our plans fluid allows for changes further down the road. In writing his books, Stephen King would first establish a situation for his story to centre around, insert a cast of characters, and then use his intuition to work from there. His question wasn't "What do I need to happen?" but instead "Given this situation, and these characters, what would they do to get around it?" He would place himself in the shoes of these characters and use his natural intuition to narrate the story right through to the end. Through this method of dynamic narration, King would describe himself as "the first reader of my books," which proved an exciting endeavour for him given his usual genre was the suspense thriller.

Learn from King's method of relying on intuition in a given situation, and you'll come up with brilliant story points you'd never think yourself capable of writing. Many writers, however, confuse this technique with being less rigorous in the planning stage—you need to avoid wandering as distractions and vague ideas pull you in all directions. Start from an outline, and iteratively build more detail into it using your natural intuition, until you have a workable story. This work is all done in the planning stage before you write the first word of your novel or screenplay. Think of it in this way: If you don't know what's going to happen yet, how will your audience do the same? Life is unpredictable, and so should your story be. To plan in this way, and get a realistic, unpredictable, and immersive story out of it is the height of strategic storytelling.

The Idiot Plot

The term "Idiot Plot" originated from science fiction author James Blish, and was popularised by the film critic Roger Ebert in his review of the 1990 film *Narrow Margin*. A story with an Idiot Plot only moves forward because all of its characters behave like idiots. Such stories are at their worst when they completely depend on a character making an idiotic decision against their personality and with no prior foreshadowing. If that character had acted like a reasonable person, or in a manner consistent with their prior choices, the ending would come a lot sooner, and there'd be little for the audience to enjoy.

The main problem with an Idiot Plot is not the irrationality itself—some of the most powerful tragic stories centre around rational characters descending into irrationality. The main problem with it lies in the unnatural contrivance and contortion of the plot. The writer has had to pull something out of the bag to make the pieces fit together, rather than let events unfold naturally. In a good tragedy, the character doesn't suddenly become an idiot and make bad choices, but they are driven to that point by some terrible act or emotional turmoil. A tragedy is all about irrationality unfolding naturally out of rationality.

The Idiot Plot, of course, is any plot that would be resolved in five minutes if everyone in the story were not an idiot.

—Roger Ebert, film critic

We've all watched that horror movie scene where the sole inciting incident is one of the main characters doing something unbelievable dumb. A deadly monster roams the house, the family are safe, hidden in a closet, silently waiting for the monster to leave. Then one of them decides to scream at the top of their lungs and run across the house. The noise alerts the monster and the character gets eaten, and their entire family are now in danger.

The scene has the potential for rising tension. The audience watch on, hands half-covering their eyes, wondering what's going to happen. So far so good. The tension rises to an unbearable level as the monster draws closer. But then all the tension is dissolved at once by the dumbass. The reactions become "Who would do that?" and "Ugh, how stupid." The audience takes the story less seriously and all investment in its resolution is rightfully gone.

The audience reacts this way because the character's action is completely unrealistic. No rational person would run out screaming like that—we'd like to think we'd keep our heads on straight in that situation, not completely lose it and put our family in danger. Such characters *disgust* the audience; they're rarely fun to watch. The audience wakes up out of any immersion they had invested, and realise they're watching a work of conspicuous fiction. You must avoid *conspicuous fiction* and instead aim for *immersive fiction* that keeps your audience's attention right through to the end credits.

Whenever you're unsure of what action your character should take in a given scene, step into their shoes. Let's imagine a new scene: Your character's in a seedy bar, surrounded by drunks. They just got dumped by their girlfriend. How would they feel? Well, they'd probably feel depressed, and more in the mood to drink than to engage with anyone. They're unlikely to want to strike up an upbeat conversation with the bartender. They're more likely to sit staring into the bottom of their glass. You can practically smell the beer in the glass. See the potential benefits to your story?

Stepping into your characters' shoes is a reliable way of keeping their actions realistic and their motivations relatable. These things might seem basic, but too many writers forget them. This believability is always important—if you feature characters that the audience develops an inherent disgust for, no one will enjoy your story. On the other hand, if you portray characters that are the kind of people that your audience will like and get behind, they'll love your story. It's that simple.

This method of radical relatability gives you the ability to chart a path for your character's actions in any given scene. You're a human being, and you have a good feeling for how you'd act in a given situation. Most importantly, you can get an accurate sense of how you'd *feel* in a given situation, and that ultimately drives how you'd act—it gives your story the reality check it needs.

> *In Chekhov's story "The Malefactor," a peasant removes the nuts from railroad ties to use as weights for his fishing lines, unaware that this comparatively trivial theft could endanger the lives of hundreds of railroad travellers. A lawyer asked Chekhov how he would have punished the peasant had he been judge at his trial. "I would have acquitted him," said Chekhov. "I would say to him: 'You have not yet ripened into a deliberate criminal. Go—and ripen!'"*
> —The Little, Brown Book of Anecdotes

Trust Your Instincts

This method's effectiveness rests on how well you can connect with the scene on an emotional level. Picture yourself in the scene and imagine how you'd feel. What are your instincts telling you? Trust them; that's what makes this method most effective. If you're struggling, just relax and ask yourself these four questions:

1. What can I see?

2. What can I hear?

3. What can I smell?

4. How do I feel?

By reflecting on these four questions, you're getting in touch with the sensory details at that moment, which will help you to dive deeper into that scene, giving you a clearer picture of the character's point of view. This enhanced perspective will help your audience connect with the character's personality, motivations, and emotions.

Therefore this method not only helps to think about realistic actions, but it also helps to think about your story's thematic tones and motivations. What would a real person feel about the overarching tone of the events happening in your story? What are the conflicts bubbling up inside your characters? Studying these questions will make your story feel more coherent and make it multidimensional.

Try not to colour these instincts with any morality, prejudice, or preconception. Every person is the hero of his own story. You must write his motivations from his perspective, not yours. What drives his actions? It's only by stepping into his shoes that you can answer that question with confidence. One key goal of this method is to bridge the gap between the audience and the character. Succeed at making the most ostensibly evil antagonist an empathetic and understandable person, and you have succeeded where most storytellers fail.

> I once heard of a professor who was being ferried across a river by a boatman, who was no scholar. So the professor said, "Can you write, my man?" "No, sir," said the boatman. "Then you have lost one-third of your life," said the professor. "Can you read?" again asked he of the boatman. "No," replied the latter, "I can't read." "Then you have lost the half of your life," said the professor. Now came the boatman's turn. "Can you swim?" said the boatman to the

professor. "No," was his reply. "Then," said the
boatman, "you have lost the whole of your life,
for the boat is sinking and you'll be drowned."
—*The Hero of the Humber* by Henry Woodcock

Take Reality Checks

Stepping into your characters' shoes also allows you to take reality checks at points in your story. That means not just stepping into your characters' minds, but also into the world around them.

In the fantasy genre, we create fantastic new worlds far away from the humdrum of our everyday lives. But history has shown us that the most successful fantasy and science fiction stories have actually focused more on character personalities and themes familiar to daily life. It's always a mistake to have worlds and characters so out of this world as to make them completely alien, as discussed in Law 5, Reflect Reality in Fantasy.

In *Star Wars*, the world is somewhat alien, but it feels real because many of the same human concepts are present in each of the stories—people dress similarly, the names are familiar, and their society suffers from recognisable issues. These things may seem superficial, but they subtly help your audience to intuitively relate to the world you've built. *Star Wars* is about family, teaming up with your friends, and facing down treacherous villains. We can all relate with these themes.

Deep empathy with your characters has the added benefit, then, of allowing you to step into your world and ask yourself if you feel confused or ambivalent about any of its aspects. If the answer is "yes" to any parts we've discussed, then you need to question its place in your story, because if you feel that way, the majority of your audience definitely will.

Relatability in Action

As discussed earlier, the audience must be allowed to relate to your characters in an intuitive way. At any point, you can ask yourself if some action your protagonist is about to take is relatable or not. Put yourself in their shoes—is that action the first reaction you have when you imagine yourself in their situation? Be sure to use the context of earlier conflicts to figure this out with added nuance.

The silly action in the horror movie we looked at earlier in the chapter could have been saved, and not made the character seem so stupid and unrelatable. In general, people pride themselves most sensitively on their intelligence. No one wants to think that they're stupid, so they're not going to relate to that one character making stupid decisions. In fact, such behaviour *disgusts* audiences.

Characters need flaws, yes, but the purpose of flaws is to make your characters more down-to-earth and likeable, and their struggles more meaningful. If your gut reaction is to dislike a character due to her unflappable arrogance or stupidity, you may need to rewrite the character's motivations behind the arrogant or stupid actions she takes. No story has ever benefited from a dislikeable character. A character's flaws are meant to be relatable and give meaning to their personal struggles—no one is going to admit relating to someone they dislike.

Of all your characters, your story's villain will benefit from intuitive flaws the most. A story is only as good as its villain, and every villain thinks he's the hero of his own story. What better way to make him relatable, then, than to step into his shoes and ask yourself why he's doing what he's doing? The audience wants to see villains like these in your stories. Your villain's methods have clear moral issues, but your audience will enjoy seeing his real, relatable motivations driving these methods (see Law 6, Make Your Villain the Hero of Their Own Story).

In *Avengers: Infinity War*, great care is taken to convey the moral cost of Thanos's actions and the heavy toll they take on him. Thanos is the main villain and his actions are in no way commendable, but his views are strongly argued, and it's precisely this attention to detail in the conflict that makes *Infinity War* such an emotionally resonant film. An understandable villain driven by relatable motivations adds untold depth to your story.

You are more like your audience than you might think, and planning your story in as intuitive a manner as possible will enhance their experience. This is also why taking the reader's perspective when reviewing your drafts is so critical. If you take the time to step into your characters' shoes, experience their viewpoint, and ask yourself if it all fits together and makes sense, and then make corrections as necessary, your audience will feel the direct benefits of this too. It's only by forcing yourself to take the inside-out perspective that you can break out of the pattern of creating flat stories that lack resonance.

Reversal

There isn't anything worse than having a character make a stupid choice for the sole reason of pushing the plot forward. Your audience will see through the ploy immediately and take your story less seriously. Step into your character's shoes to help them make the most intuitive, realistic, and character-defining choice at that moment.

While our goal is to avoid the Idiot Plot, do not forget that an irrational choice made by a character is not always a bad thing, so long as it's understandable, consistent with their personality, and that those kinds of decisions don't define your story as a whole—indeed, some of the greatest tragedies have centred on characters behaving irrationally. In William Shakespeare's *Macbeth*, the title character is driven into an accelerating spiral of mad choices only after he murders King Duncan, his friend and mentor, at his power-hungry wife's behest. This kind of negative reversion is understandable because of the terrible guilt he feels, and to us it's a natural progression since it both makes sense and comes after much foreshadowing.

Unlike an Idiot Plot propped up by an irrational choice with no basis from the prior material, a resonant tragic story has great meaning because it resolves around an irrational yet understandable choice based on sufficient foreshadowing. The former is based on laziness and a lack of planning, and the latter is a journey into the dark parts of our nature executed with purpose.

Law 18

Accord with Timeless Myths

History has shown us that the stories that come closest to humanity's timeless myths enjoy the strongest resonance with the audience, and thus the longest perennial success. Timeless myths can never be repeated too often because they touch on fundamental things about human psychology. As long as human nature ceases to change, these rules will continue to work. Accord with cultural myths and common human experiences to achieve a deep connection with your audience.

Observance of the Law

In 1984, at the Palace of Fine Arts in San Francisco, the mythologist Joseph Campbell took to the podium to deliver his address on what he called the "inner reaches of outer space." The Palace's dome accorded with the Ancient Greek style, its wondrous architecture fitting the discussion at hand. Campbell told those gathered in front of them that as humanity gazes out into the stars, it gazes into itself. "From the outer world, the senses carry images to mind, which do not become myth, however, until they're transformed by fusion with accordant insights, awakened as imagination from the inner world of the body."

In that audience was George Lucas, the film director who had recently gained worldwide fame and wealth after finishing the first *Star Wars* trilogy. Lucas had long been a fan of Campbell's work, having studied the mythologist's books for his early drafts of the original *Star Wars* story. Campbell's seminal work, *The Hero with a Thousand Faces*, laid out his blueprint for what he coined the Hero's Journey, a story motif based on adventure and personal growth. He had shared how this tale of a hero's adventure towards spiritual growth through grand challenges was common to all human cultures, indicating that this archetype lay in the core of the human psyche in general. Luke Skywalker's journey from Tatooine to destroying the Death Star, and defeating the evil Emperor, emulated the Hero's Journey and enjoyed great critical appraise, not to mention a worldwide community of millions of fans. Lucas's work had provided a well-executed proof of Campbell's theories.

After the address, Barbara McClintock, a Nobel laureate and mutual friend of both Lucas and Campbell, finally introduced the men to each other. Lucas told Campbell of how *The Hero with a Thousand Faces* had influenced *Star Wars*. Campbell hadn't seen the films, but Lucas eventually corrected that by inviting him to his home, Skywalker Ranch. The author insisted on watching all three films in one day—the world's first *Star Wars* binge was by the man who had inspired its creation.

Two years later, Campbell released the final book before his death, *The Inner Reaches of Outer Space*. Building from his discoveries of common myths and their central place in the human psyche, Campbell demonstrated that in a time of agonising literalism in politics and science, true art lay in stories and metaphors. The imagination of the mind and the potential that lay in its creativity reflected the infinite breadth of the cosmos.

Before his death, Lucas invited Campbell to Skywalker Ranch once more, this time with the PBS journalist Bill Moyers. The two men walked around the Ranch's new grounds, discussing Campbell's views on mythology and its impact on modern human culture. With Lucas's help, they caught it all on film. This footage would become the first episode of a six-part series called *The Power of Myth*. In this series and its accompanying book, Campbell demonstrated that the reason are enchanted by modern films such as *Star Wars* is because they tell us about ourselves and our sensitivity to heroic myths, rather than because of any of their exciting technology or special effects. In tribute to his friend, Lucas would go on to finance the project in its early stages, sharing the gift of Campbell's profound reflections with the world.

Interpretation

The Hero's Journey has formed the template for many of Hollywood's most successful films, as well as countless books in literature. But as Joseph Campbell demonstrated in his work, our enjoyment of these stories is not due to any particular storytelling technique— the key to the template lies within us. Humans have a special proclivity for inspiring stories about heroes who start small but become greater through the challenges they face. As they defeat the evil monster at the end of the story and return home, we each feel an innate spark of hope.

George Lucas may have understood this storytelling pattern better than any director working at the time. With *Star Wars*, he didn't just create a saga of films, or a franchise worth billions of dollars by the time he sold it to the Walt Disney Corporation—he created a global movement. Millions of fans from different cultures all over the world faithfully watch the movies over and over, all experiencing the same rush when Obi-Wan duels with Darth Vader, and when Luke uses the Force to destroy the Death Star. Understand: People from every culture, regardless of background or race, want to feel like the hero and overcome unsurmountable deeds. By telling stories like Lucas and embracing the heroic archetype, you can create that same feeling of empowerment.

J. R. R. Tolkien's *The Hobbit* is another classic piece of literature that accords beautifully with the Hero's Journey archetype. Bilbo Baggins shuns his comfortable life to take up the call of adventure, and as a result, he returns home braver, wiser, and more self-reliant. The journey awakes inside him a great courage and valour he was not aware of, and the experience changes him as much as he changes Gandalf and the dwarves around him.

No matter what setting you choose for your story, you can touch on the same sensitive, emotional points as these great works of film and literature. The lesson that Lucas took from Joseph Campbell was that people experience stories with a kind of shared group myth. They come together, marvel at the impressive movements portrayed in these stories, and beg the creators for more. The greatest stories get closest to creating these feelings and reward their creators with lifelong fans. To have your story emulate that same group mythology, with fans desperate to immerse themselves in the heroic tales you tell, is the height of storytelling.

Keys to Storytelling

When legendary mythologist Joseph Campbell published his first book to the world, it had a mixed reception. The book, *The Hero with a Thousand Faces*, was revolutionary in many ways, with tales of talking snakes and flesh-eating rituals that none of his contemporaries had studied or publicised. Campbell had long been fascinated by the sheer variety of mythologies that different cultures have created in history. Ever since his university studies, his goal was clear: to study these mythologies, compare them, and find meaningful patterns.

The Hero with a Thousand Faces was the result of nearly a decade of diligent study on this goal. In his work analysing the mythologies of these different cultures he found a definite pattern. Each of these myths when compared with one another, no matter how far apart culturally or geographically, seemed to share the same fundamental roots. Every culture had developed coming-of-age rituals, along with fantastical tales and myths to explain their significance in their respective societies. In the absence of the science and computing power we enjoy today, they had to resort to mythologies to explain grand phenomena such as the weather or the movement of stars.

A typical example would go as follows. A boy, once he'd reached a particular stage of development, was taken from his mother by the men and foisted into a frightening initiation to join them and become a man. The boy would face some trial, often harsh, designed to transform his soul from boy to man. In Jewish cultures, boys reaching the age of 13 (and more recently, girls reaching the age of 12 or 13) recite from the Torah as a way of celebrating their place in the adult community. However, more barbaric examples abound in history, most notably the manhood ritual of historic Indonesian cultures, where a young man was required to kill another man in order to marry a woman and have a child with her.

The Ancient Greeks developed their mythology to develop theories on how the world worked. The gods on Mount Olympus were at the centre of Greek mythology, each having their own story and fulfilling their role in nature. While today we have scientific explanations for events such as thunder, earthquakes, and volcanic eruptions, the Ancient Greeks did not. They developed a rationale around the gods' actions to explain these frightening and seemingly random natural phenomena. Zeus, the god of thunder, ruled over all other gods, and people interpreted a thunderstorm as the corporeal indication of his disapproval for something the humans had done. And they believed that Demeter, the goddess of agriculture, controlled all the seasons, granting the sunshine or rainfall that was best for the bountiful Greek harvests. All of these myths were attempts to explain an otherwise brutal and dispassionate world, indifferent to the needs of its fragile human inhabitants.

Because the Greeks loved myths and stories, it is no surprise that they created great works of literature. Early Greek writers produced epic poems, romantic poetry, and some of the world's most famous stories. The two most famous of these were Homer's epic poems the *Iliad* and the *Odyssey*. While on the surface the *Iliad* follows the deeds of Achilles in the war between the Greeks and the Trojans, it is really a cautionary tale about the pitfalls of arrogance and blind stubbornness, as Achilles is struck in the flesh of his ankle at the culmination of a war needlessly dragged out over ten years. So much youth is wasted as thousands of brave soldiers die over the course of ten years, all because of one king's damaged ego. Young men dying over the squabbles of their leaders is a theme that has repeated itself in both literature and real life.

And similarly, *The Odyssey* is perhaps the first popular Hero's Journey on written record. After spending a decade in *The Iliad*'s siege of Troy, *The Odyssey* details the next decade that Odysseus spends on the journey home, which is full of its own great variety of challenges. In stark contrast to the anger, power, and wrath of Achilles, Odysseus uses these challenges to display his wits, his poise, and his clear head in the face of danger. In *The Odyssey*, Homer describes how the gods respect Odysseus over all other men for his powers of foresight and planning, as average men react hastily in the moment. His intention with this great work of mythology was not just to tell a story, but to give young men an archetype to aspire to. Homer likely saw it as more virtuous to survive and conquer through wits and strategy than to die in a blaze of glory like Achilles.

In modern times, the Walt Disney Company has dominated the media industry by taking these timeless stories and turning them into popular and marketable films watched by hundreds of millions every year. Disney films and their characters have a distinctly positive and reassuring effect on their audiences. Aim for this mark for with your own stories by harnessing the same storytelling techniques that Disney uses in each of its successful films. Spend your time working on characters that your audiences will love; put them through struggles familiar to modern audiences. Try switching these myths up by placing these characters in interesting situations that give a slight twist on the ancient archetypes, just as Disney's *Treasure Planet* is Robert Louis Stevenson's *Treasure Island* in space. *Toy Story* answered a question we all wondered about as children—what did our toys get up to when we left them at home? *Hercules* is a more literal retelling of an Ancient Greek myth, just as *Beauty and the Beast* is from an old French folktale. Each of these examples from Disney's successful filmography takes an ancient myth, an old folktale, or a piece of childhood wonder, then gives it great characters and some modern film-making techniques, and turns it into a beloved story for millions of audiences to watch. See that their methodology for creating such beloved tales is easy to understand, so study them deeply.

Throughout his career, Campbell argued that myths like these aren't simply a relic of our human ancestors. They're a fundamental part of the human psyche. We may laugh at the idea of our ancestors holding rituals about talking snakes and worshipping the sun, but that part of humanity still lives in all of us today, making us flock to the newest *Star Wars* or *Avengers* movie. To humans, no matter how developed we think we are, myths in their various forms provide us with meaning.

> *Rejection of the unknown is tantamount to "identification with the devil," the mythological counterpart and eternal adversary of the world-creating exploratory hero. Such rejection and identification is a consequence of Luciferian pride, which states: all that I know is all that is necessary to know. This pride is totalitarian assumption of omniscience — is adoption of "God's place" by "reason" — is something that inevitably generates a state of personal and social being indistinguishable from hell. This hell develops because creative exploration — impossible, without (humble) acknowledgment of the un-*

known—constitutes the process that constructs and maintains the protective adaptive structure that gives life much of its acceptable meaning.
—*Maps of Meaning* by Jordan B. Peterson

In modern times, we have let mythologies fade back into the recesses of spiritual literature. As untold computing power grants us new levels of understanding of the world around us, we've shunned the mythologies that used to help us explain these things. Yes, it's probably a good thing that we don't believe the Earth is flat any more. The point is that humans naturally feel a need to come up with explanations for the scary things happening around us, and the myth fulfilled that need.

As we are told by society to follow this or that path in our development, we feel scared and often depressed. This depression is frequently due to feeling a lack of meaning in our lives. In the absence of grand myths and initiation rites, we find other ways of getting that feeling of purpose, of having a place in this vast and frightening world. In the worst cases, we numb ourselves with alcohol or resort to drugs. Often, initiation rituals provide young people with the same kind of meaning in the present day, especially in university fraternities and sororities, sports clubs, and the military. New initiates thus treat their membership as a revered honour.

> *Ultimately, man should not ask what the mean-ing of his life is, but rather must recognise that it is he who is asked. In a word, each man is questioned by life; and he can only answer to life by answering for his own life; to life he can only respond by being responsible.*
> —*Man's Search for Meaning* by Viktor E. Frankl

Campbell further argued in his television series, *The Power of Myth*, that there is a positive side to this: a re-surgence in great stories in the modern age. An epic tale of heroism, bravery, and transformative struggle taps into the same inspiration invoked by ancient myths. That is why Luke Skywalker has more in com-mon with King Arthur and the *Epic of Gilgamesh* than you might think. An immersive and exciting film gives us a powerful analogue of the same thrill our ancestors felt when their grandfathers told them the same an-cient myth that their own grandfathers passed down to them in turn. The excitement we feel when we sit down to watch *Star Wars* or *The Matrix* is no accident. Master storytellers are well aware of the power that these timeless myths have on us. As history has shown us, these stories are also perennial *sellers*. Far from receding out of cultural memory, the revenues of the original *Star Wars* saga have continued to accelerate in the decades following their release. Understand: Master storytellers accord with timeless myths. A great story that accords with ancient human myths, along with all the critical elements of storytelling, will immerse the audience and awaken that special excitement they may not often experience elsewhere. But it's not just heroic journeys or ancient myths that can make a story perennial. The key is touching on timeless human problems. We as a species have not changed much since our days of living together in caves. We have always had to deal with the deaths of loved ones, being bullied by someone and dreaming of one day defeating them, among many other diverse issues like these. They're familiar to the human experience. When a story takes us along a journey with these themes, we instantly recognise them and the associated feelings rush over us. Filmgoers and avid readers of books actively seek out such emotional rollercoasters, and master storytellers aim to fill this need.

Everyone can relate to shared human experiences such as hope, disappointment, and heartbreak. Use these emotional triggers in your own story, and your audience will connect with your characters on a deeper unconscious level. Making your characters more vulnerable and earnest in dramatic moments will multiply this effect, since such moments allow deeper connections in real-life. These emotional triggers will work on your audiences today and they'll still work in a hundred years. If you doubt that, remember that audiences watching one of Shakespeare's comedies today laugh just as hard as his original audiences in the sixteenth century. The Hero's Journey is unlikely to stop yielding success any time soon, nor are the same emotional triggers that our ancestors responded to a thousand years ago. The influential psychiatrist Carl Jung once said that "Nights through dreams tell the myths forgotten by the day." Deep down, we want dream-like myths like these. They're fundamentally part of us.

When planning your story, ask yourself the following question: If someone picks up your book or film in 30 years' time, in a different country to your own, what translates? This question might seem daunting, but it's a critical test of your work's longevity. As Ryan Holiday argued in his book *Perennial Seller*, no creator sets out to make work that fizzles out after a week, but too often relies on outside factors to make their story a success.

The truth is that evergreen success is more in your control than you might think. Look at the classic poems, plays, novels, and films—while each one might sit in a different time or place, every single one of them touches on some universal human experience. Everyone can relate to the sheer panic felt by Hamlet, everyone can relate to the excitement of an early courtship in *Pride and Prejudice*, and everyone can relate to the burning desire that Luke Skywalker feels to escape his dull life on the desert planet Tatooine. Dazzle your audience with the same grand spectacles that have always filled us with awe and satisfaction, and play the same themes that press on the same emotional triggers we've always had built within us. The ability to recognise and harness the eternal aspects of the human psyche, and then translate and interpret them for your own stories, is the height of storytelling.

Reversal

Critics of story archetypes such as the Hero's Journey argue that storytellers too often use them as cut-and-paste templates, making unoriginal and predictable stories with no creative or artistic qualities. The two common pitfalls of using ancient story patterns are that you either lazily let the myth tell the story for you, or that you overfit your story to the point of insecure obsession. According with timeless myths does not mean copying their patterns verbatim.

In creating *Star Wars*, George Lucas added many of his own themes beyond the Hero's Journey myth. First, Luke's desperation to leave the family farm reflects the same burning desire Lucas felt in his own youth, and second, setting the story as a space opera reflected the growing trend from Stanley Kubrick's *2001: A Space Odyssey* released in 1968. Do not be afraid to add your own personal touch into your stories. Never forget that in creating a story, you are building your own little universe, in which you make all the rules. All the myth does is give you a rough mould in which to pour your creative efforts—there's still lots of work to be done filling in the rest.

When using classic story archetypes, don't lose sight of the other critical elements of good storytelling—remember you always need strong characters with relatable problems, a cohesive structure from start to end, and a plot that unfolds naturally. When George Lucas came back to create the *Star Wars* prequel trilogy a decade later, he wanted to call upon the story archetype of the fallen hero, and show the dark emotions bubbling up inside Anakin as he becomes the evil Darth Vader. The success he'd found so far also gave him power and authority over every part of the film-making process.

The *Star Wars* prequel trilogy became an abundant fountain of cautionary tales on storytelling. Unlike his earlier days, where he had surrounded himself with film-making experts such as Irvin Kerschner and Gary Kurtz, each responsible for their parts of the process, he failed to do so with the new prequel production, spoiling the renditions of his desired tragic archetypes. Instead, the latent skills of his production team weren't used to their fullest, and the results speak for themselves—scene after scene of awkward, expositional dialogue, and a plot contrived to fit around his needs. Lucas had a deep knowledge of archetypes and mythology, and had used these to great effect when conceiving the original trilogy. But he didn't recognise that a sole focus on these abstract story patterns would come at such a detriment to the audience's experience. Learn from this example that archetype and myth alone cannot create a good story—the results of glibly shaping your plot around pre-ordained models speak for themselves. Audiences need strong characters to love and relate to, mutual struggles for them to face and surpass, and to see the raw emotions these challenges bring up. They should not have to rely on a literature lesson after leaving the cinema scratching their heads. Show the myth and let the audience feel it; you should never have to explain it.

The key to using this law effectively then is recognising the intentions behind it. We're trying to accord with myths, not rely on them or contrive our plot to align with their core models. It's clear when a story is merely exploiting an archetype, because all the right tropes are there but in a forced and incongruent way, and audiences don't respond well to that. Your goal is to create a story that accords with timeless human experiences, one that forms an interpretation of some ancient myth, not one that copies it beat for beat. Be less afraid of the consequences of calling on tried and tested story tropes than their misuse. In storytelling, the following metaphor applies: The bad story tries to *look like*, while the great story simply *is*.

Law 19

Build Tension with the "Bomb under the Table" Technique

Tension invariably grabs the audience's attention, and it is simple to manipulate to gain the maximum effect. Introduce a problem and let it build. Allow the tension to grow until it becomes unbearable. Your goal is to induce discomfort. At some point you must release the tension and allow your reader a chance to catch their breath, but only once the tension has been allowed to grow to a satisfactory level. This rule can be extended from single scenes right across entire series—see it as one of the most powerful tools in your storytelling arsenal.

Observance of the Law

In 2009, a director named Quentin Tarantino released his latest film, *Inglourious Basterds*, set in Nazi-occupied France during the Second World War. Lieutenant Aldo Raine leads a team of Jewish-American soldiers on a warpath through France, and their mission is to gain a reputation for gruesomely murdering Nazi soldiers and strike fear into the German forces nearby. In Tarantino's signature style, it contains plenty of two things: blood and suspense. Raine's team, called the Basterds, would use guerilla tactics to strike at German forces and scalp all the men in that unit. Each one of the Basterds takes on an informal debt of 100 Nazi scalps when joining Raine's team, and they do not disappoint.

The film's blood and suspense begins in its famous opening scene with the Basterds' ultimate foe, Colonel Hans Landa, played by the then-obscure German-Austrian actor Christoph Waltz. This scene sees Landa roll up to the cow farm owned by the LaPadite family, in search of a family of French Jews who have escaped the colonel's relentless pursuit. This family, the Dreyfuses, are, in fact, hiding underneath the LaPadites' floorboards and remained so as Monsieur LaPadite nervously leads Colonel Landa into his home. In spite of his clear authority in the situation, Landa shows an effusive, almost embarrassing humility and politeness in this man's home.

Almost like a doctor having a routine chat with his patient, Landa asks LaPadite some questions about the Dreyfus family and their rumoured whereabouts. The camera pans down below the floorboards to the Dreyfus family, each member dirty and in rough clothes. They covered their mouths as they pinned their eyes to the conversation occurring above them. Landa has offered to speak in English, knowing that LaPadite speaks the language, and that it's unlikely the Dreyfus family will as well.

The questioning continues. But this once-polite series of questions begins to show subtle signs of aggression, as Landa pulls out a large, ostentatious tobacco pipe and starts to rant, proudly comparing the Germans to eagles and the Jews to rats. Landa is twisting the knife, dragging the conversation as long as he can. He explains that the penalties for harbouring "enemies of the state" are severe, whereas there are great prizes for coming clean. LaPadite, who has kept his cool until this point, begins to show signs of nervousness, not giving Landa eye contact and shuffling in his seat. Tears started to well in his eyes, and Landa locks onto this opportunity, asking him directly, "You are harbouring enemies of the state, are you not?"

"Yes," whimpers LaPadite, those tears now streaming down his cheek.

Pointing down to the ground as his soldiers marched into the room, Landa politely excuses himself in French while giving his men the signal to fire at the floorboards. Wood, hay, and blood all exploded into the air as the bullets killed all but one of Dreyfus family. Only Shosanna, the elder daughter, manages to escape, running out from under the home and over the hill as fast as she can, herself crying at the death of her entire family. Landa spots the girl and takes aim with his pistol, but, opting to let her live, shouts "Au revoir, Shosanna!"

Interpretation

This opening scene arguably won Christoph Waltz the 2010 Academy Award for Best Actor. It not only sets a grim, bloody, and darkly comedic tone for the rest of the film, but it also keeps the audience in rapt suspense throughout. As the audience sees a Nazi colonel roll up to a peaceful farm with LaPadite and his daughters all doing their work in the hot sun, there's a palpable dread. What are they doing here? What do they want? The wife and daughters look to the father, who knows the stakes—they could get found out and killed at any moment. But if he can play it cool for an hour or so of questioning, they'll be in the clear.

Colonel Hans Landa subverts our expectations of a rude, arrogant, and brutal Nazi officer and instead presents himself to the LaPadite family with self-effacing charm and utmost politeness. He asks permission to try some of LaPadite's apparently famous cow's milk, complimenting him on its satisfying taste. This creates uncertainty around what this Nazi colonel will do; there is a palpable layer of suspense. As this conversation goes on, the audience sees a brief glimpse of the Dreyfus family hiding under the floorboards, all terrified, their eyes locked on the room above them.

This simple reveal makes the audience wonder if LaPadite will get off scot-free or if Landa indeed suspects the truth. Neither of these possibilities are clear, as the questioning continues into polite and banal small talk. Not making it clear to the audience which way the situation will go just makes the suspense even worse. It's an uncomfortable to scene to watch, and as Landa goes into his tirade on the Germans as eagles and the Jews as rats, we suspect he may know *something*, but we don't know what exactly. The tension becomes unbearable as we know something *has* to happen eventually, but we don't know what it'll be, or when, or how. When LaPadite breaks down and admits the truth, Landa has the family of Jews shot in swift, ruthless style.

In storytelling, tension and uncertainty are interlinked. Establish a scene that subtly undercuts the audience's expectations in some way. This will make them feel uncomfortable, but unable to explain why. Create a contrast similar to Landa's politeness and subtle self-deprecation in spite of his clear power in the situation and the stereotype of the brash Nazi officer. Then, the longer you can draw out this uncertainty, the longer you'll be able to heighten the suspense to an unbearable level of discomfort.

Revealing the stakes—in this case the Dreyfus family—raises the scene's stakes, creating even more uncertainty about the scene's outcome. The key is never to allow any answers or certainty until you're ready. Premature answers drain the scene of tension and defeat its purpose—maximising the discomfort. Learn from Tarantino, the master of cinematic suspense, and ruthlessly use this technique to build and release tension in the way you see fit.

The suspense is terrible, I hope it will last.
—Oscar Wilde, 1854-1900

Keys to Storytelling

There's a famous recording of Alfred Hitchcock giving some of his most valuable advice on how to build tension in a scene. Take a group of five people, all sitting around a table, talking about something mundane. Then, all of a sudden, a bomb goes off. They're all killed, and there's complete carnage in the scene.

The problem with this, Hitchcock explained, is that you get five seconds of shock and virtually no tension. Shock might stun your audience for a moment, but it's gone with virtually no side effects. It leaves nothing in its wake, nothing to work with. On the other hand, tension is insidious, building in the background—it keeps the audience's attention and makes them want to know more. The key then is a deep understanding of this distinction between shock and tension, and how to build simultaneous discomfort and interest with the latter.

Let's go back to that same scene, but at the start, *show* the audience the bomb, while keeping it concealed from the characters, who chatter on in the same manner as before. The timer is counting down from five minutes. The audience is held in suspense. They look at each other in panic and wonder at what's going to happen, and whether they'll discover the bomb. As the timer ticks to single digits, one of them sees the bomb and throws it out the window, just in time for it to explode outside.

How is this scene different? We're putting the audience through five minutes of continued suspense, instead of a brief few seconds of shock. The tension is unbearable right until the end of the ticking timer. We're putting the audience through an experience that makes them move to the edge of their seats. Now *that* is something we want for our own stories.

You'd be surprised at how reliably this tactic works for building scenes filled with tension. Film-makers such as Quentin Tarantino have built their careers on baking tension and discomfort into their storytelling. It plays on our innate human need for stability and closure because it explicitly denies them to us. As a result, we can't help but read or watch to the end.

Start Your Scene with Stability

The first step of this technique is to begin your scene with some everyday setting. People are sitting around a table eating, or there's a group of friends relaxing with a drink in a bar. Whatever the scene is, it feels relaxed. There's little to feel stressed about on first glance.

The audience won't be able to tell whether this scene had been going on for five hours or five minutes, because it's stable. There's not much movement happening yet. The audience almost expects something to happen. We create the stability to provide contrast for the unbearable suspense we're about to build.

This expectation is crucial because we're about to disrupt this stability with some juicy conflict. It's a known state that the audience has seen, that they'll want to return to once we get started.

Show the Audience the Bomb Under the Table

Now it's the time to introduce the conflict to the scene. Show the audience the one thing that's going to figuratively blow everyone to smithereens. Obviously it doesn't have to be an actual bomb, but it needs to be something that, upon seeing it, causes the audience to feel discomfort.

The point is, the audience cringes because they *know* in their bones that something bad's about to happen. We keep the knowledge from the characters, but tell the audience, so there's a mismatch of anticipation. The audience is waiting in extreme anticipation, whereas the characters aren't aware of the stakes involved.

Revealing your "bomb" raises the scene's stakes, making the consequences dire. Something *really* bad has to be threatened for this to take maximum effect. In Christopher Nolan's *The Dark Knight*, when the Joker threatens to blow up the two ferries if one of them fails to blow up the other before midnight, we cringe as the timer ticks closer to zero. We don't need to know more than the characters, because the tension is palpable.

In the opening scene of Jordan Peele's *Get Out*, a young man walks along a quiet street at night. Confused, he calls a friend to get directions. He's visibly nervous, telling himself "Everything's going to be fine" over and over. Then, a car drives up past him. Out of his sight, the car does a U-turn and slowly drives up behind the young man. What's going to happen? This scene doesn't last long, and the consequences are dire indeed, but the car's U-turn behind his back and its approach behind him build the suspense.

Stretch the Elastic Band as Far as It'll Go

We've started with a simple, stable scene. We've introduced some source of conflict, and upset the stability. The audience is uncomfortable. They know something terrible is about to happen, but they don't know when or how. Things are going well. Our job now? Nothing. Let events continue and draw it out as long as possible.

Think of it like an elastic band. We start with a loose elastic band, hanging free and relaxed. Then we pick up the elastic band in both hands and start pulling. We pull gently at first, so it only just begins to stretch. But we keep on stretching it further and further. Further and further. How long will this last? We don't know. We keep going. Further and further. Will it snap? Surely, something has to happen. Is it going to break in the next few seconds? Keep stretching it, further and further, then with a SNAP the elastic band's tension releases in a loud bang. Keep this image stored in your head—it's the key to understanding this law.

Just like an elastic band, the longer you can keep stretching out the discomfort and anticipation, the better. Never release the tension prematurely. Ever wonder why we hate random jump scares so much? It's because they're unearned. When the horror movie should keep building the suspense, it lets it all go for something as inconsequential as a cheap shock with a loud noise. And it is just that, a cheap shock. We're aiming to build something valuable. We do that by stretching out the tension as far as it'll go.

We're using human psychology to create a suspenseful experience for the audience. People want stability, which we're actively disrupting. We've disrupted it so we can keep worsening the tension until it becomes unbearable. Then, just at the point when they *need* some resolution, we keep it going a few moments longer, and then SNAP, we release it. The gunfight breaks out, the argument erupts, and the balloon pops.

Man is not equally moral at all times — this is well known. If one judges his morality by his capacity for great sacrificial resolve and self-denial (which, when it has become constant and habitual, is saintliness), man is most moral in affect; greater excitation offers him new motives, which he, when sober and cool as usual, perhaps did not think himself capable of. How can this be? Probably because of the relatedness of everything great and highly exciting: once man has been brought into a state of extraordinary tension, he can decide as easily to take frightful revenge as to make a frightful break with his need for revenge. Under the influence of the powerful emotion, he wants in any event what is great, powerful, enormous, and if he notices by chance that to sacrifice his own self satisfies as well or better than to sacrifice the other person, then he chooses that. Actually, all he cares about is the release of his emotion; to relieve his tension, he may gather together his enemies' spears and bury them in his own breast. Mankind had to be educated through long habituation to the idea that there is something great in self-denial, and not only in revenge; a divinity that sacrifices itself was the strongest and most effective symbol of this kind of greatness. The triumph over the enemy hardest to conquer, the sudden mastery of an emotion: this is what such a denial appears to be; and to this extent it counts as the height of morality.

—*Human, All Too Human* by Friedrich Nietzsche

Long-Term Tension

Tension is one of the finest ingredients for an individual scene, but it can be more satisfying to build underlying tension across an entire story. This is how we generally structure our stories: to introduce a normal world, create some conflict, and then let the pressure cooker build until the final confrontation lets the audience breathe.

The tension builds over time because the conflict we've introduced early in the story lies unresolved. We deny the audience a deciding confrontation between hero and villain until the end because we want to draw it out as long as possible. As long as that can be drawn out, and the audience's attention retained, we have the makings of a great story right there. Tension results from any conflict between characters and is necessary for an exciting story. That is why we don't allow the main hero and villain of a long saga duel it out until the last story.

> *The day drags along, you make thousands of plans, you imagine every possible conversation, you promise to change your behaviour in certain ways—and you feel more and more anxious until your loved one arrives. But by then, you don't know what to say. The hours of waiting have been transformed into tension, the tension has become fear, and the fear makes you embarrassed about showing affection.*
>
> —Paulo Coelho, author

How do we maintain the audience's attention as we build the tension? The best way to achieve this is to let a palpable anxiety grow as the story progresses and move the story forward at all times. If at any point you spend too much time dissolving the tension with an irrelevant side plot, or meaningless chit-chat, you'll lose the audience's interest.

Another time-tested way to keep the audience's investment in your story's rising suspense is to structure your acts properly. Go back and review Law 8, Structure Your Story around Change. An irreversible choice must mark each act. The hero's family are killed, then he decides to leave his home and accept his mentor's advice, and so on. Think of each act as a mini-story, each with its own mini-conflict, with a resolution that lets the audience breathe for a second. Each act is, in a way, a mini-story with its own tensions.

By letting the audience breathe at the end of every act, you're letting that act's mini-tension diffuse for the higher purpose of allowing the story as a whole to build in tension. Establish an ebb and flow to the story's pacing. We need these occasional pauses to let the audience know when the story has moved to the next stage. And the final confrontation? It's approaching, slowly but surely.

Short Chapters and Cliffhangers

Structuring your story with short scenes or chapters, each marked with a slight cliffhanger, can be an effective way to ramp up the suspense. If there's a time limit on your heroes finding the secret, what better way to illustrate this race against time than with brief, frantic scenes?

Novelist Dan Brown has used this approach to good effect in his books *The Da Vinci Code* and *Angels and Demons*. In each story, Robert Langdon and his teammates race against time to uncover some mystical secret. The chapters get shorter as the stakes get higher, signalling to the audience that Langdon is getting tantalisingly close to his goal. He often ends chapters with a question left unanswered, and the audience, desperate to know what happens next, can't help but continue reading.

The problem with this approach is that it's cheap, and seasoned audiences will not appreciate cliffhangers if they're misused. In particular, cliffhangers should never be used to deny the audience closure on the story's main plot thread. If you're writing a series, cliffhang minor plot details that will be important later on. Marvel has done this with their signature post-credit scenes hinting at the next stories in their cinematic universe. But when it comes to the central underlying tension in your current story, there can be no compromise.

Reversal

The reversal that Hitchcock mentions in the famous recording is that the audience will never forgive the storyteller if the bomb *never* goes off—in other words, the tension is *never* fully released. Just as an elastic band stretched too far will break, your scene will fail if you don't keep track of the tension. The decision to split the film adaptations of *The Hobbit* into a trilogy came with such scorn—it failed to find a natural stopping point for the second film, causing the audience to feel a sort of ambiguous confusion at the end. Keep tension under control, and know when to release it. Your audience will struggle to forgive such a denial of closure.

Law 20

Concentrate Dramatic Impact

Too much circulation makes the perceived value go down. The less of a good character you show in the story, the more valuable they are. Only give characters and scenes as much space in the story as necessary and no more. This is a common stumbling block for sequels—the storyteller or the commercial interests behind them mistakes the audience's love for a character by giving too much away and diluting their once strong impact. Avoid this fate by resisting the urge to open Pandora's box—it'll only spoil your character's air of mystery. Instead, you must work hard to build tension and potential energy all the way through your story, delivering the knock-out punch when the time comes.

Transgression and Observance of the Law

In 1979, a director named Ridley Scott released *Alien*, a horror film set in space. This film begins with the crew of the *Nostromo*, a commercial logistics vessel, on their return journey to Earth. On the way, the ship's main computer, Mother, intercepts a distress signal from the nearby moon LV-426, and wakes the crew from their extended sleep. The team follows company policy and investigates the planet, finding a derelict alien ship. It has an eerie, organic design that none of them have seen before.

Deep in the bowels of this mysterious ship, they find a dark, misty room full of alien eggs. In a horrifying scene, one of them opens, revealing a vicious creature resembling something between a squid and a scorpion. The creature latches onto Executive Officer Kane's face, knocking him out cold. After escaping with Kane back onto the *Nostromo*, the crew are confused and concerned about what has just happened. Kane seems to have normal vital signs but attempts to remove the creature don't work—cutting its skin releases a toxic acid that burns through the ship's metal hull.

The creature dies and Kane wakes up, but hours later a new creature burst out of Kane's chest. This creature seems even more vicious than the "Face Hugger" creature from before and hides away in the shadows.

All of them looked horrified at the mess that is left of Kane's body—this scene was unscripted and the actors' looks of shock are genuine. It eventually transpires that Science Officer Ash knew the creature was deadly, and he'd received a secret command from the company to bring it back to Earth, and to sacrifice the crew if necessary.

Over the space of a few hours, the crew repeatedly runs into this once tiny alien creature, and each time it is found, it's grown bigger, and brutally kills the *Nostromo*'s crew until only Warrant Officer Ripley is left. The audience does not get to see the alien much until the final confrontation, but each time it appears on screen, it is a menacing, deadly presence. Its giant, insect-like frame and disgusting shiny skin were like nothing that audiences had seen before. This horrifying creature appears out of nowhere, kills a member of the crew with ruthless efficiency, and then runs away, leaving the audience terrified about where it might come from next. Eventually, Ripley kills the alien in a frighteningly tense series of scenes that prove her wits and bravery.

In the decades following this film's release, like the alien creature, *Alien* evolved into a larger series of films. A cult following grew out of the film's world and the lore expanded—this alien was now part of a species called the Xenomorph. Audiences had a morbid curiosity for these terrifying aliens, and wanted to see more. Studios responded by completing a trilogy of films following Ripley and showing more of these aliens "interacting" with humans in a gratuitously violent fashion.

Even though the *Alien* trilogy came to a natural climax in 1992 with *Alien 3*, 1997 saw yet another addition to the franchise, *Alien: Resurrection*. Fans gave mixed responses, as many felt that Ripley's story arc had already finished and that this was yet another commercially motivated attempt from Hollywood to reboot a beloved franchise. Indeed, *Alien 3* had suffered greatly from studio interference, and this new addition was no different. Allegedly, issues arose right from the start. The odd mixture of comedic and gravely serious tones gave the film a strange, tongue-in-cheek feel, appearing to take itself less seriously than previous entries in the original trilogy. The Xenomorph creatures were given lots of screen time but shown as mere lab subjects, with scientists controlling their movements through directed blasts of ice. These once deadly creatures of immense power had been reduced to puppet characters with none of the threat of the original *Alien*. Although some audiences enjoyed the change in direction, the film flopped. The *Alien* series, with all the menace and terror fans had come to love, was over.

Interpretation

Like other films in the horror genre, *Alien* didn't have a huge budget, nor did it have many Hollywood stars in its cast. But a film rarely needs a big budget to terrify the audience or build suspense. Core storytelling techniques are simple to execute, even with two characters sitting at a table and some confrontational dialogue. *Alien* manages this by creating a terrifying creature with strange physical features that efficiently kills every living thing it comes across.

While the alien creature in the film is indeed terrifying, it is actually the mystery and uncertainty around it that keeps the suspense at such a high level. Audiences don't get to see the alien often. Until the final confrontation scene with Ripley and the alien, the creature only appears a couple of times. But each time the alien appears on screen, it's a significant event. It kills one member of the crew, hides, and then springs out of nowhere to surprise another. When the alien is not on screen, the audience feels an uncomfortable, sustained tension until it reappears.

Where later films in the *Alien* franchise went wrong was forgetting that this type of suspense was the key to the original film's success. Showing the aliens too often, showing them as lab subjects, and breaking the suspense through other means, turned the films into cheap, tensionless action romps. The original 1979 film remains a classic, and likely will do for years to come.

To achieve the same effect in your storytelling, particularly if you're writing a horror story, ration out your monster's appearances carefully, making each of these appearances count. Knock the audience flat every time the character appears, and you'll make their impact a lot greater. When your audience loves one of your characters and begs for more of them, don't take this literally and give them more on-page or on-screen time. Instead, give them more of the concentrated high-impact drama that the character provided before. Follow the classic maxim "less is more" in this regard, and you too can make characters as iconic as the Xenomorph.

The Vixen and the Lioness

A vixen who was taking her babies out for an airing one balmy morning, came across a lioness, with her cub in arms. "Why such airs, haughty dame, over one solitary cub?" sneered the vixen. "Look at my healthy and numerous litter here, and imagine, if you are able, how a

*proud mother should feel." The lioness gave her
a squelching look, and lifting up her nose,
walked away, saying calmly, "Yes, just look at
that beautiful collection. What are they? Foxes!
I've only one, but remember, that one is a lion."*

—*Aesop's Fables*, sixth century BC

Keys to Storytelling

Think back to the most impactful moments in your favourite stories: the individual scenes where a character has delivered a line, carried out some action, and left you reeling. It's likely that you're not alone in picking those moments because of the sheer strength of their impact. As a rule, quality beats quantity in the long run.

There is a central tenet of military strategy that can be summarised by the phrase "concentrate your forces." It is much better to focus all of your might on a single problem and beat it into submission, than to listen to your fears and spread your soldiers thin across the entire front. As military philosopher Carl von Clausewitz (1780-1831) wrote, "there is no higher and simpler law of strategy than that of keeping one's forces concentrated." Given a powerful force, what possible good can come from dispersing its power? Better to find the enemy's weak point and smash it with all of your might. This rule can be lifted from the battlefield and equally applied to many areas of life, from achieving our goals to winning a sports game or beating a competitor. In storytelling, the strategy's analogue is to concentrate dramatic impact and let your stars shine brightly.

However, commercial interests often violate this rule by conflating quantity with quality. They see the audience responding well to a character or theme as a signal to simply add more of them into the sequel. Their intentions aren't wrong—giving the customer more of what they respond to is a time-tested principle of business. But this often gets misinterpreted, and by adding more they actually dilute the object of focus. This is often why sequels fail to measure up—commercial interests backing the film's production try to hack their way to a better product based on some arbitrary marketing metrics.

The ability to avoid the common fate of sequels and give your audience those rich, dense, and character-defining moments is within your grasp. Make the following oath: "I shall be conservative with my best characters." Key to this is resisting the urge to give them more screen time than necessary, and instead focus on a few character-defining moments. This strategic rationing of high-impact characters is critical to creating memorable moments in your stories that your audience will never forget.

It's no great secret that too much of a good thing is itself a bad thing. The problem that a lot of writers fall into is that they listen too much to their commercial backers and take the desires of their audience too literally. Let's look at a common scenario. A writer adds a villain to his story, and though the villain doesn't mince words, he has one high-impact scene where he does something cruel to the hero and delivers a bad-ass line at the end. The audience loves that one evil villain, but he's mysterious and doesn't appear or say much in the story, so the audience begs the writer to add more of him in future stories.

The writer dutifully listens and goes on to write a three-book series all about that one character, with the focus on him at all times. That vocal minority gratefully picks up their copies of this new series, but sales tail off after the first few months, making his hard work and dedication to his audience seem of little merit. Meanwhile, in the year that's passed, the writer's original story is doing better than ever, its readership having steadily increased month-on-month.

What happened here? Let's examine the situation. The new series may have done well due to hype or pre-orders from excited super-fans, but the majority of the writer's fans didn't latch on because that original villain's impact is now completely diluted. The attention is solely on this character in a completely different light to the original story, and there's no mystery any more. Meanwhile, the thunderous drama that introduced that same villain in the original story has catapulted it to perennial glory, and mere word of mouth enabled its spread among new readers.

What neither the writer nor the audience realises is that it's precisely that character's scarcity, and the impact he delivers in those brief moments, that make him so attractive. In the original story, the writer skilfully provided a high concentration of impact associated with that character. This appearance and disappearance appealed him to the audience and got them talking. They all rave about him.

But in the new series, he takes on a different tone. It's not that these new stories are inherently bad because of this. But there is inevitably going to be a disappointing dilution of that character's impact. There's no way that the writer can deliver the same level of intensity as he did in the original story. However, in a subtle yet perverse way, he has made his original story more valuable in contrast.

The Elm-Tree and the Vine

An extravagant young vine, vainly ambitious of independence, and fond of rambling at large, despised the alliance of a stately elm that grew near, and courted her embraces. Having risen to some small height without any kind of support, she shot her neighbour to take notice how little she wanted his assistance. "Poor infatuated shrub," replied the elm, "how inconsistent is thy conduct! Wouldst thou be truly independent, thou shouldst carefully apply those juices to the enlargement of thy stem, which thou lavishest in vain upon necessary foliage. I shortly shall behold thee grovelling on the ground; yet countenanced indeed, by many of the human race, who, intoxicated with vanity, have despised economy; and who, to support for a moment their empty boast of independence, have exhausted the very source of it in frivolous expenses."

—Fables, Original and Selected by James North-

cote

The ability to deliver scenes with a high concentration of impact will significantly enhance your audience's experience, and propel you to the heights of storytelling success. Your audience will finish your story and share these impactful moments with their friends, and the memories will last for a long time.

The most common example of this is with villains that don't necessarily need many establishing scenes. They're extremely menacing, and the audience sees these characteristics from a series of impactful scenes that show him doing evil things. The villain's menace alone is enough of a character-defining moment.

The 1979 film *Alien* is one of the most suspenseful science fiction horror stories ever made, and the titular alien is rarely shown on screen. Every time the alien appears, the scene fills with uncomfortable tension. The alien appears in the horrific fashion we're familiar with, and brutally kills one of the terrified *Nostromo* crew. We are introduced to the alien when it bursts out of a crew member's chest, and an antagonist can't have more of a disturbing introduction than that.

Alien 3 completely ruined this great iconic figure of science fiction horror, as multiple aliens are shown throughout the film, fully lit in scenes devoid of any tension or discomfort. The aliens are treated more like docile zoo animals than the fearsome invincible enemies they should be, as the film's creators completely mistook the potentially dominant role of these creatures to create terrific experiences for the audience.

The aliens were handled poorly in the later films of the franchise because the creators failed to realise why audiences loved watching them in the original film. The original *Alien* was set in a futuristic space environment, but that was only the setting. The story is primarily about survival horror, with a mysterious and horrific creature brutally killing every single one of the helpless crew. *Alien 3* and *Alien: Resurrection* are emblematic of all sequels that fail to recognise why their originators succeeded.

In *Alien*, the scenes with the alien provided great impact because the stakes are high. The crew aren't some elite military soldiers, they are logistics; they have barely been trained even to defend themselves in the face of extreme danger. And here's this horrific new creature that nobody has ever seen before, that just burst out of one of the crew's chests to grow to 10 feet tall in a couple of hours. The extreme danger the crew faces creates just the level of threat we're after. Showing little of the creature on screen heightens the tension because we know that something's coming, but we don't know when or how. That makes it so much scarier when it does appear out of nowhere to brutally kill someone.

In *Star Wars*, the villain Darth Vader appears less often than you might think, and whenever he does, it's a character-defining moment. Watch the film again and study each of these moments deeply. First, he threatens someone for information. Then he chokes a high-ranking officer. After that, he interrogates a young woman, made even worse with our later knowledge that the woman is actually his own estranged daughter. There's no fluff; each one of these scenes delivers a characteristic, highly concentrated dose of evil, and you would do well to emulate that in your stories.

In the prequel story *Rogue One*, Darth Vader only appears on screen in two sequences, the first when he summons Director Krennic to his retreat on Mustafar. We catch a glimpse of Vader's deformed body in the bacta tank, but not enough to see his whole face or body, teasing the audience. After Vader suits up, Krennic looks up to be greeted by the imposing figure as he enters, dramatically strolling through billows of steam. Vader towers above Krennic as he gives him a verbal thrashing. When a desperate Krennic asks for a meeting with the Emperor, a disappointed Vader, sick of his politicking gives him with his signature Force-choke.

Darth Vader next appears at the film's climax, emerging out of the darkness to mercilessly slaughter an entire group of Rebel guards. It's a short yet dramatic scene that shows how easily he can cut through a terrified group of trained guards, and the dispassionate manner in which he can do so. Vader only appears in these two scenes, but the audience sees how powerful and evil he is.

Darth Vader was handled expertly in *Rogue One* by preserving the mystery and power surrounding his character. It wouldn't have been possible to achieve this if he'd appeared more often in the film. But many critics and audiences did complain that Vader wasn't in the film more. This criticism was short-sighted because doing so would have lessened his impact. Above all, he wasn't actually the story's main antagonist, and having more of him in the film would have drawn too much attention away from Director Krennic. Vader's purpose in the film is solely to give a menacing context for the events in the story with an added dash of fan service.

The conservatism with which Vader was treated in *Rogue One* is extreme, and should not be the road to take when establishing your main villain for the first time. For the main villain, two sequences won't suffice; he needs to appear more often to provide some meaningful conflict for the hero. The point of all of this is that you need to step back and examine how you're presenting your best characters in each scene. If it isn't a character-defining moment, rewrite it. Use the alien creature in *Alien* and Darth Vader in the original *Star*

Wars as your models in this regard—they are emblematic of cinema's greatest villains. Think of your best characters as stars emitting a limited amount of light—err on the side of shining brightly in a few scenes. Don't dilute them by letting them shine dimly throughout the whole story.

Reversal

Conservatively rationing out your most impactful, resonant moments is a great way to make your stories stick in your audience's minds forever. But never lose sight of the overall structure of your story. Don't make your story merely a series of interconnected awesome moments. Zack Snyder's 2016 film *Batman v Superman: Dawn of Justice* suffered from this fate, and while its awesome individual scenes acted as great marketing fodder in the pre-release stage, creating a lot of hype, critics and audiences gave the film only mildly positive reviews. *Batman v Superman* is so invested in these little moments that it fails to accord with any discernible act structure, making it feel boring.

What makes a story truly memorable is the inspiring character arc that spans the entire story. The themes that you explore. The rising conflict that lasts from start to finish. Learn to step back and examine your story as a whole. Don't rewrite any of it just to fit around that one awesome scene you're dying to write. Memorable moments will pack a punch and establish your character's best traits, but they must always work alongside the main thread of your story.

Law 21

Description Is Telepathy

The most common mistake writers make when describing a character or a place is to exhaustively list every detail about them in as literal a way as possible. Contrary to intuition, this actually fails to convey the most important details because it constrains the reader's imagination. The best way to describe is to make your descriptions as brief and intuitive as possible. Give your audience a tidbit, and let them decide for themselves what the characters look like. That will help them to take ownership of the story and feel invested in its outcome. Unleash the raw cosmic power of your audience's imagination.

Observance of the Law

In 1974, a 26-year-old English teacher named Stephen King was struggling financially. To make some money he decided to write and release his first published novel, which he called *Carrie*. It was not taken well by agents at first, but eventually, after dozens of rejections, the book found its first publisher. After years of writing short stories for magazines, *Carrie* was King's first full novel to get published to a wide audience. The story follows the main character Carrie White's struggles through high school as she develops strong telekinetic powers. Carrie's schoolmates bully her relentlessly, and she receives further physical and mental abuse at home from her mother, a raving Christian fundamentalist.

Carrie is introduced to the reader as she showers with the rest of her class after a sports lesson at school —in itself a humiliating scenario for any high school student—only to suddenly get her first period in front of her fellow students. The stress and confusion of this event not only fills us with the same nightmarish embarrassment one would naturally feel in this situation, but in the story it also triggers her telekinetic powers, as she knocks over the main bully, Chris Hargensen. After the teachers accordingly ban Chris from the prom for bullying Carrie, she vows revenge and eventually gets it.

In writing *Carrie*, King peppered news reports and academic journal entries throughout the novel, with detailed observations of Carrie's supernatural abilities as they develop. These descriptive pieces complement the conventional story narrative by creating a kind of mystery documentary beyond the scope of its high school drama. This application of the writing axiom Show, Don't Tell piques the reader's interest, making them immersed in the story in a way that a simple one-dimensional narrative could not have achieved alone. The audience feels like they are a part of an ongoing investigation:

> *From* The Shadow Exploded *(p. 54): Carrie White's mother, Margaret White, gave birth to her daughter on September 21, 1963, under circumstances which can only be termed bizarre. In fact, an overview of the Carrie White case leaves the careful student with one feeling ascendant over all others: that Carrie was the only issue of a family as odd as any that has ever been brought to popular attention. As noted earlier, Ralph White died in February of 1963 when a steel girder fell out of a carrying sling on a housing-project job in Portland. Mrs White continued to live alone in their suburban*

> *Chamberlain bungalow. Due to the Whites'*
> *near-fanatical fundamentalist religious beliefs,*
> *Mrs White had no friends to see her through her*
> *period of bereavement. And when her labour*
> *began seven months later, she was alone.*
>
> —*Carrie* by Stephen King

King's use of description in *Carrie* shows the difference between his signature style and those of most other authors. The character and scene descriptions flow in a way that few authors have managed to recreate since. In one early scene, just after the shower incident, King describes Carrie's religion-induced shame as she returns home. What the average reader might regard as familiar interests for a teenage girl in fact fill Carrie with revulsion and anxiety—her religious-fanatic mother has deliberately not given her the "birds and the bees" talk, and so Carrie feels like she has no one to turn to. In one simple scene, a little more of Carrie's personality reveals itself, establishing a significant portion of the story's conflict as follows:

> *She went into her tiny bedroom. There were*
> *many more religious pictures here, but there*
> *were more lambs and fewer scenes of righteous*
> *wrath. A Ewen pennant was tacked over the*
> *dresser. On the dresser itself was a Bible and a*

plastic Jesus that glowed in the dark. She un-
dressed—first her blouse, then her hateful knee-
length skirt, her slip, her girdle, her pettipants,
her garter belt, her stockings. She looked at the
pile of heavy clothes, their buttons and rubber,
with an expression of fierce wretchedness. In the
school library there was a stack of back issues of
Seventeen *and often she leafed through them,*
pasting an expression of idiotic casualness on
her face. The models looked so easy and smooth
in their short, kicky skirts, pantyhose, and frilly
underwear with patterns on them. Of course
easy was one of Momma's pet words (she knew
what Momma would say to a question) to de-
scribe them. And it would make her dreadfully
self-conscious, she knew that. Naked, evil,
blackened with the sin of exhibitionism, the
breeze blowing lewdly up the backs of her legs,
inciting lust. And she knew that they would
know how she felt. They always did. They
would embarrass her somehow, push her sav-
agely back into clowndom. It was their way.

—*Carrie* by Stephen King

In his memoir, *On Writing,* King admitted that "I didn't
know jack-shit about high school girls" and relied

heavily on the advice of his wife Tabitha, who advised him on the struggles that girls go through in their teenage years. This help assisted him in creating the perspectives of characters such as the young teacher Miss Desjardin, who tries to feel sympathy for Carrie, but only finds herself feeling a visceral irritation at her cluelessness. King also worked hard to picture Carrie's perspective by putting himself in the shoes of "the two loneliest, most reviled girls in my class—how they looked, how they acted, how they were treated." This unusual attention to detail on the social struggles that girls face helped King treat his audience to rich descriptions of Carrie's whirlpool of emotions as she descends into uncontrolled rage.

Carrie's initial readers may not have realised it at the time, but they were reading the seminal work of a writer who would continue to create some of the world's best-known books in this same style: eerie mystery through documentary-style narration and conservative descriptions that let the reader form their own images of the troubled characters. With *Carrie*, this unique style creates the fascinating and immersive experience that would earn King his first six-figure publication deal—in 1970s dollars—allowing him to quit his job as an English teacher and become a full-time author.

Interpretation

Stephen King is perhaps the best-selling author of all time. But forgetting the legend surrounding his career, let us examine why *Carrie* was such a success. King's style is not to allow excessive description or prose to bog down the reader and slow down the flow of the story's events. Descriptions are a central component of his books and never sparse, but they're written in the right measure and in a way that creates visceral images in his readers' minds. He narrates in a way that creates mystery and tension, through a sort of collaborative documentary. In his memoir, *On Writing*, King would later explain that he liked to let the narration fold naturally out of an odd situation, putting the reader at the point of least knowledge and working forward from there with the reader.

When reflecting on this book, King wrote that "If I tell you that Carrie White is a high school outcast with a bad complexion and a fashion-victim wardrobe, I think you can do the rest, can't you? I don't need to give you a pimple-by-pimple, skirt-by-skirt rundown." His point is that his job as the novelist is to create a character description that forms a link of recognition in the reader's mind. Nearly all of us have gone to high school, we've all felt like the outcast, and we've all made these passing summaries of our peers. King uses that to reach out to the reader and transmit that image from his mind to theirs. When King was asked what writing is, his response was delivered in his signature down-to-earth style: "Telepathy, of course."

Stories require immersion, and good descriptions are the most reliable means of letting the reader into the story. Achieving good descriptive skill is therefore vital to the storyteller, and although it appears simple, it requires time and practise. You must become a voracious reader, working to find and learn from the moments that we feel immersed in without any effort on our part as the audience. In a way, you must be able to notice this happening and snap yourself awake, noting down how and why you think this happened. This might seem odd and disruptive, but its effects are critically effective: to gain the ability to transmit what you want the audience to experience into a digestible written form. Whatever scene you need to transmit, you need to be able to visualise it clearly and write it so that your story will, as King put it, "cause your reader to prickle with recognition." Add that to your list of writing mantras. As stated this technique is not easy but it is powerful; you will have to train this ability to create these images, and transfer them into words that cause that moment of instant recognition. Understand: Description's aim is not to exhaustively list and describe every physical feature of your characters, or every thought that pops into their heads—its purpose is to transfer recognisable images to the audience in a seamless manner. That is the height of storytelling.

> *Strip a writer to the buff, point to the scars, and he'll tell you the story of each small one. From the big ones you get novels, not amnesia. A little talent is a nice thing to have if you want to be a writer, but the only real requirement is that ability to remember the story of every scar. Art consists of the persistence of memory.*
>
> —*Misery* by Stephen King

Keys to Storytelling

Philip K. Dick waited until the last chapter of *Do Androids Dream of Electric Sheep?*—later adapted into the *Blade Runner* films—to reveal that the main character is bald. This late revelation divides readers of the classic novel, not because he's bald, but because it is an oddly specific detail that shatters many people's mental image of Officer Deckard without providing any value to the story.

People have read all the way through Dick's thought-provoking crime mystery novel, immersing themselves in the post-apocalyptic Earth it depicts. The audience has developed a mental image of this world in their mind's eye. So why did Dick decide to reveal this strange detail about the main character?

It's a mistake to think that your readers want picture-perfect descriptions of characters, especially if they're the story's main protagonist. Unless your audience shares every physical detail with that character, they'll struggle to identify with them. This is an error that will limit your audience's immersion.

A better approach is to ensure that as many people as possible can identify with your story's characters. That means that anyone can pick up your story and see themselves as the main character. They can place themselves in the world you've created and not feel off-put. Video games often do this by allowing the player to customise the main character's appearance directly.

J. R. R. Tolkien fought to ensure his stories weren't made into films in his lifetime because he sincerely believed in letting his readers develop their own images of Middle-earth and all of his beloved characters. He cared deeply about the world he'd created, and a film adaptation with specific actors and locations would make it difficult for audiences to create any other mental picture of his stories.

It is an obvious fact of film that you need to show your characters to your audience, so there's no hiding of appearances or mannerisms. You have to pick an actor to play the role, after all. But that's doesn't preclude you from following this law when writing. The key is in allowing people to see themselves in your characters, and to not err too strongly in any direction when it comes to physical descriptions. If your own Carrie needs black hair, give her black hair, but stop there and don't get too specific—will yet another detail about her nose and face add anything to the story?

Your audience also needs to feel like they can imagine themselves in your story's world, so this law ties in well with Law 5, Reflect Reality in Fantasy. Keep character and place names similar to those in the real world, don't make them too alien. A world filled with alien concepts and unpronounceable names isn't going to endear itself well to anyone. Audiences felt immersed in the dirty, gritty Los Angeles of *Blade Runner* because it was such a believable look into the near future—Ridley Scott was notorious for his use of practical effects and his attention to detail, so study his films deeply.

The key to storytelling here is that when you tell your story to your audience, you want them to have an experience that's unique to themselves. They experience your story in their own unique way because you let them develop their own mental image of your story.

The ability to do this, then, can provide untold benefits for your stories due to the vastly enriched experiences you can convey to your audience. Let us examine some examples that illustrate the steps to gaining this ability.

The *Twilight* saga of books gained wide readership in part because the author Stephenie Meyer let readers see themselves in the main character Bella. Meyer makes it easy for anyone to find something to relate to in Bella's character by being vague about her appearance and refusing any details of where she has come from.

While Bella's love interest Edward is described in intricate detail, from the style of his hair down to his unique mannerisms, Meyer was intentionally vague about Bella's appearance. Everyone reading *Twilight* can relate to being the new kid in school, lonely and scared in a strange environment. But also, everyone wants to meet a new exciting person who opens up a whole new world you didn't even know existed—for Bella, this is Edward.

Like *Twilight*, you have an advantage if you're writing a book and not a film, because you can allow your audience to form their own ideas about what characters look like and how they act. You instead *show* the audience a character's defining features through the actions they take, how they interact with other characters. When it comes to character descriptions however, err on the side of letting the audience fill in the blanks.

This strategy is best reserved for your story's main protagonist because the person at the centre of your story has to be relatable, and you must not take any narrative choices that stop your audience from seeing themselves in your hero. It might work best then to use minimal descriptions of your main character's appearance to avoid this risk. Don't worry about being too vague; your audience will create their own mental image of them all by themselves.

The problem with going overboard on character descriptions is that you inevitably dump a load of exposition on the reader, never an enjoyable experience. Take a different approach and show your character's nature and backstory through choices, actions, and feelings. Take up the same narrative space that you would have used to describe your main character with exposition, and have them *do* something that displays a personality trait instead.

Using this technique will give your audience a much clearer picture of what your character is actually like, compared to just listing superficial physical features. Why is it so important for your main characters to look a certain way, when it'll just alienate half your readers? The fascinating part of storytelling is character development, how people adapt to events and either improve or regress. It's characterisation over personalisation.

A common reason why audiences don't connect with a story's protagonist is that the writer has failed to write a character the audience can root for. Your story's protagonist must show traits that the reader aspires to and holds in high regard. Make them do heroic things, rescuing their friends in danger, and improving upon their weaknesses. Everyone wants to see themselves as the hero of their own story, so why not let them?

Writing less virtuous characters is a little more nuanced. When writing a scene where your main character betrays his friends, tread carefully. It can provide a more interesting multidimensional type of character development to your story. But any morally questionable actions you make your characters take must threaten the stakes in a meaningful way, and you must foreshadow them. The audience can still like a character that makes bad choices, as long as the character shows some capacity for embracing honour and treating people around him well. Han Solo in *Star Wars* is ostensibly selfish when he abandons the Rebel Alliance with his cash reward. But when Luke is the last Rebel fighter left to destroy the Death Star, Han returns at just the right moment to help his friend deliver the final blow. In this critical moment, our love for this rogue solidifies because he pulls through when his friend needs him.

Audiences will empathise with a flawed character if his flaws are understandable. Everyone can empathise with imperfection, and we've all messed up and made bad choices. And to see that reflected in a character is endearing.

In *Les Misérables*, the main character Jean Valjean starts the story serving two decades in prison for stealing a loaf of bread for his sister's starving child. He's relieved at finally being granted parole, but he can't find any work as an ex-convict. But then Bishop Myriel, finding him shivering and beaten, takes him into his church and gives him some food and a bed for the night. Valjean betrays this kind man by stealing his silverware, only to be caught the next morning and brought in to face the bishop. The bishop, seeing the potential in this moment, tells the police officers that he voluntarily gave the silver to Valjean, so they leave him alone. But he sternly looks Valjean in the eye and tells him that he must use the valuable silver to become an honest man, that he has "bought his soul for God." A shame-filled Valjean hates what society has driven him to become and vows to take a different path.

Why do we like Valjean so much after stealing a kind old man's silver? It's a deplorable act in the face of his benefactor's charity and generosity. But Valjean knows he is wrong, and he is driven to stoop to this level by a society that has cast him out and beaten all the faith and goodness out of him. The bishop doesn't take his theft personally and sees in this turn of events an excellent opportunity to wake Valjean up and put him on course for his positive character arc. Valjean ends the story as a saint, having positively impacted the lives of dozens of repressed people around him.

We have all messed up and done things we're ashamed of—we look back on these experiences, cringe, and vow never to repeat them. So embrace the strength of these emotions and let your characters do the same thing. You can harness this truth by emulating the Jean Valjean revelation in your story, and use that vulnerability to give your audience reason to identify with your main character. The key is to later allow the moments of virtue shine through when times get more difficult. We all imagine ourselves like this in our own lives, and designing your character arcs in this way is a subtle but effective way to let your audience identify with your story.

LAW 21

Reversal

There is a fine balance to narrative description, and the key is in the extent of its use. Describe too much, and you leave most readers overwhelmed, if you haven't bored them to tears. Describe too little, on the other hand, and you leave readers confused and turning back through the pages to remind themselves who characters A, B, and C are. Your audience must connect with your characters to enjoy your story, so leaving your descriptions too sparse will put this connection in danger. Understand: The most common failure of storytellers is to give their characters detailed physical descriptions but no actual characterisation, no rough edges to hold onto—it's these character traits and moments of emotional resonance we most often grasp onto and remember, not superficial details.

To achieve this balance, master storyteller Stephen King told aspiring authors to use as intuitive and visceral descriptions as possible. His primary technique was to sprinkle in some brief details familiar to the human experience, allowing the reader to use their own experiences to form a fuller picture in their minds. This technique doesn't come naturally to everyone; it requires training your use of empathy and deep intuition. But practise enough, and you'll be able to quickly come up with simple character descriptions that give the audience an instant, visceral, and personalised image of that character with maximum efficiency.

To strike the optimal balance, you also need to take your genre and your audience into consideration. Rich character descriptions are often encouraged in high fantasy stories, while they're unusual in action thrillers. J. R. R. Tolkien wrote entire chapters describing his characters, and his readers delight in the juicy details he revealed about their habits and personalities. But he also knew that his characters' true personalities would never be adequately conveyed to the audience through some clever descriptive phrase—as in any story, and real life for that matter, you can only discern someone's true nature through their actions. As Stephen King said, "spare me, if you please, the hero's 'sharply intelligent blue eyes' and 'outthrust determined chin;' likewise the heroine's 'arrogant cheekbones.' This sort of thing is bad technique and lazy writing, the equivalent of all those tiresome adverbs."

Your audience may well have similar tastes to those of Tolkien's, but the only way to find out for sure is to ask your most loyal readers and get a feel for what they respond to best—don't make it too public, ask your closest friends if you need to. This humbling exercise is always useful because it'll give you insights you might not have thought of by yourself. Your audience provides you with an infinite well of perspectives, all unique. Always keep in mind though that *you* are the storyteller, and your audience *wants* to surrender to your vision. That doesn't mean you should ignore advice, but it means that just because that one reader said she wanted more descriptive detail on characters X, Y, and Z doesn't mean that's the best direction for your story, and you need to discern the right answer. People are almost always correct in whether they like or dislike something, but rarely are they ever correct on why that is.

> *Thin description leaves the reader feeling bewildered and nearsighted. Overdescription buries him or her in details and images. The trick is to find a happy medium. It's also important to know what to describe and what can be left alone while you get on with your main job, which is telling a story. I'm not particularly keen on writing which exhaustively describes the physical characteristics of the people in the story and what they're wearing (I find wardrobe inventory particularly irritating; if I want to read descriptions of clothes, I can always get a J. Crew catalogue). I can't remember many cases*

where I felt I had to describe what the people in a story of mine looked like—I'd rather let the reader supply the faces, the builds, and the clothing as well. If I tell you that Carrie White is a high school outcast with a bad complexion and a fashion-victim wardrobe, I think you can do the rest, can't you? I don't need to give you a pimple-by-pimple, skirt-by-skirt rundown. We all remember one or more high school losers, after all; if I describe mine, it freezes out yours, and I lose a little bit of the bond of understanding I want to forge between us.

—*On Writing* by Stephen King

Law 22

Great Dialogue Is About What's Not Said

Dialogue is the best way to illustrate conflict. Friction between characters is vital to any story, and one of the best ways to show it is through dialogue rich with conflicting motivations. Dialogue is not a reporting device, it is a manifestation of that character's state, and it must therefore rely on subtext. Use dialogue to encourage your audience to discern feelings and facts, not merely to explain facts or plot details.

Transgression of the Law

The *Star Wars* prequel trilogy built up a long tally of storytelling blunders, but dialogue was a particular problem. In *The Phantom Menace*, exchanges of dialogue between Jedi, politicians, and Tatooine traders all suffer from the same problems: characters explained things in literal terms to each other, showing little emotion and providing no characterisation. There is no conflict in any of these exchanges, nothing to draw the slightest bit of interest in the characters' problems. Instead, the dialogue only serves as a device to explain and further the plot.

In *Attack of the Clones*, Obi-Wan and a teenage Anakin are introduced to the audience recounting one of their past adventures. They meet with Padmé and her security detail, but Anakin argues with his master over his abilities as a Jedi apprentice. The intention behind this clash was to show the conflict growing between master and apprentice before the latter's fall to the dark side, which thematically makes sense—Lucas always had a clear understanding of mythology. The problem is that instead of showing the beginnings of dark unrest, it shows Anakin as a moody, unlikeable, and petulant teenager arguing with his master.

The dialogue problems continue into the romance portion of the film. *Attack of Clones* is meant to be the love story for Anakin and Padmé, but bizarre and stilted dialogue fails to show any romantic tension between the characters. Anakin spends most of their exchanges whining about how Obi-Wan treats him. Even surrounded by vast, beautiful (and entirely computer-generated) scenery, the audience cannot feel the romance between these people supposed to be falling deeply in love. So when, just before the colosseum scene, Padmé confesses her deep love for Anakin, the audience is left confused and sceptical. Unlike in *The Empire Strikes Back* where Han and Leia's love blossoms out of a genuine romantic tension throughout the film, *Attack of the Clones* fails to set up any palpable romantic tension for the audience to believe in this revelation of Anakin and Padmé's supposed love.

The final instalment, *Revenge of the Sith*, shows improvements. A standout performance by Ian McDiarmid as Chancellor Palpatine, robust computer-generated sequences, and genuinely funny moments with beloved characters such as Master Yoda, all showed that Lucas relished his chance to finally tell the tragic fall-of-the-hero story he'd been trying to tell all along. While a marked improvement on the previous two films, *Revenge of the Sith* suffers from many of the same dialogue issues. Characters walked in front of pure blue-screen scenes, explaining the plot to each other without emotion or conflict. And when it attempts conflict, it comes across as awkward at best and cringeworthy at worst. When Obi-Wan challenges Anakin before their final duel, lines such as "I do not fear the dark side as you do!" and "I have brought peace and justice to my new empire!" fall flat in embarrassing fashion and have become ongoing jokes.

Interpretation

The purpose of dramatic dialogue is not to serve as an extension to the narration. Dialogue's purpose is to express the motivations of and conflicts between the characters in a way that makes optimal use of subtext. It expresses feelings, shows motives, and drives the story forward in a subtle, indirect way. The most common failure that writers make when writing dialogue is to use it as a mere explicative device to explain the plot and everyone's motives literally, while neglecting its potential for emotional power.

Unfortunately, Lucas made that precise failure in the *Star Wars* prequels, and the results speak for themselves. The films are nowhere near as entertaining as the original trilogy, and no one can attach any distinct qualities to the characters, making them all forgettable. Characters are remembered for their true nature, the qualities that make them individual. Dialogue is the easiest way to let characters express these personal qualities through subtextual motivations. The central part of the movement in any piece of dialogue should be, like an iceberg, under the surface. Any on-the-nose references will leave the tension flat and do nothing for the characters. Failure to recognise this will make your characters little more than plot mouthpieces.

> *If dialogue is the fastest way to improve a manuscript, then the fastest way to improve your dialogue is to amp up the conflict and tension. The dullest exchanges are those between two people on the same wavelength, with nothing gripping to talk about. I call these "sitting-down-for-coffee scenes." Watch out for them. If you do have two friends or allies sitting down to talk, don't make it just about feeding the reader information. Make some trouble.*
> —*How to Write Dazzling Dialogue* by James Scott Bell

Observance of the Law

Among its plethora of shining examples of masterful storytelling, Christopher Nolan's *The Dark Knight* uses dialogue at critical moments to convey the conflicting motivations of each of its characters. One of the film's central themes is the battle between order and chaos, and this is where the main characters all butt heads. This conflict is most clearly on display in two key scenes.

The first of these scenes comes after the mob accountant Lau successfully escapes Gotham with his clients' funds. Police Lieutenant Jim Gordon makes a colossal blunder by raiding a mob bank vault, only to find it left empty by the mob. Angry with Lieutenant Gordon, District Attorney Harvey Dent tricks Batman into meeting with him by using Gordon's Bat-Signal on top of the police building. Gordon, knowing he didn't make the signal, stumbles upon the meeting gun in hand suspecting the worst, but finds Dent and Batman.

All three of these characters walk into the scene primed for conflict. Dent is frustrated at Gordon's secrecy and his secret alliance with Batman, a known vigilante. Gordon is frustrated at his failures to beat the city's ruthless mob. Bruce Wayne as Batman is most concerned about getting these two men to work together so they can all achieve their common goal.

> Dent: Lau's halfway to Hong Kong—if you'd asked, I could have taken his passport—I told you to keep me in the loop.

Gordon: Yeah? All that was left in the vaults were the marked bills—they knew we were coming. As soon as your office got involved, there's a leak—

Dent: —My office? You're sitting down here with scum like Wuertz and Ramirez... (Dent pauses, looks away) Oh yeah, Gordon, I almost had your rookie cold on a racketeering beef.

Gordon: Don't try to cloud the fact that clearly Maroni's got people in your office, Dent.

Dent: We need Lau back, but the Chinese won't extradite a national, under any circumstances.

Batman: If I get him to you, can you get him to talk?

Dent: I'll get him to sing.

Gordon: We're going after the mob's life savings. Things will get ugly.

Dent: I knew the risks when I took this job, lieutenant. Same as you. (Turns to Batman) How will you get back anyway? (Batman has disappeared into thin air. Shocked, Dent turns to smirk at Gordon nervously.)

Gordon: He does that.

—*The Dark Knight*, 2008

Notice that this conversation isn't comfortable or pleasant. It's short, but it's full of conflict: Dent's frustration at being kept out of the loop, Gordon's defensiveness about his police force's capabilities, and their shared discomfort around Batman's silent yet imposing presence. But the real genius behind this dialogue is that it's the film's most explicit display of each character's individuality and core motivations. Dent wants to beat the mob through legal means, but he can't do that without the police's cooperation. Gordon wants to beat the mob in his own way, using Batman's detective skills to his advantage in spite of his official party line. Bruce Wayne as Batman has no such political motivations, instead wanting to unite these two men and the forces at their disposal, while he solves the problem in his signature lone wolf style.

Our second example of dialogue in the film is the famed interrogation scene between Batman and the Joker. This meeting of the film's hero and villain comes at the film's halfway point, so the pent-up tension means both characters are primed for an excellent piece of confrontational dialogue. By this point, the Joker has tried to manipulate Batman into revealing his identity by killing five people in live news broadcasts. Bruce Wayne as Batman has taken the public disgrace on the chin and feels immense pressure to stop the killings at any cost.

Batman: *You wanted me. Here I am.*

The Joker: I wanted to see what you'd do. And you didn't disappoint... (laughs) You let five people die. Then you let Dent take your place. Event to a guy like me, that's cold—

Batman: Where's Dent?

The Joker: Those mob fools want you gone so they can get back to the way things were. But I know the truth—there's no going back. You've changed things. Forever.

Batman: Then why do you want to kill me?

The Joker: (Laughs maniacally) Kill you? I don't want to kill you. What would I do without you? Go back to ripping off mob dealers? No, you... you complete me.

Batman: You're garbage who kills for money.

The Joker: Don't talk like one of them—you're not, even if you'd like to be. To them you're just a freak like me... they just need you right now. But as soon as they don't, they'll cast you out like a leper. Their morals, their code... it's a bad joke. Dropped at the first sign of trouble. They're only as good as the world allows them

to be. You'll see—I'll show you... when the
chips are down, these civilised people... they'll
eat each other. (Grins) See, I'm not a monster...
I'm just ahead of the curve.

(Batman suddenly grabs the Joker and pulls
him up to his face. The Joker grins with relish.)

—*The Dark Knight*, 2008

Here, the Joker expertly pushes all the right buttons, provoking Batman into a rage. This provocation defines the Joker's primary motivation—to show that anyone, but especially the most virtuous person, can be brought down to his level. Batman's signature rule is never to kill, and the Joker turns this on its head by claiming that Batman had indirectly caused those people's deaths through his own need to keep his identity secure. Evidently, the Joker killed those people, but throughout *The Dark Knight*, he forces Batman into dilemmas that put an intense strain on his firm set of guiding principles. This interrogation scene is so good because its dialogue compresses the film's primary conflicts into a single piece of confrontational dialogue that successfully amps the tension up to feverish level.

Interpretation

The Dark Knight's greatest success as a story is in the clarity of its character conflict, and the way it uses dialogue to raise that conflict to as high a level as possible. Had Nolan written scenes with characters bickering back and forth about each other's literal intentions, it would not have worked. Understand: Good dialogue is about what's not said. The two examples of dialogue described above clearly express each character's core motivations with absolute efficiency. Your goal should be to emulate this combined feat of economy and effectiveness with your own story's dialogue.

Great storytelling can often be boiled down to creating a cast of characters who inherently disagree with each other, and going from there. Not every conversation in your story needs to be an argument, but for the beginner, it's a good start. The key is to use these interactions to show, not tell the audience the characters' distinct motivations. Regardless of what strategies you use to build your characters and structure your plot, your sharpest tool is always dialogue that indirectly conveys the conflicting motivations and goals. Master this combination, and you will create dialogue that excites, inflames, and inspires your audience.

Keys to Storytelling

Burn the following mantra into your brain: Great dialogue is about what's *not* said. When we listen to people talk in real life, we don't just hear the information being exchanged; we naturally infer all sorts of things about the people involved—their personalities, their interests, and their values. This presents an opportunity for you to convey many things before your characters actually do anything. We always say that "actions speak louder than words," and this is most correct, but that's not to say you can't convey anything through words, quite the opposite in fact. Dialogue is an opportunity for you to lay bare everything about your characters' conflicts, and present the grey moral differences between your hero and villain.

When Ben Kenobi teaches Luke about his "dead" father and how they'd bravely fought together as noble Jedi Knights, using the Force, and expertly flying spacecraft, this isn't just expository dialogue. Ben is laying out a potential adventure for Luke to embark on, away from his rural farm life. The scene also lays bare who each character is at that moment—it shows that Ben isn't a crazy old hermit, but actually a brave hero, who has left his life of adventure behind him. He is offering Luke the chance to prove his potential. Luke is excited at the opportunity for an adventure but his refusal shows that he feels resigned to a life he has little control over. Thus, in a few short lines of dialogue we learn everything we need to know about each character's true personality, forming the base for each character's arc. Ben, a wise hermit, comes out of hiding to pass on the baton to a new generation and achieve true transcendence in the Force while facing down his old pupil. Luke, an adolescent longing for adventure, finally becomes the hero he's always known himself to be.

Use this strategy in the following manner: Chart out arcs for your main characters, and write a simple scene just before the story's inciting incident, where they all show their motives. This technique gives the audience an opportunity to connect with your characters right before the event that makes the real story begin. On the other hand, the *Star Wars* prequels fail because they don't use the subtler effects of dialogue on characterisation and story. Every other scene has dialogue whose only role is to describe the plot to the audience. Instead of conveying feelings, characters literally explain their feelings. Instead of presenting the conflict, they literally explained the conflict. This completely drains all tension.

Do you see the difference in each of these cases? Good dialogue conveys and presents, while bad dialogue literally explains. Each piece of dialogue is an opportunity to let your audience feel your characters. In real life, people's outward appearances often reflect their inner opposites. The same is true in great stories. The chronically shy are actually desperate for attention. The overtly superficial long for others to take their intelligence seriously. When a character arrogantly brags about his achievements, the audience senses that he might be insecure and covering up some sensitivity. But when the character's father explains that he's arrogant, we shrug our shoulders and nod along. We believe them, but we never see it, so it's never made real for us. In *Attack of the Clones*, Obi-Wan walks along slowly with Yoda, explaining that his apprentice Anakin's new powers have made him arrogant. At no point have we seen Obi-Wan and Anakin fight together, so how are we supposed to believe this? A far more effective approach would have been to start the film with a fight scene where Anakin brashly fights off some foe but puts himself and his master in danger.

Whenever you encounter a weak piece of dialogue like the above, you must think of how you can express the information through action instead of words. What information is it explaining? How can we more subtly present that information to the audience? Does the audience even need the information? Working to find the right answers to these questions will solve most of your issues with weak dialogue and provide untold benefits to your story's entertainment value.

> *Great dialogue begins before you write a line. It starts by creating a cast of characters who differ from each other so there is always the possibility of conflict or tension.*
>
> —*How to Write Dazzling Dialogue* by James Scott Bell

Quentin Tarantino and Confrontational Dialogue

The film director Quentin Tarantino is famous for the way he directed and wrote the confrontational dialogue in the films *Pulp Fiction*, *Inglourious Basterds*, and *Django Unchained*. Film students often spend months dissecting these scenes, trying to reverse-engineer the master director's skill. Tarantino's mastery of story dialogue is simpler than you might think, and attaining it is two-fold.

First, Tarantino tries to bury exposition in minutiae. When *Pulp Fiction*'s Jules and Vincent drive to the job, they chat about Vincent's time in Europe, showing the audience that Vincent is a loyal employee of their boss Marcellus Wallace. Jules jokes about Vincent's apparent sexual insecurities when they discuss whether a foot massage constitutes a sexual act. Their later gossip about whether their boss threw a man out of the window conveys to the audience that he is not a man to disappoint. This piece of gossip both establishes Wallace's fearsome reputation and foreshadows the story's later conflict.

This technique is useful because it's also entertaining—we all love the "Royale with Cheese" anecdote. But by being lulled into this fun exchange, we learn more about the plot and the characters by osmosis. We feel Jules's and Vincent's personalities. Vincent is loyal, quiet, and well-travelled. Jules is genuine, tough, and thoughtful. We also learn about their jobs and how their boss is an uncompromising man.

This dialogue all happens while they're doing stuff that advances the plot, since Jules and Vincent talk to pass the time while they drive to the hit job. They continue talking to relax and relieve the tension before they go in and shoot the young men. Not only do these scenes serve a purpose, but they feel natural. We've all chatted to our co-workers to pass the time at some point. The point of this technique is to inform the audience of necessary facts without them knowing it. The contrast between the relaxed banter and sudden threat of shooting the young men dead in the next scene also shows their professionalism and how they've grown used to such acts of extreme violence.

Tarantino's second technique is to use confrontational dialogue to ramp up the suspense. As discussed in Law 19, Build Tension with the "Bomb under the Table" Technique, tension is best built up by disturbing a scene's sense of stability with some threat and then continuing to stretch out that scene as far as possible. In the opening sequence of *Inglourious Basterds*, Colonel Hans Landa calmly interrogates Monsieur LaPadite about Jews suspected to be in the local area.

Landa is ostensibly polite and respectful, as he asks for a glass of milk and calmly explains his predicament to LaPadite in a routine way. We are then shown the Jewish family hiding underneath the floorboards, so we know that there's a high risk that LaPadite will get found out. As Landa reads the tension on LaPadite's face, he turns the screw by explaining the different animals that each race embodies, referring to the Jews as "rats" and noting the indignities that people will put themselves through when in hiding. The audience is made aware that there are heavily armed German soldiers who could enter and kill them all at the snap of Landa's fingers.

By this point, the discomfort is at its highest and LaPadite can barely hold himself together. Landa's kind demeanour disappears, and he directly asks LaPadite, "You are harbouring enemies of the state, are you not?" "Yes," whimpers La Padite, tears rolling down his face. We knew this was coming. The suspense is unbearable. The tension is finally released as Landa's soldiers burst in and brutally execute all but one of the Dreyfus family. See that nothing more than a simple reveal of the high stakes and some uncomfortable dialogue can take the audience on an emotional roller coaster, setting the tone for the rest of the film.

Expressing Theme and Symbolism

If your story has a pervading theme or message, you can also use a specific tagline to express it at pivotal moments. In *The Godfather*, the tagline "I'm going to make him an offer he can't refuse" is used to convey the passing of the baton from Don Corleone to his son Michael as the unlikely new head of the family. It's a single sentence with a profound impact. When Michael says the line at the ending, it signals his transformation from a wide-eyed young man into a powerful and ruthless crime boss.

More repetitious symbolism in dialogue can also affirm a central theme, so long as it's expressed at natural moments and not overtly beaten over the audience's head. It doesn't have to be a single tagline. Each instance can be an interesting variation of a central theme. The theme in *The Dark Knight* is tragic heroism. Lines of dialogue such as "You either die a hero or see yourself become a villain," and "I took Gotham's White Knight and brought him down to our level," stick in our minds because they naturally flow with the tone and feeling of the story.

These lines of dialogue don't feel forced, because they're consistent with what's going on in the story. Bruce Wayne has to give up the mantle of Batman, there are threats to justice everywhere, and the Joker looks like he's going to win for most of the film. Because they also foreshadow the ending, it makes it feel all the more inevitable when Batman drives into the distance, taking the blame for all of Harvey Dent's murders.

One Last Thing

If you're writing dialogue for a novel, try this technique: Write each participant's dialogue in turn, without embellishment. No "he said," or "she said," just write the words being spoken from beginning to end. Finish the dialogue and then go back to add the intermittent thoughts, actions, and gestures. Using this technique will help your dialogue flow better from the reader's perspective. It'll also stop you from focusing on embellishments when you should be thinking solely about the maximising that subtextual conflict between the participants. Picking smart descriptors for your dialogue is far less critical than immersing your reader in the conversation.

> *The day I proposed to Alma she was lying in an upper bunk of a ship's cabin. The ship was floundering in a most desperate way and so was Alma, who was seasick. We were returning to London from Germany. Alma was my employee. I couldn't risk being flowery for fear that in her wretched state she would think I was discussing a movie script. As it was, she groaned, nodded her head, and burped. It was one of my greatest scenes—a little weak on dialogue, perhaps, but beautifully staged and not overplayed.*
>
> —Alfred Hitchcock, 1899-1980

Reversal

No possible good can come from glib dialogue. However, while creating a story based solely on dialogue has been done many times to great effect, it comes with the caveat that it must express each character's conflicting motives. A story full of dialogue but little action has to excel at this use of interpersonal conflict to an even greater degree than usual. Never snub the value of action, it can be doubly powerful in its subtextual power. The warning here is to pay attention to the balance between dialogue and action, and to consider whether some real action can improve your dialogue-heavy story.

Law 23

Write Proactive Characters

Just as in real life, there is nothing more irritating than a character who acts like a wimp, giving up at the slightest difficulty, and doing nothing about the challenges that face them. Audiences relate to characters who are proactive. Make characters who act to create the plot, not the other way around. Great characters make your reader look up, not down. Leave your audience feeling more inspired than when they first pressed "play" on your story.

Observance of the Law

In 1985, when Stephen King wrote his novel *Misery*, he planned to release it under the pseudonym Richard Bachman. At the time, releasing multiple novels in the same year was frowned upon in the publishing industry. Publishers wanted to focus attention on the launch of each new novel and didn't want to saturate the market. King, however, was a prolific writer and made a compromise with his publisher to allow him to pen his new titles using the pseudonym. King's voracious and excited attitude to writing seeped into his novels' characters, often finding themselves in some mystic situation and working their way out of it using their initiative.

Misery follows Paul Sheldon, the author of a popular series of Victorian romance novels starring Misery Chastain. Paul has a tradition of finishing the first draft of every one of his novels in the same room of a hotel in Colorado, and his latest is no different. In celebration, he drives in a jubilant drunken mania through the Colorado mountains instead of flying straight home to New York City. This joyride ends in a bad car crash during a snowstorm, shattering both his legs and leaving him unconscious inside his car.

Annie Wilkes, a former nurse, finds Paul in the car wreckage and rescues him. Annie happens to be a massive fan of Paul's work and recognises him, and so she puts him up in her home's guest bedroom rather than taking him to a hospital. Though grateful at first for Annie's help, Paul begins to feel a sense of unease at her strange, obsessive manner. His suspicion is confirmed when, upon reading his latest finished draft, she violently berates him for its profane language. As "punishment," Annie force-feeds Paul with medication, washing it down with soapy water. This horrific torture, however, is only the beginning. Annie bursts into yet another fit of rage at Paul, this time disappearing from the house without warning, leaving him bedridden without any food, water, or painkillers. He spends two days in agony, his body writhing in pain, hunger, and withdrawal symptoms.

After this ordeal, Paul realises that Annie is not only socially weird but also dangerously disturbed, and resolves to escape the house in any way he can. Close to death, Paul still uses every mental resource available to him. He decides to submit to her commands for the time being and writes a new Misery book that brings the character back from the dead, biding his time until he regains the strength to leave by his own accord. He plays along with her sweet manner, complimenting her food and nursing skills. Each eager mouthful of soup, each letter on the typewriter, and each sweet, false smile as she walks in the room is another step towards freedom. Though Paul suffers horribly at the hands of his sadistic captor, he gains lasting satisfaction in his eventual escape.

> *She left and returned with a steaming bowl of soup. There were vegetables floating in it. He was not able to eat much, but he ate more than he thought at first he could. She seemed pleased. It was while he ate the soup that she told him what had happened, and he remembered it all as she told him, and he supposed it was good to know how you happened to end up with your legs shattered, but the manner by which he was coming to this knowledge was disquieting—it was as if he was a character in a story or a play, a character whose history is not recounted like history but created like fiction.*
>
> —*Misery* by Stephen King

Interpretation

As with many of Stephen King's stories, *Misery* starts off innocuously enough with a familiar-seeming protagonist in a difficult situation. We identify with them and start to like them. But events unfold to reveal horrifying truths through a series of increasingly brutal acts. The audience can identify with Paul due to the stark contrast made with the deranged Annie, but the most significant impact comes from his undying determination to *get the hell out of there*. In the same situation, we would feel terrified and want an escape in any way possible, and from the moment she makes him gargle and swallow that soapy water, we need to know how he gets out in the end.

Had Paul quietly sat in his bed feeling sorry for himself, submitting to Annie's blows and not acting on his burning desire for revenge, the book wouldn't offer much of a story. Paul's will against Annie's entrapment drives the story forward. He isn't a wimp, and we're shown that he consistently sees his goals through to the end when he finishes his latest novel. So when he decides to find any way he can to escape, we're invested, because we believe that he will find a way. Paul proves his credentials as an active character, and, accordingly, we put our trust in him. Those who have read *Misery* to the end know that this trust is rewarded.

Keys to Storytelling

Editor and book reviewer Rose Fox tells aspiring novelists that "protagonists need to protag." Celebrated characters have strong motivations and make choices that reveal those desires. A submissive doormat who gives up on their goals is never an appealing character. Such people in real life irritate us, mainly because we want to grab them and get them to do something about their problems. Audiences view story characters in the same way. Once a character is conceived and their motivations clear, let them go to work. Picture yourself holding an energetic household pet above the ground, desperate to weave their way out of your hands. Once released on the floor, they dart off into the distance. That is the image to use when creating an active character.

An active character has an explicit goal, and proactively works towards pursuing it. Your story must have at least one active character, usually the main protagonist or the villain. This character shapes the events of the story by pushing towards his goal, generally creating conflict by rubbing up against other less active characters' goals.

Readers quickly lose interest in characters who sit back and refuse to take the reins. At their low points, we can all feel sympathy for a character, but only momentarily. We expect them to get up, dust themselves off, and get back to work. Some of the worst, dislikeable characters have been whiny brats whose only purpose is to flail about hysterically to provide some perverse comic relief. Never write a character with such passive tendencies, unless they have a positive change arc later in the story. Otherwise, audiences will ask why this character is even in the story, and this question is illustrative. Why include a character who relents under pressure and does nothing?

We often fall into the trap of creating passive characters, usually by writing a plot first and the characters second. This is a bad approach to writing stories. The better strategy is to think character arc first, and plot setting second. Think less "How do I get my hero to do this?" and more "What would my hero do next?"

An active protagonist character works best when it's the audience's first introduction to that character. This order fits well within a positive change arc. The hero states a goal, she goes after it, and creates friction with the hostile force, and thus the conflict that drives the story. This proactivity on the hero's part links tightly to the arc they need to take. In other words, they initially chase after what they think they want, not what they actually need. There is no requirement on the goal being right; it's just a target that the character is explicitly working towards.

> "Ask, and it will be given to you; seek, and you will find; knock, and the door will be opened to you. For everyone who asks receives, and the

one who seeks finds, and to the one who knocks
it will be opened. Or which one of you, if his son
asks him for bread, will give him stone? Or if he
asks for a fish, will give him a serpent?"

—Matthew 7:7-10

Here is how their chasing usually goes: The hero has a goal, they make plans, they take their first steps, and BAM, they're hit squarely in the face by the antagonistic force. They realise that their first idea wasn't right, and the choices they make to adjust and drive forward yet again are a chance to show his character development. An active protagonist story, then, is the best opportunity to show your audience that your hero, while strong-willed, is imperfect, and needs to do some serious learning before he can become the hero he needs to be. He falls down in some way, he realises his old approach wasn't right, and he thrusts forward yet again after reflection and further training.

The plainest modern example is Marvel's *Thor* film from 2011. Thor begins the story believing in the lie that he is invincible and that he has an unconditional place on the throne of Asgard. He goes to the ice planet Jotunheim, wanting to prove his strength, but all that achieves is getting his friends into perilous danger and ruining a fragile peace treaty. Not very kingly behaviour. His father, the king of Asgard, punishes him by sending him to Midgard (Earth) and depriving him of his immortality. Crucial to the plot, Odin deprives Thor of his hammer Mjolnir, which he can only lift again once he proves himself worthy. This is Thor's lowest point. Accordingly, he spends the majority of the plot trying and failing to pursue his lost hammer. His brash, ill-thought-out pursuit of Mjolnir ends in repeated failure, and he learns that he can't solve every problem with brute force.

Thor ends the story as a wise and patient leader, having realised that it's more important to protect your friends than to charge in all guns blazing. He drives the plot forward by hastily attacking his goal, but his failure to carefully think beyond his fists makes him realise he needs more than just brute force to achieve his goals. It is only through protecting his friends and using their scientific knowledge that he proves himself worthy of Mjolnir.

The challenge to your hero's active pursuit of the goals has to mean something. It must expose the flaws he needs to shake off to become the real hero. If your character achieves their goal without making it happen because of what they've done, the reader is going to feel cheated at the end of the story. The active protagonist makes his own choices, and he's not buffeted around by the ever-increasing conflict. There are times he has to react to situations, but even then, he still explores which options fit best with his explicitly stated goal. He influences the plot, not the other way around.

> *If a character doesn't want something, they're passive. And if they're passive, they're effectively dead. Without a desire to animate the protagonist, the writer has no hope of bringing the character alive, no hope of telling a story and the work will almost always be boring. Aaron Sorkin put it succinctly, "Somebody's got to want something, something's got to be standing in their way of getting it. You do that, and you'll have a scene."*
>
> —*Into the Woods* by John Yorke

Storytellers often think solely of the protagonist when it comes to writing active characters. But that doesn't always have to be the case. History has shown us that the best stories have had proactive, empathetic villains that dictate events for the hero, who spends most of the plot reacting to his foe's bold initiative.

Indeed, a protagonist erring more towards the passive side can work in such a case. But there is a strong caveat you can't ignore: While your hero doesn't have to be active, he does need to react strongly in his own way. The conflict created by the proactive villain causes stress for the hero, and this shows the audience how he acts under pressure. The choices he makes under this pressure show who he is. Therefore the proactive villain strategy is best at providing characterisation for your hero.

If you go down this route and choose to create a proactive villain, then one technique you can use is to show events from the hero's perspective. We only see through the eyes of the hero as the villain does terrible things to the people he loves. The hero is the underdog, a role that most people trust. We feel sympathy for the hero as the villain exerts untold terror on him and his friends. There is a risk here, though—show too little from your villain's perspective and he'll fail to be empathetic. Balance this out by starting the story right in the action from your villain's perspective, and then transitioning to your hero once you've made this establishing character moment for the villain.

One more caveat with this approach is that your hero must have the guts to fight back. The point of this technique is to give your hero the opportunity to go one level up. He has to be stronger than ever to defeat this villainous force. We see his vulnerability, we see his flaws, and we see him pull together friends, former enemies, and his inner strength to make it a fair fight.

The obvious example of this technique is *The Dark Knight*, whose villain the Joker is the primary active character—he explicitly states his goal right from his first sequence all the way to the end. He wants to upset the established order and show that Gotham's heroes can be brought down to his level. He has a flawed yet very strongly argued motivation. The Joker relentlessly pursues this goal, creating all of the challenges that Batman has to face.

In *The Dark Knight*, Bruce Wayne as Batman is a reactive character. He spends the bulk of the story reacting to the Joker's manipulative schemes, but he doesn't wallow in self-pity for too long. Wayne adapts his suit, his methods, and he trains his detective skills. The Joker stretches his moral code to the limit, and he barely keeps his head above water. In threatening Batman's identity, the Joker makes Bruce Wayne choose between his rule to never kill and his own secret identity. In forcing him to choose between Rachel and Harvey, he once again force him to choose between his love and his mission to protect Gotham. In each case, the Joker compels Batman to show his true virtue in the face of impossible dilemmas.

The Joker's plan breaks Bruce Wayne down, but it creates the ultimate stage for him to show his true colours. And from a broader perspective, that's a good thing, and it's what makes the story great. The terrible conflict brought about by the Joker forces Batman to become the tragic hero that Gotham needs: the Dark Knight.

This kind of storytelling can work very well for the second story of a three-part series. We've spent the first story investing in the protagonist in a straightforward Hero's Journey arc, meaning that when we cruelly beat him down in the second story at the hands of a ruthlessly proactive villain, the protagonist's rise has deep emotional resonance.

In 1984, ahead of Apple's launch of the first Macintosh computer, Steve Jobs addressed his engineers over the various developmental issues they were facing. The engineers told him they needed two weeks to iron out all the bugs to make it ready for launch. Jobs calmed them down and said to them that if they could do it in two weeks, they could do it in one. There was little difference in those timeframes. They would have to work extra hard, putting in days' worth of overtime. Apple's engineers overcame the obstacles, and the product was yet another success of industry-redefining proportions.

How did that story make you feel? It likely made you feel inspired, aware of new possibilities, and impressed by the calm optimism that Jobs could inspire in his staff. So tell a story like that one. Resigning yourself to defeatist attitudes only lets the problems creep further and further. Had Jobs and those engineers not inspired such a pervasive culture of proactivity, Apple would not have repeatedly redefined what was considered possible in the technology space as they have done. People find such stories inspiring because they open up opportunities, and the power to take those opportunities lies within us; there's no magic secret, there's only proactivity and the open mind required to see those opportunities in the first place. When we see these challenges played out in stories, we instinctively root for the characters and hope they succeed. The proactive character must win, regardless of whether they're the hero or villain.

> *"But my nose is running!" What do you have hands for, idiot, if not to wipe it? "But how is it right that there be running noses in the first place?" Instead of thinking up protests, wouldn't it be easier just to wipe your nose? What would have become of Hercules, do you think, if there had been no lion, hydra, stag or boar—and no savage criminals to rid the world of? What would he have done in the absence of such challenges? Obviously he would have just*

rolled over in bed and gone back to sleep. So by snoring his life away in luxury and comfort he never would have developed into the mighty Hercules. And even if he had, what good would it have done him? What would have been the use of those arms, that physique, and that noble soul, without crises or conditions to stir him into action?

—*Discourses* by Epictetus

Reversal

What possible good can come from writing whiny characters who submit to the whims of fortune and let the antagonist trample all over them? There can be no reversal to this critical law; do not bother looking for one.

Law 24

Point Everything to the End and Beyond

The best stories move with a deliberate pace. Not every story has to move fast, but every part of the story must build to the crescendo of your ending. The most lasting part of your story is the impression it leaves in the audience well after they've read the last page or left the cinema. You can achieve this most powerful of effects through the use of subtext—it is always better to leave the juiciest details unsaid and leave your audience thinking.

Part I: Point Every Beat Towards the Ending

Write your story in a way that confidently takes your audience on a clear path to the ending. Stories that succeed in creating a deliberate pace will immerse the audience, making them forget themselves. This success depends on bringing together all the elements of structure and conflict into a single cohesive journey that unapologetically directs the audience to a natural crescendo.

Observance of the Law

Christopher Nolan adapted his 2006 film *The Prestige* from Christopher Priest's book of the same name. *The Prestige* follows the rivalry between stage musicians Alfred Borden and Robert Angier, which rapidly escalates out of control with deadly consequences. In the opening sequence, the magicians' set designer John Cutter demonstrates the stages of a magic trick to a little girl:

> *"Every magic trick consists of three parts, or acts. The first part is called the Pledge; the magician shows you something ordinary. The second act is called the Turn; the magician takes the ordinary something and makes it into something extraordinary."*

> —*The Prestige*, 2006

Veteran actor Michael Caine's performance as Cutter piques the audience's curiosity, and afterwards the audience is introduced to the two main characters, Borden and Angier, at the grim conclusion of their rivalry. Borden watches Angier drown in a water tank, smashing his fists against the solid glass. Their rivalry well-known to the public, Borden is convicted of Angier's murder and sentenced to death.

Flashing back to when these two men first met, the film returns to the start of their journey. Both Borden and Angier work as shills for a stage magician, planted audience members in on all of their boss's magic tricks. The plot jumps back and forth in time as the two men read one another's journals, tracking the progress in their careers in an attempt to understand the other's magic tricks, and maybe achieve some closure from the horrible fallout of their rivalry.

This mutual obsession with outdoing each other drives them to new heights in their respective careers. Both men gain wealth and huge followings, although deep down Angier is desperate to replicate Borden's repeated masterpieces, most of all the "Transporting Man" sequence that so mystifies and delights his audience. Through the struggles and pain these men bring upon themselves and each other, the audience finds repeated jaw-dropping mystic plot twists that escalate the tension right through to the ending.

Not only does the plot move fast, but the ending stares the audience in the face right from Cutter's opening scene. The entire film is an elaborate magic trick that beautifully unfolds as the audience is treated to the explosive conflict between Borden and Angier. With its nonlinear plot, tragic twists, and unexpected actor performances, *The Prestige* is a masterpiece in strategic storytelling.

Interpretation

The Prestige indirectly establishes its own ending right from the first two scenes. Cutter's monologue on the three stages of a magic trick, followed by Angier's tragic death, is itself the Pledge, promising the audience a cautionary tale on the dangers and potential fallout of competitive rivalry when it spirals out of control. From that moment on, the film forces the audience's sights on this "ending," much like when a magician distracts their audience with some shiny object of focus. But the real answer stares the audience in the face the entire time, and it's given in part by Cutter's opening monologue.

The plot drives forward at a tireless pace by the apparent conflict between Borden and Angier. These two men's motivations are in stark contrast, providing a powerful engine for moving the story forward at an ever-accelerating speed. Borden's tricks become more daring, with deadly consequences for his assistants and friends. Angier's emotional agony drives him to match Borden's increasing fame by going to America, where he meets a historical figure played by an unexpected actor. The audience happily submits to this whirlwind of events and the emotional rollercoaster created by the plot.

Replicating *The Prestige*'s success is two-fold, and a lot like the setup of a magic trick. First, you must lock your audience's attention on the story's goal. You need a dramatic scene that grabs the audience by the scruff of the neck and demands their attention—usually the more painful this is for the characters, the better. Holding their attention like this tricks them much like a red herring does with foreshadowing—it distracts them from the true movements happening under the surface.

Second, your story must have a multitude of characters with directly opposed motivations and beliefs. This design can only result in conflict, which you must see as your story's engine. Conflict shown through repeated arguments and acts of mutual cruelty will inevitably advance the story at a pace that cannot slow down. That means you must not slacken the story's underlying tension. Stories must *advance*, and they can only advance through ever-heightening conflict. Heighten the discomfort, and your audience will beg you for a resolution.

In the nineteenth century, the legendary escape artist Harry Houdini would extend his death-defying stunts, holding himself locked underwater for longer than necessary, as his audiences gasped and held onto their chairs. Right at the last second, Houdini would escape to rapturous applause, the audience sighing in relief. Houdini was able to deliberately heighten the drama through his devotion to hard work and endless practise. Studying the mechanisms of locks and ancient sleight-of-hand tricks gave his stage appearances the drama and heroism they're remembered for today.

Similar to Houdini's masterful escape tricks, this law of storytelling demands intense work in the planning stage. To make your story unfold with the elegant beauty of *The Prestige*, every piece of the puzzle must fit together perfectly. An ad hoc approach to writing can never achieve that same level of congruity in story structure. Hard work, endless practise, and an eye for grand strategy will give you the same roller coasters of satisfying drama created by legendary performers such as Houdini and masterful stories such as *The Prestige*.

*Every writer is surprised anew when a book, as
soon as it has separated from him, begins to take
on a life of its own. He feels as if one part of an
insect had been severed and were going its own
way. Perhaps he almost forgets the book; perhaps he rises above the views set down in it;
perhaps he no longer understands it and has lost
those wings on which he soared when he devised
that book. Meanwhile, it goes about finding its
readers, kindles life, pleases, horrifies, fathers
new works, becomes the soul of others' resolu-
tions and behaviour. In short, it lives like a being fitted out with mind and soul—yet it is
nevertheless not human. The most fortunate
author is one who is able to say as an old man
that all he had of life-giving, invigorating, up-
lifting, enlightening thoughts and feelings still
lives on in his writings, and that he himself is
only the grey ash, while the fire has been rescued
and carried forth everywhere. If one considers,
then, that a man's every action, not only his
books, in some way becomes the occasion for
other actions, decisions, and thoughts; that
everything which is happening is inextricably
tied to everything which will happen; then one
understands the real immortality, that of*

> *movement: what once has moved others is like*
> *an insect in amber, enclosed and immortalised*
> *in the general intertwining of all that exists.*
> —*Human, All Too Human* by Friedrich Nietz-
> sche

Part II: Create Impact Beyond the Ending

If a story's ending leaves the biggest impression on your reader upon putting your book down or leaving the cinema, then the power of its subtext leaves an even greater impression for the days, weeks, and months afterwards. Master the art of making things unsaid yet clear. Don't try to force your story's most important themes through glib, on-the-nose pieces of dialogue; they should ooze out of the gaps between the lines.

Observance of the Law

The planned sequel to the 1982 film *Blade Runner* spent 15 years in development hell before finally being released as *Blade Runner 2049* in October 2017. *Blade Runner 2049* is a neo-noir science fiction film carrying on from the world built by the classic *Blade Runner* film with Harrison Ford. In this world, humanity has created what are called "replicants," a type of artificial human with enhanced capabilities. They can run faster, lift more, and think faster than "organic" humans and, accordingly, are subjugated by the latter as slaves. The ability to create a near-unlimited supply of obedient super-humans has allowed humanity to colonise new worlds beyond Earth. *Blade Runner* not only tells an entertaining story within a believable universe, but it raises interesting ethical questions around this concept. Are these synthetic humans just as human as us? Are their lives worth as much? Do they feel the same way we do?

The 2017 sequel *Blade Runner 2049* follows Officer K, a "blade runner," whose job is to "retire" (kill) replicants designed to old specs who have gone rogue. At the start of the film, a fight between K and a rogue replicant reveals that K is himself also a replicant. The furious betrayal seethes out of the rogue replicants' face as he braces himself against K's powerful, superior blows. K, used to this reaction and unaffected by this routine job, finds out something at the rogue's farm that completely changes his perspective on his own kind: the rogue took care of a female replicant who seems to have died during a caesarian section. This revelation implies that replicants can breed and self-replicate—an incredible discovery that if true could cause riots between humans and replicants, and K's concerned boss Lieutenant Joshi tasks him with finding and destroying any related evidence.

The rest of *Blade Runner 2049* proceeds in this manner, revealing more information and character exploration in an understated way. We as the audience don't know any more details than K does, and his journey to explore the real potential of his replicant kin unfolds accordingly. At no point does its director Denis Villeneuve shove the associated themes of sentience, reality, or free will in our faces. There are no glib thesis statements, nor are there any on-the-nose lines of dialogue. These themes are *shown* to the audience, whether through a fellow police officer hurling abuse at K, or the condescending yet mothering manner that his boss treats him with, or the sudden explosion of pent-up rage he releases when his deepest fears are confirmed. Roger A. Deakins' masterful cinematography that finally earned himself an Academy Award caps off this masterpiece of cinema by successfully hypnotising the audience, drawing us into the fascinating story that *Blade Runner 2049* tells us.

Interpretation

On its initial release, *Blade Runner 2049* could have been seen as a flop in financial terms. General audiences called it boring, with a lot less action than the trailers appeared to promise. But just as its popularity rose and it reached greater heights of critical acclaim,

Blade Runner 2049's central feature is its gradual and understated build up. Had this film had been put together by a less skilled team, it would have been filled with obvious on-the-nose references to its themes surrounding the rights of replicants, action sequences that added nothing to the story, and suffered endless cuts.

Keeping your audience engaged does not require a plot that moves at any specific level of speed. Your story must have deliberate forward movement, and it must achieve this with conflict and a growing undercurrent of tension to keep your audience engaged. *Blade Runner 2049* builds slowly, but in a way that unfolds like a lotus before the audience. These conflicts, such as the frustration K feels, and the general fear and unfairness that replicants have to endure, are revealed to the audience through actions and subtle dialogue. These emotional chords aren't pushed at the audience, because they don't need to be; instead, the story *induces* these feelings. This distinction is what art is all about. To those who appreciate unfolding pieces of information and the slow build of tension, *Blade Runner 2049* is a beautiful work of art.

Ridley Scott's original *Blade Runner* created a cult following in the decades following its release, and that is illustrative. But it didn't just spawn fan fiction and further world-building; it also influenced countless other storytellers to embrace the power of imagery, theme, and subtext. It opened a debate on the film's themes— what if we had access to such untold power? How should we treat artificial humans if we had the ability to create them? These themes were repeated, reinterpreted, and extended in further beloved stories. That is why you need to embrace the potential that such subtext gives to your own stories. If your story has something to say, then leave it unsaid, but in a way that the audience *gets* it. Your story will stay in their hearts for the rest of their lives.

> *Our existence has no foundation on which to rest except the transient present. Thus its form is essentially unceasing motion, without any possibility of that repose which we continually strive after. It resembles the course of a man running down a mountain who would fall over if he tried to stop and can stay on his feet only by running on; or a pole balanced on the tip of the finger; or a planet which would fall into its sun if it ever ceased to plunge irresistibly forward. Thus existence is typified by unrest.*
>
> —Arthur Schopenhauer, 1788-1860

Keys to Storytelling

It is a common maxim of storytelling that every scene must contribute to moving the plot forward at all times. It holds true for screenwriters of big blockbuster action films because the premise is usually quite simple: Character A tries to achieve an objective but character B blocks A in some way, and dramatic gun-fights ensue.

Most of Dan Brown's novels have succeeded by providing a non-stop journey of mystery where the tension rises higher at every moment. Short, punchy chapters punctuated by cliff-hanger questions succeed in making the audience wonder what'll happen next. Each of his books generally has some mystery that the heroes seem to get closer and closer to, and the audience feel like there's some tangible payoff as they carry on reading. Try this approach of dangling bait in your stories and you'll hook readers all the way to the ending.

In action-oriented stories like these, derailing an exciting, fast-paced plot with an irrelevant scene can feel like an abrupt interruption of the pacing. The critical distinction to make here is whether a scene contributes to the *plot* or to the *message* of the story. On the face of it, one might question the validity of this rule, and how it could apply to their less fast-paced drama story.

In Marvel's *Thor*, not every scene with the title hero on Earth is a visible movement of him towards getting his all-powerful hammer Mjolnir back. The diner scene where he throws about coffee mugs and asserts his dominance over others is to illustrate why he needs to shed his brash, headstrong attitude to become the leader that Asgard needs. He outwardly displays arrogance but his actions make his later character development stick in the audience's mind.

In the 1972 film *The Godfather*, the horrific scene where the elderly businessman awakes to his prize horse's severed head staring right back at him indeed grabs the audience's attention, but one might ask how this moves the plot forward. Well, it doesn't. But if this scene had been cut, we'd have a less clear picture of the grisly world that Michael has chosen to enter. There isn't as much value in his character arc. See how this scene leaves the plot different to how it started? It has a strong implication on how the audience sees the characters.

Keeping that example in mind, let us revise a more reliable representation of that storytelling axiom we started with: that each of your story's scenes must have an implication to its core message. It's a more flexible form of the principle because you adapt its application around on the type of story you want to tell. An action-oriented story can use it in both of these ways—first, through overt plot movement, and second, through subtler undertones.

Jane Austen's *Pride and Prejudice* is a clearer counter-example to the every-scene-a-rush principle, instead using each scene to meticulously build the relationships and conflicts between the characters. The relationships between the characters are so complex that university literature courses on Austen's book provide students with an interconnected web diagram to chart them all out. This complexity may seem unnecessary, but once it's built and the conflicts are all primed, the scene is set for the rich emotional confrontations that we're looking for.

Different audiences see this type of slow-moving story in different ways. More action-oriented audiences might see it as boring because it's thin on the action side, whereas the more relationship-and-drama-oriented camp find it a fascinating web of unravelling interpersonal conflict and tension. Genre and cultural tropes both exert a powerful influence on an audience's expectations of a story, so pay attention to these (though on occasion you should gleefully subvert these expectations and catch the audience off guard, as discussed in Law 9, Subvert Expectations).

The 1968 film *2001: A Space Odyssey* has a minimal plot because Stanley Kubrick's vision was instead to create an immersive futuristic experience. It's more an anthology of the perils of the human race's immense progress, and it's a timeless message that will never go stale. Each scene is meticulously filmed to contribute to the rich escapism Kubrick wanted audiences to feel. Decades after its original release, it continues to achieve this goal. What's different about it, then? It doesn't have any character arcs, nor does it have any obvious plot, so does it transgress this law? No, because it has a stated goal and reaches for it—humanity itself is the film's protagonist, and the film casts a dim light on the potential dangers of relentless progress. But more importantly, *2001*'s genius is in how it enraptures its audience and has influenced countless future film-makers. Kubrick deliberately kept the true meaning of *2001*'s cryptic ending a secret to his grave, meaning that audiences have continued to argue and speculate for decades after its release. Far from relying on constant action, *2001* masterfully hypnotises the audience with its ambiguous plot and mesmeric cinematography—a brilliant application of this law.

Christopher Nolan's *The Dark Knight* moves forward at a relentlessly fast pace, with exciting and impressive action set-pieces. But the less action-oriented scenes that rely more on drama provide obvious messages about what the film is trying to convey to you. The Joker is violent for a reason, and you leave the cinema screen with a very clear understanding of what that reason is. Christopher Nolan's works consistently achieve this mark because each of his stories has a clear message to convey, and considerable effort is put into planning their intricate structures. Every scene that you see in his films points in the direction of the ending.

Follow Nolan's example, then, and cut scenes that don't appear to contribute to your story's structure. Think deeply about your story's core message and the tensions and character arcs required to convey it to the audience. Concentrate your hard work into this area, and you'll gain a clear sense of what should happen in the plot to convey that message.

Following archetypal story models such as the Hero's Journey can indeed make this step easier because there is an established structure for your plot to move along. The path is waiting in front of you, and it's not hard to identify which scenes don't push your plot forward in the literal sense: The hero appears, she has a need, she goes to fulfil that need, she searches for the need, she finds the solution, she takes the solution, she returns, and she's now a master of both the inside and outside worlds. Each jump concludes with a choice that illustrates her character development, and any movement in between is to convey any further messages you want to tell.

> *Perhaps the immediate opportunity lies in more careful and more intelligent treatment of film stories. The American film directors under their commercially-minded employers have learnt a good deal about studio lighting, action photographs, and telling a story plainly and smoothly in moving pictures. They have learnt, as it were, to put the nouns, verbs and adjectives of the film language together. But even if we conceive the film going no further as an art, it is obvious that what we must strive for at once is the way to use these film nouns and verbs as cunningly as do the great novelist and the great dramatist, to achieve certain moods and effects on an audience.*
>
> —Alfred Hitchcock, 1899-1980

Reversal

Do not take this law at face value. You can rarely go wrong with a fast-paced story, but the speed itself isn't the key. The key is to have a stated, firm goal for your plot to deliberately work towards. This can only come through structure and rigorous planning. This law, more than the others, gives you more latitude in how you use it to immerse your audience. Do you need to push forward at all times at a breathless pace? Or would you rather create a work of art that builds a beautifully satisfying character arc? There's no right answer. But there is a common thread to all approaches involved: that at either end of the spectrum, these options involve creating a plot with a goal.

Author's Note

Let me take this opportunity to thank you for taking the time to read and finish this book. I hope you have enjoyed the experience, and that there is something in these pages that helps you in your storytelling journey. As a faithful reader of my book, I want to offer you something in return:

For a supplementary guide on how I wrote this book, and my extended recommended reading list, just send me an email at jon@24lawsofstorytelling.com. You can also visit the website at www.24lawsofstorytelling.com.

My goal with this book has always been to help at least one storyteller—whether they are an author, screenwriter, or one of the countless other professions that require the ability to tell a great story. If you feel like you've gained something from this book, then please consider leaving a review.

I hope we can continue this conversation about how to make great, awe-inspiring stories that immerse our audience in a world of delight—and I look forward to hearing of any and all successes you've had creating your own.

Jonathan Baldie, September 2018

Appendix

Spoilers

Story spoilers are listed below by chronological appearance in each chapter.

Law 1: Be Cruel to Your Characters

- *Ben-Hur*, 1969 film. Directed by William Wyler and produced by Sam Zimbalist for Metro-Goldwyn-Mayer

- *Star Wars: The Empire Strikes Back*, 1980 film. Story by George Lucas, directed by Irvin Kershner, and produced by Gary Kurtz for Lucasfilm Ltd.

- *To Kill a Mockingbird*, 1960 novel by Harper Lee. Published by J. B. Lippincott & Co.

- *Star Wars: The Last Jedi*, 2017 film. Directed by Rian Johnson for Lucasfilm Ltd.

Law 2: End Quickly at the Moment of Catharsis

- *Star Wars*, 1977 film. Directed and written by George Lucas for Lucasfilm Ltd.

- *The Dark Knight*, 2008 film. Directed, produced, and story co-written by Christopher Nolan. Based on characters appearing in comic books published by DC Comics

– *The Prestige*, 2006 film. Directed by Christopher Nolan. Based on *The Prestige* by Christopher Priest, a 1995 novel

Law 3: Trust Flaws More Than Strengths

– *Superman*, 1978 film. Directed by Richard Donner, story by Mario Puzo. Based on characters appearing in comic books published by DC Comics

– *Die Hard*, 1988 film. Directed by John McTiernan. Based on *Nothing Lasts Forever* by Roderick Thorp, a 1979 novel

Law 4: Show, Don't Tell

– *Star Wars: The Phantom Menace*, 1999 film. Directed, produced, and story co-written by George Lucas for Lucasfilm Ltd.

– *Star Wars: Attack of the Clones*, 2002 film. Directed, produced, and story co-written by George Lucas for Lucasfilm Ltd.

– *Gone Girl*, 2012 novel by Gillian Flynn. Published by Crown Publishing Group

– *Pride and Prejudice*, 1813 novel by Jane Austen

Law 5: Reflect Reality in Fantasy

- *The Silmarillion*, 1977 book by J. R. R. Tolkien. Published by George Allen & Unwin

- *The Hobbit*, 1937 novel by J. R. R. Tolkien. Published by George Allen & Unwin

- *The Lord of the Rings*, series of novels by J. R. R. Tolkien published between 1954 and 1955. Published by George Allen & Unwin

- *Iron Man*, 2008 film. Directed by Jon Favreau for Marvel Studios. Based on Iron Man by Stan Lee, Don Heck, and Jack Kirby

- *Thor*, 2011 film. Directed by Kenneth Branagh for Marvel Studios. Based on Thor by Stan Lee, Larry Lieber, and Jack Kirby

Law 6: Make Your Villain the Hero of Their Own Story

- *Black Panther*, 2017 film. Directed by Ryan Coogler for Marvel Studios. Based on Black Panther by Stan Lee and Jack Kirby

- *Fahrenheit 451*, 1953 novel by Ray Bradbury. Published by Ballantine Books

- *The Lord of the Rings*, series of novels by J. R. R. Tolkien published between 1954 and 1955. Published by George Allen & Unwin

- *Othello*, c. 1603 play by William Shakespeare

- *Heat*, 1995 film. Directed, written, and co-produced by Michael Mann

- *Harry Potter*, series of novels by J. K. Rowling published between 1997 and 2007. Published by Bloomsbury Publishing

Law 7: Weave Foreshadowing Seamlessly into the Plot

- *Great Expectations*, 1861 novel by Charles Dickens. Published by Chapman & Hall

- *The Dark Knight*, 2008 film. Directed, produced, and story co-written by Christopher Nolan. Based on characters appearing in comic books published by DC Comics

- *Romeo and Juliet*, c. 1591-1595 play by William Shakespeare

- *The Hound of the Baskervilles*, 1902 novel by Arthur Conan Doyle. Published by George Newnes

- *Star Wars: The Force Awakens*, 2015 film. Directed, written, and co-produced by J. J. Abrams for Lucasfilm Ltd.

- *Star Wars: The Last Jedi*, 2017 film. Directed by Rian Johnson for Lucasfilm Ltd.

Law 8: Structure Your Story around Change

- *Star Wars*, 1977 film. Directed and written by George Lucas for Lucasfilm Ltd.

- *Thor*, 2011 film. Directed by Kenneth Branagh for Marvel Studios. Based on Thor by Stan Lee, Larry Lieber, and Jack Kirby

- *Seven Samurai*, 1954 film. Directed, edited, and co-written by Akira Kurosawa

- *Pulp Fiction*, 1994 film. Directed and written by Quentin Tarantino. Based on a story by Quentin Tarantino and Roger Avary

Law 9: Subvert Expectations

- *Get Out*, 2017 film. Directed and written by Jordan Peele

- *Alien*, 1979 film. Directed by Ridley Scott and written by Dan O'Bannon

- *The Hound of the Baskervilles*, 1902 novel by Arthur Conan Doyle. Published by George Newnes

- *Watchmen*, 2009 film. Directed by Zack Snyder. Based on *Watchmen* by Dave Gibbons and Alan Moore

Law 10: Conflict Is Everything—Guard It at All Costs

- *All My Sons*, 1947 play by Arthur Miller

- *Star Wars: The Empire Strikes Back*, 1980 film. Story by George Lucas, directed by Irvin Kershner, and produced by Gary Kurtz for Lucasfilm Ltd.

Law 11: Characters Must Learn from Their Mistakes

- *Fifty Shades of Grey*, series of novels by E. L. James published between 2011 and 2017. Published by Vintage Books

- *Star Wars: The Force Awakens*, 2015 film. Directed, written, and co-produced by J. J. Abrams for Lucasfilm Ltd.

- *The Matrix*, 1999 film. Directed and written by the Wachowskis

- *The Dark Knight*, 2008 film. Directed, produced, and story co-written by Christopher Nolan. Based on characters appearing in comic books published by DC Comics

Law 12: The Hero and Villain Must Share the Same Goal

- *Batman Begins*, 2005 film. Directed, produced, and story co-written by Christopher Nolan. Based on characters appearing in comic books published by DC Comics

- *Avengers: Infinity War*, 2018 film. Directed by Anthony Russo and Joe Russo. Based on *The Avengers* by Stan Lee and Jack Kirby

- *Star Wars: The Force Awakens*, 2015 film. Directed, written, and co-produced by J. J. Abrams for Lucasfilm Ltd.

- *Captain America: Civil War*, 2016 film. Directed by Anthony Russo and Joe Russo. Based on Captain America by Joe Simon and Jack Kirby

Law 13: Series Are a Right, Not a Privilege

- *Fantastic Four*, 2015 film. Directed by Josh Trank. Based on The Fantastic Four by Stan Lee and Jack Kirby

- *Harry Potter*, series of novels by J. K. Rowling published between 1997 and 2007. Published by Bloomsbury Publishing

- *Iron Man*, 2008 film. Directed by Jon Favreau for Marvel Studios. Based on Iron Man by Stan Lee, Don Heck, and Jack Kirby

- *Marvel's The Avengers*, series of films released between 2012 and 2018 at the time of writing. Based on *The Avengers* by Stan Lee and Jack Kirby

- *Star Wars: The Force Awakens*, 2015 film. Directed, written, and co-produced by J. J. Abrams for Lucasfilm Ltd.

- *Star Wars: The Empire Strikes Back*, 1980 film. Story by George Lucas, directed by Irvin Kershner, and produced by Gary Kurtz for Lucasfilm Ltd.

- *Star Wars: Return of the Jedi*, 1983 film. Story by George Lucas, directed by Richard Marquand, and produced by Howard Kazanjian for Lucasfilm Ltd.

- *The Dark Knight Rises*, 2012 film. Directed, produced, and story co-written by Christopher Nolan. Based on characters appearing in comic books published by DC Comics

- *The Lord of the Rings,* series of novels by J. R. R. Tolkien published between 1954 and 1955. Published by George Allen & Unwin

Law 14: Make Bold Choices

- *A Game of Thrones,* 1996 novel by George R. R. Martin. Published by Voyager Books

- *Harry Potter,* series of novels by J. K. Rowling published between 1997 and 2007. Published by Bloomsbury Publishing

- *Avengers: Infinity War,* 2018 film. Directed by Anthony Russo and Joe Russo. Based on *The Avengers* by Stan Lee and Jack Kirby

- *The Great Escape,* 1963 film. Directed by John Sturges. Based on *The Great Escape* by Paul Brickhill, a 1950 novel

- *Sophie's Choice,* 1979 novel by William Styron. Published by Random House

Law 15: Tighten with Relentless Rigour

- None

Law 16: Humour Is Always Welcome

- *To Kill a Mockingbird*, 1960 novel by Harper Lee. Published by J. B. Lippincott & Co.

- *Casablanca*, 1942 film. Directed by Michael Curtiz. Based on Murray Burnett and Joan Alison's unproduced stage play *Everybody Comes to Rick's*

- *Batman Begins*, 2005 film. Directed, produced, and story co-written by Christopher Nolan. Based on characters appearing in comic books published by DC Comics

- *Pirates of the Caribbean: Dead Men Tell No Tales*, 2017 film. Directed by Joachim Rønning and Espen Sandberg and written by Jeff Nathanson

Law 17: Write along the Line of Greatest Intuition

- *Angels and Demons*, 2000 novel by Dan Brown. Published by Corgi Books

- *Star Wars: The Phantom Menace*, 1999 film. Directed, produced, and story co-written by George Lucas for Lucasfilm Ltd.

- *Star Wars: Attack of the Clones*, 2002 film. Directed, produced, and story co-written by George Lucas for Lucasfilm Ltd.

- *Star Wars: Revenge of the Sith*, 2005 film. Directed, produced, and story co-written by George Lucas for Lucasfilm Ltd.

- *Avengers: Infinity War*, 2018 film. Directed by Anthony Russo and Joe Russo. Based on *The Avengers* by Stan Lee and Jack Kirby

- *Spider-Man 3*, 2007 film. Directed by Sam Raimi. Based on Spider-Man by Stan Lee and Steve Ditko

- *Macbeth*, 1623 play by William Shakespeare

Law 18: Accord with Timeless Myths

- *Star Wars*, 1977 film. Directed and written by George Lucas for Lucasfilm Ltd.

- *The Hobbit*, 1937 novel by J. R. R. Tolkien. Published by George Allen & Unwin

- *The Odyssey*, c. eighth century BC epic poem by Homer

Law 19: Build Tension with the "Bomb under the Table" Technique

- *Inglourious Basterds*, 2009 film. Directed and written by Quentin Tarantino

- *The Dark Knight*, 2008 film. Directed, produced, and story co-written by Christopher Nolan. Based on characters appearing in comic books published by DC Comics

- *Get Out*, 2017 film. Directed and written by Jordan Peele

Law 20: Concentrate Dramatic Impact

- *Alien* franchise of films released between 1979 and 1997. Created by Dan O'Bannon and Ronald Shusett

- *Rogue One: A Star Wars Story*, 2016 film. Directed by Gareth Edwards for Lucasfilm Ltd. Based on a story by John Knoll and Gary Whitta

Law 21: Description Is Telepathy

- *Carrie*, 1974 novel by Stephen King. Published by Doubleday

- *Twilight*, series of novels by Stephenie Meyer published between 2005 and 2008. Published by Little, Brown and Company

- *Les Misérables*, 1862 novel by Victor Hugo. Published by A. Lacroix, Verboeckhoven & Cie.

Law 22: Great Dialogue Is About What's Not Said

- *Star Wars: The Phantom Menace*, 1999 film. Directed, produced, and story co-written by George Lucas for Lucasfilm Ltd.

- *Star Wars: Attack of the Clones*, 2002 film. Directed, produced, and story co-written by George Lucas for Lucasfilm Ltd.

- *Star Wars: Revenge of the Sith*, 2005 film. Directed, produced, and story co-written by George Lucas for Lucasfilm Ltd.

- *The Dark Knight*, 2008 film. Directed, produced, and story co-written by Christopher Nolan. Based on characters appearing in comic books published by DC Comics

- *Star Wars*, 1977 film. Directed and written by George Lucas for Lucasfilm Ltd.

- *Pulp Fiction*, 1994 film. Directed and written by Quentin Tarantino. Based on a story by Quentin Tarantino and Roger Avary

- *The Godfather*, 1972 film. Directed by Francis Ford Coppola, produced by Albert S. Ruddy. Based on *The Godfather* by Mario Puzo, a 1969 novel

Law 23: Write Proactive Characters

- *Misery*, 1987 novel by Stephen King. Published by Viking

- *Thor*, 2011 film. Directed by Kenneth Branagh for Marvel Studios. Based on Thor by Stan Lee, Larry Lieber, and Jack Kirby

- *The Dark Knight*, 2008 film. Directed, produced, and story co-written by Christopher Nolan. Based on characters appearing in comic books published by DC Comics

Law 24: Point Everything to the End and Beyond

- *The Prestige*, 2006 film. Directed by Christopher Nolan. Based on *The Prestige* by Christopher Priest, a 1995 novel

- *Blade Runner*, 1982 film. Directed by Ridley Scott, written by Hampton Fancher and David Peoples. Based on *Do Androids Dream of Electric Sheep?* by Philip K. Dick, a 1968 novel

- *Blade Runner 2049*, 2017 film. Directed by Denis Villeneuve, written by Hampton Fancher and Michael Green. Based on characters from *Do Androids Dream of Electric Sheep?* by Philip K. Dick, a 1968 novel

- *The Godfather*, 1972 film. Directed by Francis Ford Coppola, produced by Albert S. Ruddy. Based on *The Godfather* by Mario Puzo, a 1969 novel